Finding Family

The Salty Key Inn Series
Book - 4

Judith Keim

BOOKS BY JUDITH KEIM

THE HARTWELL WOMEN SERIES:

The Talking Tree – 1
Sweet Talk – 2
Straight Talk – 3
Baby Talk – 4
The Hartwell Women – Boxed Set

THE BEACH HOUSE HOTEL SERIES:

Breakfast at The Beach House Hotel – 1
Lunch at The Beach House Hotel – 2
Dinner at The Beach House Hotel – 3
Christmas at The Beach House Hotel – 4
Margaritas at The Beach House Hotel – 5
Dessert at The Beach House Hotel – 6
Coffee at The Beach House Hotel – 7
High Tea at The Beach House Hotel – 8 (2024)

THE FAT FRIDAYS GROUP:

Fat Fridays – 1
Sassy Saturdays – 2
Secret Sundays – 3

THE SALTY KEY INN SERIES:

Finding Me – 1
Finding My Way – 2
Finding Love – 3
Finding Family – 4
The Salty Key Inn Series Boxed Set

THE CHANDLER HILL INN SERIES:

Going Home – 1
Coming Home – 2
Home at Last – 3
The Chandler Hill Inn Series – Boxed Set

SEASHELL COTTAGE BOOKS:

A Christmas Star
Change of Heart
A Summer of Surprises
A Road Trip to Remember
The Beach Babes

THE DESERT SAGE INN SERIES:

The Desert Flowers – Rose – 1
The Desert Flowers – Lily – 2
The Desert Flowers – Willow – 3
The Desert Flowers – Mistletoe and Holly – 4

SOUL SISTERS AT CEDAR MOUNTAIN LODGE:

Christmas Sisters – Anthology
Christmas Kisses
Christmas Castles
Christmas Stories – Soul Sisters Anthology
Christmas Joy

THE SANDERLING COVE INN SERIES:

Waves of Hope – 1
Sandy Wishes – 2
Salty Kisses – 3

THE LILAC LAKE INN SERIES

Love by Design – 1
Love Between the Lines – (2024)
Love Under the Stars – (2024)

OTHER BOOKS:

The ABCs of Living With a Dachshund
Once Upon a Friendship – Anthology
Winning BIG – a little love story for all ages
Holiday Hopes
The Winning Tickets (2023)

PRAISE FOR JUDITH KEIM'S NOVELS

THE BEACH HOUSE HOTEL SERIES

"Love the characters in this series. This series was my first introduction to Judith Keim. She is now one of my favorites. Looking forward to reading more of her books."

BREAKFAST AT THE BEACH HOUSE HOTEL is an easy, delightful read that offers romance, family relationships, and strong women learning to be stronger. Real life situations filter through the pages. Enjoy!"

LUNCH AT THE BEACH HOUSE HOTEL – "This series is such a joy to read. You feel you are actually living with them. Can't wait to read the latest one."

DINNER AT THE BEACH HOUSE HOTEL – "A Terrific Read! As usual, Judith Keim did it again. Enjoyed immensely. Continue writing such pleasantly reading books for all of us readers."

CHRISTMAS AT THE BEACH HOUSE HOTEL – "Not Just Another Christmas Novel. This is book number four in the series and my introduction to Judith Keim's writing. I wasn't disappointed. The characters are dimensional and engaging. The plot is well crafted and advances at a pleasing pace. The Florida location is interesting and warming. It was a delight to read a romance novel with mature female protagonists. Ann and Rhoda have life experiences that enrich the story. It's a clever book about friends and extended family. Buy copies for your book group pals and enjoy this seasonal read."

MARGARITAS AT THE BEACH HOUSE HOTEL – "What a wonderful series. I absolutely loved this book and can't wait for the next book to come out. There was even suspense in it. Thanks Judith for the great stories."

"Overall, Margaritas at the Beach House Hotel is another wonderful addition to the series. Judith Keim takes the reader on a journey told through the voices of these amazing characters we have all come to love through the years! I truly cannot stress enough how good this book is, and I hope you enjoy it as much as I have!"

THE HARTWELL WOMEN SERIES:

"This was an EXCELLENT series. When I discovered Judith Keim, I read all of her books back to back. I thoroughly enjoyed the women Keim has written about. They are believable and you want to just jump into their lives and be their friends! I can't wait for any upcoming books!"

"I fell into Judith Keim's Hartwell Women series and have read & enjoyed all of her books in every series. Each centers around a strong & interesting woman character and their family interaction. Good reads that leave you wanting more."

THE FAT FRIDAYS GROUP :

"Excellent story line for each character, and an insightful representation of situations which deal with some of the contemporary issues women are faced with today."

"I love this author's books. Her characters and their lives are realistic. The power of women's friendships is a common and beautiful theme that is threaded throughout this story."

THE SALTY KEY INN SERIES

FINDING ME – "I thoroughly enjoyed the first book in this series and cannot wait for the others! The characters are endearing with the same struggles we all encounter. The setting makes me feel like I am a guest at The Salty Key

Inn...relaxed, happy & light-hearted! The men are yummy and the women strong. You can't get better than that! Happy Reading!"

FINDING MY WAY- *"Loved the family dynamics as well as uncertain emotions of dating and falling in love. Appreciated the morals and strength of parenting throughout. Just couldn't put this book down."*

FINDING LOVE – *"I waited for this book because the first two was such good reads. This one didn't disappoint.... Judith Keim always puts substance into her books. This book was no different, I learned about PTSD, accepting oneself, there is always going to be problems but stick it out and make it work. Just the way life is. In some ways a lot like my life. Judith is right, it needs another book and I will definitely be reading it. Hope you choose to read this series, you will get so much out of it."*

FINDING FAMILY – *"Completing this series is like eating the last chip. Love Judith's writing, and her female characters are always smart, strong, vulnerable to life and love experiences."*

"This was a refreshing book. Bringing the heart and soul of the family to us."

THE CHANDLER HILL INN SERIES

GOING HOME – *"I absolutely could not put this book down. Started at night and read late into the middle of the night. As a child of the '60s, the Vietnam war was front and center so this resonated with me. All the characters in the book were so well developed that the reader felt like they were friends of the family."*

"I was completely immersed in this book, with the

beautiful descriptive writing, and the authors' way of bringing her characters to life. I felt like I was right inside her story."

COMING HOME – *"Coming Home is a winner. The characters are well-developed, nuanced and likable. Enjoyed the vineyard setting, learning about wine growing and seeing the challenges Cami faces in running and growing a business. I look forward to the next book in this series!"*

"Coming Home was such a wonderful story. The author has a gift for getting the reader right to the heart of things."

HOME AT LAST – *"In this wonderful conclusion, to a heartfelt and emotional trilogy set in Oregon's stunning wine country, Judith Keim has tied up the Chandler Hill series with the perfect bow."*

"Overall, this is truly a wonderful addition to the Chandler Hill Inn series. Judith Keim definitely knows how to perfectly weave together a beautiful and heartfelt story."

"The storyline has some beautiful scenes along with family drama. Judith Keim has created characters with interactions that are believable and some of the subjects the story deals with are poignant."

SEASHELL COTTAGE BOOKS

A CHRISTMAS STAR – *"Love, laughter, sadness, great food, and hope for the future, all in one book. It doesn't get any better than this stunning read."*

"A Christmas Star is a heartwarming Christmas story featuring endearing characters. So many Christmas books are set in snowbound places...it was a nice change to read a Christmas story that takes place on a warm sandy beach!" Susan Peterson

CHANGE OF HEART – *"CHANGE OF HEART is the summer read we've all been waiting for. Judith Keim is a master at creating fascinating characters that are simply irresistible. Her stories leave you with a big smile on your face and a heart bursting with love."*

Kellie Coates Gilbert, author of the popular Sun Valley Series

A SUMMER OF SURPRISES – *"The story is filled with a roller coaster of emotions and self-discovery. Finding love again and rebuilding family relationships."*

"Ms. Keim uses this book as an amazing platform to show that with hard emotional work, belief in yourself and love, the scars of abuse can be conquered. It in no way preaches, it's a lovely story with a happy ending."

"The character development was excellent. I felt I knew these people my whole life. The story development was very well thought out I was drawn [in] from the beginning."

THE DESERT SAGE INN SERIES:

THE DESERT FLOWERS – ROSE – *"The Desert Flowers - Rose, is the first book in the new series by Judith Keim. I always look forward to new books by Judith Keim, and this one is definitely a wonderful way to begin The Desert Sage Inn Series!"*

"In this first of a series, we see each woman come into her own and view new beginnings even as they must take this tearful journey as they slowly lose a dear friend. This is a very well written book with well-developed and likable main characters. It was interesting and enlightening as the first portion of this saga unfolded. I very much enjoyed this book and I do recommend it"

"Judith Keim is one of those authors that you can always

depend on to give you a great story with fantastic characters. I'm excited to know that she is writing a new series and after reading book 1 in the series, I can't wait to read the rest of the books."!

<u>THE DESERT FLOWERS – LILY</u> – "The second book in the Desert Flowers series is just as wonderful as the first. Judith Keim is a brilliant storyteller. Her characters are truly lovely and people that you want to be friends with as soon as you start reading. Judith Keim is not afraid to weave real life conflict and loss into her stories. I loved reading Lily's story and can't wait for Willow's!

"The Desert Flowers-Lily is the second book in The Desert Sage Inn Series by author Judith Keim. When I read the first book in the series, The Desert Flowers-Rose, I knew this series would exceed all of my expectations and then some. Judith Keim is an amazing author, and this series is a testament to her writing skills and her ability to completely draw a reader into the world of her characters."

<u>THE DESERT FLOWERS – WILLOW –</u> "The feelings of love, joy, happiness, friendship, family and the pain of loss are deeply felt by Willow Sanchez and her two cohorts Rose and Lily. The Desert Flowers met because of their deep feelings for Alec Thurston, a man who touched their lives in different ways.

Once again, Judith Keim has written the story of a strong, competent, confident and independent woman. Willow, like Rose and Lily can handle tough situations. All the characters are written so that the reader gets to know them but not all the characters will give the reader warm and fuzzy feelings.

The story is well written and from the start you will be pulled in. There is enough backstory that a reader can start here but I assure you, you'll want to learn more. There is an ocean of emotions that will make you smile, cringe, tear up or outright cry. I loved this book as I loved books one and two. I am thrilled that the Desert Flowers story will continue. I highly recommend this book to anyone who enjoys books with strong women."

Finding Family

The Salty Key Inn Series
Book - 4

Judith Keim

Wild Quail Publishing

wildquail.pub@gmail.com
www.judithkeim.com

Published in the United States of America by:

Wild Quail Publishing
PO Box 171332
Boise, ID 83717-1332

ISBN# 978-1-959529-98-9

Dedication

In loving memory of my parents, Charles and Dorothy Schott, who provided me with the best, the kindest, the most loving family any lucky child could have.
I still hold you close to me.

CHAPTER ONE

SHEENA

Sheena Sullivan Morelli stood outside Gavin's, the new restaurant at the Salty Key Inn on the Gulf Coast of Florida, feeling as festive as the mini-lights wound around the trunks of the palm trees that softened the outline of the building. She was dressed in her finest on this unusually warm, mid-December night, and the tropical Gulf breezes felt good as they caressed her skin.

From among the hibiscus planted around the perimeter of the restaurant, lights twinkled like the stars in the inky sky above and lent a sense of peace to the area. That, and the fact that Petey, the pesky peacock Rocky Gatto had rescued and brought to the hotel, had decided not to bother with this celebration and was hanging out down by the bay.

"Let's make this an evening to remember!" said Sheena, giving her younger sisters, Darcy and Regan, an encouraging smile.

Named after their uncle, the restaurant would, they hoped, bring in enough revenue for them to be considered successful in meeting the terms of his will. With less than a month before their final meeting with Gavin's estate lawyer in Boston, they were trying their best to prove to him that they had succeeded in beating the challenge of turning his rundown hotel into a profitable operation within one year. Winning meant they would inherit Gavin's sizable estate along with the hotel. More than that, it would determine how they'd spend the rest of their lives.

Sheena brushed an imaginary crumb off her blue linen dress and studied her sisters. Darcy was wearing a green sheath that offset her red curls nicely. And Regan, beautiful as ever, even with the scar on her face she couldn't quite hide, had chosen a violet, flowy dress that matched her striking eyes. Funny, Sheena thought, how she hadn't really known her sisters until the three of them had been forced to live and work together at the hotel. And when Regan and Brian Harwood, now her fiancé, were in a serious motorcycle accident a few months ago, frightening everyone, they'd become even closer.

"I hope everyone likes what they see," Regan said. "Mo and I did our best decorating the interior with the budget we had."

"Don't worry. It's gorgeous," said Darcy, giving Regan an impish nudge with her elbow.

"The restaurant is stunning," said Sheena, "and the food is great. We were lucky to get Graham Howard as our chef." She turned as a stream of people headed their way from the parking lot, which was filling up fast.

"Here we go! Make it good," said Sheena softly, prompting Darcy and Regan to roll their eyes at the big-sister moment Sheena couldn't help.

They'd invited county commissioners, members of nearby city and town councils, other government officials, news people, owners and managers of other hotels in the area, and even the governor of Florida to join them for this grand opening. It had been a bold move on their part, but it had already paid off in publicity, even though the governor and some county commissioners had politely declined. The fact that Darcy had been writing a column for a local newspaper helped them. She was acquainted with the ins and outs of generating publicity and had invited several writers of local social columns, travel blogs, and magazines.

Sheena was soon swept up greeting people and ushering them inside to enjoy drinks and to taste the delicious-looking food displayed in the bar and on a long buffet in the dining room.

The dark wood paneling on the walls of the main dining room supplied a rich background for the brass and crystal wall sconces that spread a soft glow along the room's edges. Crystal chandeliers hung from the ceiling, casting their own warm light. White linen cloths covered the tabletops, which were set with sparkling wine goblets and silverware that reflected the light from the chandeliers and sconces. Flickering battery candles sat among tasteful, holiday greenery, adding a pine perfume to the mouth-watering aroma of the hors d'oeuvres being passed by staff.

Upstairs, the large function room held another bar and more food to sample, drawing people through the entire restaurant. A buzz of conversation enhanced the sense of excitement. The crowd was a pleasing mixture of people who, hopefully, would be a source of future business.

Kenneth Cochran, better known as Casey, was a Cornell Hotel School grad and manager of the restaurant. Tall and thin, he was a natural at his job with his ever-present smile and alert blue eyes. Tonight, he seemed to be everywhere, overseeing staff, and greeting people. Sheena observed him with satisfaction as guests responded to his attention. If she and her sisters won the challenge, they hoped to hire Casey as the hotel manager to help Sheena, who would remain an active overseer of the property.

Sheena looked up as her husband, Tony, appeared with their two children. Tears stung her eyes when she noticed the effort Michael, at eighteen, and Meaghan, at fifteen, had put into their appearance. After initially being against her plan to come to Florida, they now embraced their new lives and were proud of all she was doing.

"Hi, Mom," said Michael. His brown eyes, so like Tony's, sparkled. "Okay if I help myself to some of the food?"

She laughed at the typical, teenage hunger of a still-growing, young man. "Of course. Enjoy."

"You look pretty, Mom," Meaghan said. "Thanks for letting me wear your necklace. It's great with my new holiday dress." She twirled in front of Sheena. Her auburn hair, like Sheena's, swung above her shoulders and brought out the hazel in her eyes.

"You look pretty, too, sweetheart," Sheena said. Her little girl was growing into a beautiful young woman.

Tony gave her a smile that warmed her heart. His smile had been one of the reasons their marriage had been prompted by the unexpected creation of Michael all those years ago. And though they'd always loved each other, their relationship had grown even stronger during their time in Florida.

He kissed her. "See you later. I'm going to mix with the crowd a little. Brian and I are hoping to pick up some new business."

She gave him a heartfelt smile. Following Brian Harwood's motorcycle accident with Regan, Tony had agreed to become a partner in Brian's construction company and was now settled into his new life in Florida. As Tony walked away, Sheena noticed Blackie Gatto headed in her direction.

Blackie was Uncle Gavin's financial advisor and a great supporter of her and her sisters as they attempted to do as their uncle wished by transforming what had been a small, run-down, family hotel into the upscale, full-service resort property he'd envisioned.

"Welcome to Gavin's," Sheena said to him, giving him a quick hug. "I'm so glad you could make it."

"I wouldn't miss it for the world," he replied, lifting her

hand, and kissing it in a gallant gesture. He indicated their surroundings with a sweep of his arm. "I think Gavin would be very pleased with this."

"We hope it brings in enough new business and revenue for us to complete our challenge here at the Salty Key Inn."

He nodded and settled his gaze on her. "I hope so, too. The downside of borrowing the money from Gavin's estate to complete the restaurant could be difficult for you and your sisters if you fail."

Sheena's stomach curled inside her, but she didn't want Blackie to see how worried she was. For the sake of her sisters and her family, she had to remain upbeat. With only a few weeks remaining to accomplish everything they had left to do, self-doubt could ruin them.

"I probably shouldn't warn you, but a special guest is going to appear this evening," Blackie said mysteriously.

"What? Who?" Sheena said and turned when Tony joined them.

"How are you, Blackie?" Tony said.

Sheena smiled as they shook hands. At one time, Tony had thought she and Blackie had something going on between them. With his Italian temper rising, he'd even yelled at Blackie to keep away from her. Now, they all could laugh about it.

"Heard you bought into Brian's company," Blackie said to Tony. "A good investment, if you ask me. The two of you guys can make a real go of the construction business in this part of the state."

"Thanks," said Tony. "Brian is still recovering from his motorcycle-accident injuries, but he's able to do more each day in the field."

"Nice to keep it all in the family," said Blackie. He waved to a gentleman in the crowd. "Well, guess I'd better go say hi to a few other people."

After he left, Tony wrapped an arm around Sheena. "You look beautiful, Mrs. Morelli."

She smiled at him. "Thanks. When you entered the restaurant with the kids, I could hardly believe how grown up they looked."

"Just a couple more years and we'll be on our own." Tony gave her a sexy grin that sent a gleam to his dark brown eyes. "It's gonna be great. Really great."

Sheena's laugh came from deep inside her. She loved that Tony still found her so desirable.

Darcy approached them holding Austin Blakely's hand. Engaged now, they were, Sheena thought, a darling couple. And well suited. Darcy tended to be a bit impetuous, and Austin, though not the least bit boring, was a calming influence.

"What's up?" Darcy asked.

"We're talking about the future," said Sheena. "The kids will be gone before we know it."

Tony grinned. "It's going to be really nice to be alone. What's going on with you two?"

"Looking around at all the preparations for this party, I'm starting to get a little nervous about my wedding," said Darcy. "I hope I can get everything done the way I want."

"All I care about is saying 'I do.' I don't need all the fancy stuff associated with it," Austin said in his usual, good-natured way.

"Whoa!" said Sheena. "We're counting on you two to set the standard for weddings here at the hotel. It's a big reason why we're going after the wedding business."

"What about Regan's wedding?" Darcy said to her. "Are she and Brian going to get married here? I've asked her, but she says she doesn't know."

Sheena laughed. “She’ll figure it out. I think her engagement to Brian is still a surprise to her.”

At the sight of the manager of a nearby hotel, Sheena excused herself and went to greet him. They needed as many friends as possible to help pull off the restaurant’s success. In truth, they probably should have waited to build Gavin’s. Now, all she could do was hope it would prove to be a risk worth taking.

CHAPTER TWO

REGAN

Regan mingled with the crowd, telling herself it would be good practice for when she'd begin filming as spokeswoman for Arthur Weatherman's restaurant chain. After her accident with Brian, she'd been certain Arthur would rescind his offer, but he and his wife, Margretta, had surprised her by keeping to their agreement. She'd always be grateful to them for helping her realize her beauty was perceived by her actions and how she felt about herself as a person. Growing up, she'd been considered the "looker" in the family—and the dumb one.

Being here in Florida, working on the hotel, had been the beginning of a whole new life for her, one she'd vowed never to leave. Her gaze searched for Brian Harwood. He was across the room leaning on his cane while he talked easily with a group of people. Even with his injuries, he still looked like a poster boy for Florida tourism with his sun-bleached brown hair and buff, tanned body. Love for him surged through her. Of all the good things that had happened to her, finding love with him was the best.

As if he knew what she was thinking, he looked over at her and smiled, making her feel warm inside.

"I heard you two got engaged. Congratulations!" said a voice behind her.

Regan whirled around. "Nicole! I'm so glad you made the trip!" She gave Darcy's old roommate, Nicole Coleman, a quick hug. She looked fabulous in a red sheath that offset her blond hair. "Have you seen Darcy yet?"

"No. I just walked in." Nicole's blue eyes lit. "Where is she?"

Regan pointed her out in the crowd. "She'll be so glad to see you."

"I was sorry to hear about the accident, but you look great, Regan." Nicole lifted Regan's hand and studied the diamond ring winking on her finger. "I'm so happy for you. And for Brian too. I had the chance to talk to him when I visited in September. He's a nice guy, and you two are great together."

"Thanks. I think so too," said Regan. She was still surprised sometimes when people told her how good she and Brian were together. For a long time, she'd been sure Brian would be nothing but trouble for her.

As Nicole left to find Darcy, Regan watched her walk away. Life sometimes seemed to be one surprise after another. In this case, she was glad Nicole had suddenly decided to leave her job in Boston, sell her new condo, and move to Florida. She suspected it had everything to do with Graham Howard. It was a good thing for Gavin's because Nicole had promised to help them with publicity for the restaurant, and they needed all the help they could get.

"Hello, Regan," came a smooth, low voice.

Regan turned to find Arthur and Margretta Weatherman standing near her. She felt a smile, still crooked from injuries she'd endured in the accident, spread across her face.

"Hello, Arthur! Margretta! I'm so glad you could come to our opening." She held out her hand, and they each shook it.

"Glad to be here," said Arthur. He glanced around. "I like what you've done here. You and Mo do good work together."

"We can't wait to have you and your business partner get started on our restaurants," said Margretta.

"Thanks," said Regan. She and Mo had bid on redoing six

of the Weathermans' family restaurants in their Florida's Finest Restaurants chain. The smile left Regan's face as she suddenly fought tears. "I want to thank you both again for allowing me to be your spokesperson. As you can see, the scar under my chin and onto my jawline is now a part of me, along with a lip that may or may not completely recover from nerve damage."

Margretta, a tall, beautiful brunette, gripped Regan's hand. "We talked about it a lot before deciding, and we're very happy you'll represent us. You're a beautiful woman as you are. It's important for young girls to realize they don't have to be perfect. None of us is."

"That's why I agreed to do it," said Regan. "It was a scary thought at first, but I'm comfortable with it now."

"We'll be in touch about the filming schedule. Probably next week. We need you to start the New Year off right for us," said Margretta.

"I hear congratulations are in order on your engagement," said Arthur. "I've known Brian for some time. He's a good man. I'm happy for both of you." He glanced around the room. "Ah, I see Blackie. I'd better go say hello."

"Thanks again," said Regan. "Be sure to enjoy the refreshments. Graham has done a wonderful job with them."

After they left her side, Regan decided to check the food displays. As she was walking through the main dining room, she saw Mo talking to a gentleman who looked vaguely familiar. She hurried over to them.

"Mo! I'm so glad you came!" She hugged him and turned to his companion. "I almost didn't recognize you, Kenton! Glad you could join us too." Kenton Standish, a robust man with sandy-colored hair and fine features, was wearing tinted, thick-rimmed glasses that disguised his blue eyes. His ordinary blue blazer and green turtleneck hid the muscular, bare chest women were used to sighing over on his television show. On screen, he played a heroic Scottish fighter. In reality, he was a kind, soft-spoken person who was Mo's partner. Ordinarily, they took great care not to be noticed, so Regan knew it was a tribute to her and her sisters for them to be here in this crowd.

"You look fabulous," Mo said. His brown face softened with affection, and his dark eyes shone with admiration. "Love that dress on you!"

"Thanks. You look pretty dapper yourself," Regan said, admiring the subtly checked gray blazer and the bold, red holiday tie he wore. "Have you spoken to Arthur and Margretta?"

"Yes," said Mo. "They're very excited about what we've designed. I can't wait for us to set our work in motion." He smiled at Kenton. "And then, we'll begin work on Kenton's house."

Regan smiled at them both. "It's going to be so much fun to do that. I've already got some ideas in mind."

Mo smiled. "Me too. Black and white ... like Kenton and me ..."

"... with bold colors," said Regan.

Mo laughed. "Exactly."

Regan loved how closely their minds worked. Since meeting Mo and working with him on a few projects, her whole world had come alive with color and texture, drawing out her artistic side.

"I understand you and Brian are engaged," said Kenton. "Congratulations."

They all turned as Brian approached.

"Here he is now," said Regan, beaming at the man who'd finally won her trust along with her heart.

Brian smiled and put an arm around her. "Hi, Mo! Good to

see you. Thanks for the books you sent to me. It's frustrating to be laid up, so it was nice to have them to read."

"Brian, I want you to meet Kenton," Mo said. "Kenton, this is Brian Harwood."

Brian and Kenton shook hands.

"I understand you're in construction," said Kenton. "I'm wondering if I could talk to you sometime about doing some work on my house. I want to upgrade the kitchen and do a few extra things with it."

"Thanks. Tony Morelli, my new partner, and I would be pleased to meet with you." He handed Kenton a business card. "Give either one of us a call, and we'll set up a time. Now, if you two don't mind, I'm going to whisk Regan away to meet some of my old friends."

"We don't mind at all," said Mo. "In fact, we're here just to congratulate you, and then we're driving to Cyndi and Tom's house for a holiday event."

"Have fun, and say hi to them for all of us here," said Regan. Kenton's sister, Cyndi Jackson, and her husband, Tom, were the hotel's first official guests, who'd taken advantage of the hotel's special, military discount plan. Since then, they'd been instrumental in steering new guests their way.

As Brian led her through the crowd, Regan gazed at her friends and family, wondering what the coming weeks would bring. The last few had been full of surprises, including her own engagement.

CHAPTER THREE

DARCY

Darcy looked around the crowded restaurant seeing more than just people—she saw faces behind which lay stories. Writing a newspaper column for several months had prompted her to view people in a whole new way. Everyone had stories—some good, some bad. With Austin's encouragement, she was even putting them together for a book. She hadn't told him or anyone else she was planning to submit her idea to a New York publisher. Secretly, she hoped to present her success to Austin as a special Christmas gift.

"There you are!" said a voice behind her.

Darcy turned to see Nicole heading her way. She opened her arms to her old roommate and hugged her tightly. "I'm glad you decided to ditch Boston and come to Florida after all."

Nicole smiled at her. "As soon as I discovered my so-called promotion at work was fake, and Rick was seeing someone else on the side, I decided to pull up roots like you did."

"And?" Darcy said, knowing the answer.

A smile broke out on Nicole's face. "And Graham encouraged me to come. After our two dates in September, I decided he was worth getting to know better. And, Darcy, I want to help you and your sisters with marketing or in any other way."

Darcy grinned at her earnestness. "Thanks. Just a few more weeks until we learn if we've met my uncle's challenge. And then I've got my wedding."

Nicole gazed around and turned to her. "There are a lot of nice things about this restaurant that we can easily publicize. You've advertised having holiday celebrations here, haven't you?"

"Yes, but because we're so new, it's been difficult to get people signed up."

"We'll talk tomorrow," Nicole assured her. "I need to go back to the kitchen to say hello to Graham, and then I'll probably need to get out of his way."

Darcy laughed with her. Graham was an excellent young chef who was serious about his work.

As Nicole left, Austin came over to her. "Hi, honey. How are you doing?"

"Good, but, Austin, I hope my sisters and I have done the right thing by borrowing money to open this restaurant. I realize how gutsy that was. We have just a few weeks to make a go of it."

Austin put his arm around her. "The restaurant is beautiful, and the food is delicious. What more do you want?"

"Reservations," Darcy said promptly.

"That's my girl. Right to the point," he said, laughing. "Well, let's mingle and see what we can do to help them along."

With Austin at her side, Darcy felt as if she could do anything.

CHAPTER FOUR

SHEENA

When Sheena saw Archibald Wilson cross the threshold, her knees went weak. Blackie had mentioned a special guest, but Sheena had no idea it would be Archibald. As a courtesy, they'd invited Gavin's lawyer in Boston to the grand opening, but they'd never suspected he'd attend it.

She hurried over to him. "Welcome, Mr. Wilson! We're so glad to have you here." It was a lie. If he didn't like what he saw, they were doomed. Not only would they fail the challenge, they'd also have to pay back the two hundred fifty thousand dollars they'd borrowed.

A tall, distinguished-looking man with white hair, he bobbed his head courteously. "I was so pleased to be invited. Now, how about showing me just what you three Sullivan sisters have been up to with this restaurant." His blue eyes twinkled. "Gavin would love what you named it."

"We wanted to do something to honor him," Sheena said.

As they passed through the crowd, Sheena caught Darcy's eye. At the sight of Archibald, Darcy's face blanched. She hurried over to them.

"Mr. Wilson, how are you? We didn't expect you to make the trip, but I'm so glad you came," she ended on an upbeat note.

"Why don't you show him around while I get Regan?" Sheena said, giving Darcy a smile that hid her fear.

She desperately needed to find the restroom and put a cold

compress on her forehead, where a headache was quickly forming. In her role as the financial person of the group, she'd pressed her sisters to accept the idea that if they wanted to open the restaurant before Christmas, they had to borrow the money. Now, it seemed a dangerous decision.

On her way, she waved Regan over. "Go find Darcy. She's with Archibald Wilson. I'll be there as soon as I can."

Regan's eyes rounded. "Archibald Wilson here? Oh my God! What are we going to do?"

Sheena laid a hand on Regan's shoulder. "We're going to show him a good time. Be sure he gets a drink and lots of delicious food."

Regan hurried on her way.

As Sheena entered the restroom, she absently thought Tony had done a great job of finding interesting plumbing fixtures at a good price. The fancy, fish-shaped faucets suited the room with its cream marble countertops and dark-blue tile floor.

After wetting one of the terry handcloths, Sheena squeezed the cold water out and pressed the cloth to her head, reminding herself to calm down. Lately, she'd been so tired, so emotional. She knew come mid-January the challenge would end, but that was no reason, she told herself, to lose the drive that had brought them this far.

She drew a deep breath and straightened. Time to act the calm, cool character she wished she was.

Sheena found her sisters sitting at a table with Archibald, deep in conversation with him. As she approached, he looked up and smiled at her. "Have a seat," he said, indicating the empty chair next to him.

He studied her. "I'm not here to judge what you're doing.

That won't happen until I see all the figures in January. I'll let them speak for themselves; I'm here to have a good time. Your uncle would like that."

"Where are you staying?" Sheena asked. "We might be able to move one of our reservations to another location." To draw people in, they'd given away free rooms to some of the more prominent VIPs.

Archibald waved his hand in dismissal. "That won't be necessary. I'm staying with Blackie."

Sheena pressed her lips together. Blackie could have told her, had said he wanted to, but then he'd left her side without giving her this very important piece of information.

"Can I get you a glass of wine?" Darcy asked her, getting to her feet.

Sheena's stomach curled at the thought. "No, thanks."

"I'll have another drink," said Archibald. He held up an empty plate. "And more of whatever is being served. The food is delicious."

Darcy smiled. "Glad to do that. I'll be right back."

After Darcy returned to the table and Archibald had another drink and sampled more of Graham's food, he entertained them with stories of Boston.

When Sheena couldn't avoid it any longer, she got to her feet. "Thank you for coming, Archibald. I have to see to our other guests. But don't leave without saying goodbye."

Sheena immediately went to find Blackie.

He smiled at her when she approached.

"Blackie, may I speak to you for a moment?" she asked, receiving frowns from the three women who surrounded him.

"Excuse me, ladies," he said.

Sheena led him to a quiet corner and faced him. "Blackie, our special guest was Archibald Wilson? You should have told me."

"Ah, don't worry about it. He's here to have a good time."

"He seems to be doing so, but what is it going to mean to our challenge?"

"Nothing," said Blackie firmly. "He's a nice guy, but a bit of a stickler. You'll have to wait until January to find out. His having fun here won't affect the result at all."

Sheena's shoulders slumped. "Okay. Guess it's just a wait-and-see game."

He shrugged noncommittally. "Wish I could help you, but I can't. We're not to discuss it at all during his stay with me. That's an agreement we made before he arrived."

Fighting an urge to cry in frustration, Sheena simply nodded.

The next morning, Sheena sat with her sisters in the kitchen of the suite she and her family were using temporarily. Temporarily, that is, unless they failed to meet her uncle's challenge. Then, they'd either be living here or out on the street. She and Tony had taken all the money they had set aside for a new house and had invested it into Brian's business securing a partnership for him. The money she and her sisters had borrowed to finance the completion of the restaurant was another worry as well. Sheena felt tired just thinking about the consequences of failing.

"What do you think, Sheena? Did we pull off the party at the restaurant last night?" said Darcy. "Like I told Austin, we have to have reservations to keep things going."

"Arthur Weatherman and his wife reserved the private dining room upstairs for New Year's Eve," said Regan proudly." Casey told me about it."

"They're such nice people," Sheena commented. "Any word on other group reservations?"

Darcy and Regan shook their heads together.

"The new social columnist at *West Coast News* promised to give us a lot of space in the next issue," said Darcy. "And the editor of *Florida Coast Magazine* is planning to put all the photographs they took of various people into their social section, along with a blurb about the restaurant. The travel blogger from *Places to Visit* was at the bar talking to people and enjoying herself."

Sheena gave her sister a nod of approval. "Good job, Darcy. How about the *Tampa Tribune*?"

"I spoke to their photographer," said Regan. "He was taking a lot of pictures."

"And the reporter said she'd give us some space," added Darcy.

"Is Sally handling the registration office?" Sheena said, holding back a yawn. At Regan's nod, she got to her feet. "Time for our meeting at Gavin's."

She followed her sisters out of the Sandpiper Suites Building and stood with them a moment, studying the restaurant across the parking lot. The simple, stucco exterior belied the elegant, wood-paneled interior, lush carpeting, and fine finishes throughout. In recognition of the bright, funky colors and decorative schemes of the commercial buildings and houses in the surrounding neighborhoods, the wood trim outside was painted turquoise, and a carved-wooden, pink flamingo stood watch outside the entrance. Were Gavin here to see it, Sheena was certain he'd approve.

"Thank God the pink house is gone," said Darcy. "I couldn't believe that's where we were supposed to live together for one year."

"And with only one old-fashioned bathroom," Regan said, shaking her head.

"I was scared to pieces when the kids were caught in the

fire that destroyed the building. Thank heavens, they were spared even if the house turned out to be a total loss." A shudder marched across Sheena's shoulder, sending chills down her spine. In her mind, she could still see flames shooting out the windows of the house and hear herself screaming for her children.

They entered the restaurant to find Casey, Graham, and Nicole sitting at a table waiting for them.

"Good morning," Sheena said.

"You all look bright and beautiful," said Casey, smiling at them. He pushed back a lock of brown hair that was falling on his brow. "How about some fresh coffee to wake you up?"

Sheena smiled happily. "Great. I could use another cup."

After he served them all coffee, Casey cleared his throat. "The party was very well received. Several people made reservations for the holidays, and others said they'd do so."

"Good," said Darcy. "We need to show we're at least going in the right direction if Archibald Wilson is to agree we've met the challenge."

"You and I can work on an online ad blitz," said Nicole.

"I sent out notices to Mo's clients," Regan said. "Some of them told us they'd check out the restaurant."

Nicole wrote that information down and smiled. "Every little bit helps."

"How did you do with the staff?" Sheena asked Casey.

"Quite well. A few mess-ups, but not bad. However, when we book parties, we'll need to add to our wait staff. So, as we move forward, expenses will likely be going up."

"The kitchen staff needs a little more coordination and practice to come together as a team, but overall we did fine," said Graham. "We can call it a learning experience."

"Your food was just delicious," gushed Regan. "Everyone said so."

"And we now have a new hostess," said Casey, turning to Nicole and smiling.

"Nicole?" said Sheena, surprised.

Nicole made a little bow. "At your service. Casey and Graham talked me into it, and I'm going to give it a try."

"What about your marketing business?" Darcy said.

"I'm going to do some consulting jobs for marketing on my own and see how it goes," said Nicole. "My severance pay will carry me for a while."

"Very good." Sheena studied Graham, Casey, and Nicole, the three people who were essential to the successful launch and operation of the restaurant. "After the first of the year and our meeting with Mr. Wilson, we hope to be able to make some adjustments to your salaries. For now, think of yourselves as part of the family willing to make this work."

Everyone laughed with good nature. Sheena hoped it would last. She'd been told restaurants were difficult for so many reasons—management of staff principal among them.

Sheena was working on financials for the restaurant when she received a call from Michael.

"Hi, Mike! What's up?"

"I need to talk to you, Mom," he said in a troubled voice. "Where are you?"

"I'm at home going over financials. Why?"

"Can you meet me down by the waterfront? We'll have more privacy there."

Sheena's stomach squeezed with worry. "What's wrong?"

"I'll meet you there," said Michael. He hung up, leaving her to wonder what could be so terribly wrong. He'd sounded as if he were crying.

She hurried across the hotel grounds toward the bay and

sat in one of the wooden chairs on the grassy area beside the water. Her mind raced. *What had happened? Her son was strong. He didn't often cry.*

She didn't have long to wait for him to show up at the hotel. From a distance, she could see Michael moving across the lawn toward her, his head down, his shoulders drooping.

Her heart thudded to a halt and then sprinted in sickening beats. She knew her child, and he was in distress. She rose to greet him.

Michael's face was pale.

"Michael, Michael, what's wrong, honey?" she said, putting her arms around him and holding him close.

His shoulders shook, and then he pulled away and gazed at her with tear-streaked cheeks. "It's Kaylee. She says she's pregnant."

Sheena felt the blood leave her face and fought to get her balance. "Is she sure?"

"As sure as she can be. One test said positive. Another said negative. She's waiting for the results of a different brand of test." He slumped.

Sheena sucked in a deep breath. "How far along is she?"

"Only a few weeks, I guess," he said. "I don't know how it could've happened. I was so careful."

Sheena took his arm. "Let's sit down. No one else is nearby, so we can talk."

She led him to one of the Adirondack chairs they'd placed on the lawn next to the bank of the bay and collapsed into it, her pulse pounding with dismay.

Michael slumped into a chair next to hers. "What am I going to do?" He ran his hands through his dark curls so like Tony's.

"First of all, we don't know for sure she is pregnant. Until then, we're not going to panic," Sheena said, lying through her teeth. She was so panicky she felt dizzy.

"What's Dad going to say?" asked Michael in a small voice that sent Sheena's thoughts back to the time when she'd had to break the news to Tony of Michael's unexpected presence. Tony had been marvelous then, but she knew he wouldn't be happy about this.

"He's probably going to be pissed," Sheena said honestly. "Dad and I have both spoken to you about the risks of being intimate with Kaylee."

Michael's eyes flooded once more.

Sheena reached over and patted his hand. "We certainly understand raging hormones, but you're both only in high school and with the most challenging and exciting years still ahead of you. I hate for you to be caught in this situation."

"But what if she's pregnant?" said Michael. "How am I going to support her? And the baby? I'm not ready to be a father. I don't even know what in the hell I'm doing myself."

"No matter the situation, we'll get through this, Michael. All of us together." Sheena's voice was shaky, but she meant every word of it.

Michael lowered his head. "The worst part is that Kaylee is blaming me." He looked up at her with an anguished expression. "I swear to you, I never pushed her to do anything she wasn't willing to do. Sometimes, I even had to fight her off, if you know what I mean."

"I believe you, son. I've seen how she was with you. And she does realize, I'm sure, it takes two people to make a baby."

Sheena recalled the first time she'd met Kaylee, who hadn't favorably impressed her. But more than her appearance, it was Kaylee's lack of goals and her willingness to blow off school Sheena had found upsetting. But no amount of honest talk with Michael had succeeded in his breaking off the relationship. Something he, no doubt, seriously regretted.

"So, I just have to wait to find out?" Michael all but wailed.

"For the time being. And sometimes, early pregnancies end quickly on their own. I've had a couple of false starts myself."

Michael's eyes widened. "You have?"

"Yes," Sheena said, thinking back to both the relief and sadness those incidents had given her. She and Tony didn't want more children than they could handle while he was building his business and she was helping him.

"What can I do for you, Michael?" Sheena asked, giving him a steady look.

"Just be like this." Once again, his eyes filled. "I love you, Mom."

"I love you too." Sheena felt her own eyes water. It had been a while since Michael had spoken to her with such affection.

They sat quietly for a while, looking out at the bay. An onshore breeze formed little whitecaps on the waves that roughed the surface of the water. Her life seemed the same way.

"Will you tell Dad?" Michael said into the silence.

"If I get the chance to talk to him, I will. But that's something you need to do, Michael, regardless of my conversation with him. It's important for you to talk to him yourself, like a man."

"Yeah, I guess you're right."

Sheena drew a breath and said, "All right. There's no need to say anything to anybody else until we know for sure what's going on. How does Kaylee feel about this? You said she was blaming you, but how is she handling it? After all, most of the burden falls on her."

"She likes the idea of our being married and told me she wants to live here at the hotel. She thinks it's glamorous, especially because her life at home isn't that happy. That's another thing. Her mother drinks too much, and her father is gone a lot driving his truck. I wouldn't want to raise a baby in that house."

Sheena was pleased Michael was thinking of both Kaylee and the baby. Though she was proud of him for that, she prayed all his worries would come to nothing.

That afternoon after arriving home from school, Meaghan pulled Sheena aside. "Can I talk to you?"

"Sure." Sheena had a very good idea what this was about. High school rumors found their way into every corner of the building.

Meaghan plopped down into a kitchen chair and faced her mother. "Today at school, I heard something about Michael, and I don't know whether to tell you."

"If you're talking about Michael and Kaylee's situation, he's already come to me. He's very upset about it, so I wouldn't say much to him at this stage. And please don't say anything to your father about it until Michael and I have had the chance to talk to him privately."

"But what do I say to the other kids? They're saying he made her do ... 'it.' But, Mom, I know what Kaylee is like around here, and I don't believe that's true."

"Neither do I. But I think you should be mindful about how you defend him. The less said, the better. It would only make matters worse for the two of them."

"Okay." Meaghan gave Sheena a worried look. "Is Michael going to be all right?"

"I hope so, sweetie. I really do."

That afternoon, Sheena waited until after Meaghan had gone next door to Regan and Darcy's suite and Michael had gone for a run on the beach. Then, she drew Tony inside their bedroom. "I need to talk to you."

As she told him about Michael's predicament, Tony's reaction was as expected. He went from shock to outright anger before settling down to a posture of worry. The situation was made more awkward because of their own history.

"I tried to tell him," said Tony, shaking his head. "What's he going to do about college?"

Sheena put a restraining hand on Tony's arm to stop his pacing. "One day at a time. We don't even know for sure she's pregnant."

A knock on the bedroom door stopped their conversation.

Tony went to the door and opened it. "Come in, son. We were just talking about your dilemma."

Michael walked into the bedroom and plopped down on the bed. Looking up at Tony, he said, "I'm sorry, Dad. You tried to tell me ..."

"Your mother and I both did," Tony said shortly. "I think you'd better think seriously about how you're going to handle this. Brian and I can always use you at the company. That will give you some income. And I suppose you could get a second job here at the hotel."

"What about school?" Michael said, his eyes so wide they looked much too big for his young, handsome face.

"You could probably take some online courses, get a start to your college career."

Michael curled up into a ball on top of the bed. Sheena wanted to go to him, but as she started to move, Tony gave her a warning look that told her to back off.

"Michael, I'm sorry this happened," Tony said. "I hope it isn't true. If it is, we'll help you. But make no mistake, it won't be easy for someone your age."

Michael sat up and gave them a glum look. "Guess that's all

I can expect."

"Let us know the minute you find out anything," said Sheena. "And if it's true, let Kaylee know we'll be there for her too."

Michael got to his feet and lumbered out of the room, looking like a much bigger version of the little boy they loved.

Sheena was left in the room with Tony and a nagging question. She studied him. He'd been there for her through everything—from the unexpected pregnancy to finally accepting the move to Florida.

"Tony, how did you feel when I told you I was pregnant?" She braced herself for the truth.

He wrapped his arms around her. "You don't know after all these years?" He gazed down at her with tenderness. "I felt then, and I've always felt I was the luckiest guy around."

Tears sprang to her eyes. It had been such an emotional day, and this was exactly what she'd needed to hear. She reached up and cupped his cheek. "Love you, Mr. Morelli."

He grinned. "I know. Say, maybe a little later you could show me."

Laughing, she gave him a playful push.

CHAPTER FIVE

REGAN

When Mo called her to meet him at Kenton's new house a few days after Gavin's opening, Regan stopped reading the promotional material for Florida's Finest Restaurants chain and rushed out the door. She couldn't wait to see Kenton's home!

Following directions, she drove south on Gulf Boulevard and, after some distance, pulled her car through a gated entrance Mo had opened for her, stopping in front of a palatial, three-story, white-stucco house. A small circle planted with colorful impatiens sat in front of the building. On each side of the circle, sweeping staircases led up to the second-story entrance, making Regan think of two curving stairs rising to heaven.

Mo stood at the top of them waving at her. She felt a smile spread across her face as she climbed out of the car. He looked perfect standing there in white linen slacks and a purple, Hawaiian-print shirt.

As she climbed a set of stairs, she gazed at the large expanse of land surrounding the house. That alone was worth a lot of money.

"Hello, welcome to my palace," teased Mo, giving her a hug. "Kenton is away, but he left me here to work on some ideas for the house. I thought you'd like to see it."

He opened the carved-wooden door stained a rich walnut and ushered her inside to a white-tiled entrance. Tall ceilings rose above them, and behind her, above the door, a round window let in light, making her feel as if she'd entered a refreshing winter scene. From the foyer, chestnut-colored hardwood floors stretched in all directions, setting off the white walls.

"Where should we begin?" asked Mo.

"How about here?" Regan walked to the right into what she realized was a private study. Bookcases surrounded a fireplace on an outside wall. Green leather chairs faced an enormous modern desk. She gave Mo a questioning look.

"Kenton likes to read, and he's a whiz at online investing," said Mo. "He's been helping me with some investments."

He led her out of the room, stopped to indicate a powder room with a fancy sink, and ushered her into a huge living area. Here again, high ceilings gave a sense of openness and space. In the center of the room, a gas-lit fireplace, exposed on three sides, added interest. Regan could see a large dining room beyond the fireplace,

As they walked to the far end of the room, she stopped to gaze at the magnificent view. A double set of sliding glass doors led to a small deck outside, which overlooked a stunning, Olympic-size, infinity-edge pool with the blue water of the Gulf beyond it.

"Beautiful place for a deck," Regan murmured.

"That's just a small observation area. The screened-in porch and main deck are on the other side of the kitchen. Follow me."

Regan trailed Mo into a modern kitchen that would tempt any person to take up classical French cooking—a la Julia Child. Gleaming, stainless-steel appliances, a huge Viking range, a magnificent central island with a huge double sink, and equipment of every kind added a professional look to the gray-granite countertops and white cabinetry.

As promised, a large, screened-in porch lay on the other side of the kitchen, along with another powder room and the deck Mo had mentioned.

"Well, what do you think?" Mo asked, beaming at her.

"It's gorgeous," said Regan. "I've never seen anything like it."

"You haven't even seen the bedrooms. We can either take the elevator or climb the stairs. There are two sets of stairs, one in front for guests and the back stairs here for staff. We can take the back stairs if you wish."

"Okay. Let's do it."

The four guest bedrooms upstairs were finished nicely and had either a private bathroom or, for two of them, a shared Jack-and-Jill bathroom. The master bedroom was an entirely different matter. Lovely couldn't begin to describe it. An open fireplace sat between the bedroom and the massive master bathroom. As Regan stepped into the bathroom, she noticed the huge spa tub butted up close to the fireplace. An enormous, two-person shower took up space in one corner. The entrance to a large walk-in closet and dressing room was on the wall opposite from the spa. It was a scene of decadent comfort, she mused, turning and going to the window in the bedroom to look out at the Gulf below. For a moment, she could believe she was on a cruise ship. She turned to Mo with a smile.

"Amazing! To think some people live this way!"

His delighted laughter matched her own. "Now, we have to make it even better."

"But it's gorgeous!" she protested.

"Yes, but it's not warm and personal. Kenton doesn't want to live in a palace; he wants to live in a comfortable, relaxing home." His eyes shone. "This is going to be fun, Regan. And I want you to help me."

"Do we have a budget?"

"Of course. But I want to do it as inexpensively as we can while keeping it top quality. That is going to be how we'll build our business. Many other designers find it easy to spend other people's money. I believe that's why Arthur chose us to do his restaurants."

Regan smiled. "Good. I like that idea. Let's get started. I'm not due on the registration desk until late afternoon."

They went back downstairs to the front entrance and walked outside and down the stairway, so they could appraise the house as any stranger would. As they stood gazing up at the house, an egret flew by, causing Regan to turn her head.

She noticed a small building to the left, partially hidden from view by foliage.

"What's that?" she asked Mo, pointing to it.

"That's the guest cottage—three bedrooms, two-and-a-half baths, and a nice kitchen. Eventually, Kenton wants to rent it out, so there's someone on property year-round."

Regan grabbed hold of Mo's arm and gave him a searching look. "This all seems like a fantasy. But it is serious between you and Kenton. Right?"

Mo smiled and nodded. "Yeah. We have a real friendship going."

Regan's sigh was full of happiness for her best friend. "It's so exciting! Sure you're not going to disappear on me?"

"Kenton knows I'm serious about being independent. He's all for my working in my own business and eventually with you."

Regan's lips curved at the idea of being in business with Mo. It could happen. All she needed to do was to help her sisters win the challenge.

"Okay, let's begin," said Mo.

They climbed the stairs and went through the house room

by room, taking photos of them and writing detailed notes about what changes to décor they might suggest to Kenton. They took a quick break for lunch and continued critiquing the rooms until it was time for Regan to leave.

Her head spinning with possibilities, Regan left the house and headed for the hotel.

Driving through the entrance to the Salty Key Inn, Regan realized that, even though they were able to fix up the property, it would never be glamourous, and they were right to keep it attractive in a simple way.

She swung into the parking lot behind the Sandpiper Suites Building. Climbing out of Gertie, Gavin's classic, '50s Cadillac convertible, Regan smelled the delicious aromas emanating from Gavin's, the restaurant they'd keep as elegant as it was designed to be.

When she appeared in the registration office, Darcy greeted her with a smile. "Arthur Weatherman left a message here for you to call him. He has something to discuss with you."

"Wonder what he wants?" Worried, Regan accepted the note with Arthur's telephone number.

Darcy gave her an encouraging smile. "He sounded very upbeat. Bet it's something good."

Fighting nerves, Regan went into the office and placed the call. In the back of her mind, she still couldn't believe the Weathermans wanted her to be spokesperson for them.

When her call was finally transferred to Arthur, he answered with a cheery, "Hello."

"This is Regan Sullivan. You called?"

"Yes, Margretta and I decided we want to introduce you as our spokesperson before the New Year. We wonder if you would do an ad campaign for us for Christmas and the New Year. We're looking for a child to help with the ad for Christmas."

An image of Emily, a little girl whom she'd met in the plastic surgeon's office, appeared in Regan's mind. "I have the perfect candidate for you. Emily Gregg is a little girl around four years old whom I met at the doctor's office. Her face was being treated for several small burn areas. She and her mother call her scars, her 'stars.' She's full of life and personality, and she has a killer smile. I think she'd make a darling Christmas angel."

Arthur chuckled softly. "I knew we were right to hire you. How do I get in touch with her?'

"Through Dr. Milford's office. And, Arthur, from my first impression of them, I think they could use the money."

"Perfect. I'll call you back with the dates and times for filming." He hung up.

Regan smiled as she disconnected the call. Maybe this whole business of being spokesperson for Florida's Finest Restaurants would be a good way to help kids in more ways than one.

CHAPTER SIX

SHEENA

Sheena was alone in the kitchen when Michael burst into the room. She looked at his flushed face and set down the spoon she'd been using to stir the sauce she'd just made.

"What is it, Michael?"

He plopped down into a kitchen chair and looked at her with tears in his eyes. "It's Kaylee."

Sheena's blood froze in her veins. "What happened?"

"She lost the baby. Now she doesn't want anything to do with me, and she's telling everyone I'm a pig who took advantage of her." Tears spilled down his cheeks, sliding past the growth of whiskers emerging on his face. "I didn't, Mom. It's almost like she's telling everyone I raped her, and I didn't. I didn't!"

Sheena went to him and placed a steadying hand on his shoulder. "I believe you, son. And I think people who know both you and Kaylee will believe you too. Have you tried talking to her about it?"

He shook his head. "No, but I talked to the coach, and he's working with the guidance counselor to put a stop to it. He believes me too."

Emitting a sigh, Sheena sank down into a kitchen chair opposite him. "I'm so sorry this has happened, Michael. How do you feel about the baby?"

He lifted his shoulders and let them drop. "I dunno. Relieved, I guess. But, it's sad too, you know?"

"Let's find a professional you can talk to. This is a big deal, Michael. It's best to handle this now, so the future isn't a problem for you." Sheena held her breath, expecting Michael to blow up at her, but he simply nodded.

Relieved, she got to her feet. "How about something to eat? Would that help?"

He shook his head. "Maybe later. I'm going to run on the beach."

After he went into his bedroom to change, Sheena went to her computer and looked up the number of someone who could help Michael. She, herself, was feeling sick about the situation.

A few days later, Sheena sat in her kitchen, sipping coffee. She intended to use the morning to do a little Christmas shopping. Their budget was tight, but lots of sales were going on, and she wanted to take advantage of having Tony and the kids away from the suite. She made a list of ideas and was about to head out to the mall when she let out a long sigh. Maybe, she thought, I'll just rest a minute. Every bone in her body felt as if it weighed a ton.

Stretched out on the bed, she realized how tense she'd been about getting the restaurant opened. Between Tony's new commitments and her own with the hotel, there were times when she felt trapped by all that was happening to her. More than her sisters, she would feel responsible if they weren't able to meet the challenge and ended up with the debt from the restaurant. She gritted her teeth. Failure was not an option. Failure would mean hurting her kids and the rest of her family.

###

Sheena awoke to someone shaking her.

"Hey! I thought you were going shopping." Darcy looked down at her with concern. "Are you feeling all right?"

Sheena sat up and rubbed her eyes. "What time is it?"

"Two o'clock."

"Damn! I guess I was more tired than I'd realized. I'll have to go shopping tomorrow if you and Regan will give me some time off." She rolled to her side and placed her feet on the floor, still feeling groggy.

"Sure, we'll work something out," said Darcy, giving her another look of concern.

Sheena waved her hand in dismissal. "Don't worry about me. I'm fine. Just a little stressed."

"Aren't we all," said Darcy. "I was talking to Nicole about our ad campaign, and she reminded me it takes a while to build a business. So, I hope you don't mind. I sent in an ad to run in a special, holiday bridal section of the *Tampa Tribune*. I know we're watching our money, but I think it might be worth it."

"Let's hope so," said Sheena rising to her feet. "Let's go check on Gavin's. There's a big holiday party scheduled for tonight."

They walked outside and headed for the restaurant.

"Hey! Wait up for me!" said Regan running over to them. She smiled at Sheena. "How'd the Christmas shopping go?"

"It didn't." Sheena shook her head. "I lay down for a few minutes and fell asleep. Guess I've been more stressed out than I'd realized. I'll have to try again tomorrow."

Regan gave her an understanding look. "Yeah, these last few weeks are going to be the toughest, not knowing whether we're going to make it or not."

The three of them entered Gavin's.

Sheena gazed around at the holiday decorations and felt

better. Against the backdrop of rich wood, the simple holiday decorations gave her a renewed sense of hope. They and their guests would celebrate this holiday and many others here.

She followed her sisters up the stairs to the function room. A client of Mo's was hosting a cocktail reception for his one hundred or so employees. Standing at the entrance to the room, Sheena admired its versatility. She hoped they could get some publicity out of this party by having a staff member offer to take photographs. She'd already thought of giving discounts to brides who allowed the Salty Key Inn to use photographs and other mementos of their weddings as promotional material.

Casey joined them. "We're all set for tonight. I was able to hire a couple of extra people for this event. I know that brings your margins down, but we have to make an excellent impression with service above and beyond the norm."

"The pricing should accommodate that issue. How's the kitchen going?"

Casey's brow furrowed. "It's going to take some time for Graham to get accustomed to his larger staff. He's used to doing most everything himself. But it's all good. His sous-chef understands and is helping. And Graham's such a likable guy I'm sure it'll work out."

"Whatever he's making smells delicious," said Darcy. "I think I'll meander down there."

Casey held up a hand to stop her. "I wouldn't if I were you. Like I said, it's pretty tense right now."

"Well, then, let's go to Gracie's," said Regan. "I could use a cup of coffee. I told Sally I'd be back to close up at six, and I could use an extra jolt of caffeine." Gracie's, the informal restaurant at the entrance to the property, served breakfast and lunch and had a large, loyal following for a very good reason—Gracie was a fabulous cook.

"Okay," said Sheena. "A quick cup of coffee sounds good." Sally, one of Gavin's people, was happy to help out in the office anytime, but they didn't want to take advantage of her good nature.

Sitting in Gracie's, Sheena took a sip of her coffee and set the cup down. Her stomach was protesting the acid in the java.

"What's the matter?" Regan asked her.

"I think I've caught the bug Meaghan had the other day. I swear she catches everything that comes along and then passes it on to me. The timing couldn't be worse."

Darcy placed a hand on her shoulder. "You've got to stop worrying so much. We've come this far. We'll make it."

Sheena couldn't stop the frustration she felt building inside. "Even if we don't make it, you've got plans moving forward—a lovely wedding, writing your book, a new life with Austin." She turned to Regan and snapped, "You too! You've got your new life with Brian and working with Mo. What do I have? Nothing if I can't continue working at the hotel."

Regan's eyes widened. "Wow! I didn't know you felt that way."

"Me too," said Darcy. "I understand you're the one who wants to continue overseeing the hotel, and I'll help in any way I can. But I want to get on with my life."

Sheena blinked rapidly to quell the sting of tears in her eyes. "Sorry. I don't know why I'm so riled up about it, but the thought of going back to the way it was before, catering to teenage children who will soon leave home is pretty upsetting."

Regan clasped her hand. "Listen, Sheena; we'll do everything we can to succeed. And then you can take it from there with support from Darcy and me. Right, Darcy?"

"Damn straight," Darcy said, giving her an encouraging smile.

A short time later, they left Gracie's, and Sheena went back to her suite. Alone, she perused some online shopping sites and then started preparations for dinner. Tony was usually hungry when he came home, and the kids liked to eat early too. It cut into her day but gave her time in the evenings to go over figures for both the hotel and Gavin's.

Later, folding laundry while her children did homework, Sheena wondered why she'd been so sad earlier about the idea of her children leaving home. With them gone, she and Tony would have the opportunity to travel, to eat anytime they wanted, to make love.

She was still smiling when Tony came into their bedroom.

"What'cha doing?" He came over to her and wrapped his arms around her. "Almost time for bed," he whispered in her ear.

She turned to face him. "Love you, Tony, but tonight isn't happening."

He rubbed his palms up and down her back in soothing strokes. "Darcy told me she's worried about you. I don't want you to wear yourself down over the hotel. Things will work out. They always do."

"I know," she murmured. "Just a few more weeks until we know, and then I'll relax."

CHAPTER SEVEN

DARCY

Darcy sat in the office studying the screen of her computer with a frown. How did one go about submitting a proposal to a publisher? She'd done a little investigation online, but every source gave different advice. Some said to be friendly; others said it should be strictly business. She could talk about her newspaper experience, but then it would be discovered she was with the newspaper for only a few months. Not good.

Unsure what to do, but eager to get a letter out, Darcy was resigned to simply doing her best. She began typing a brief letter explaining she'd come to believe in angels and wanted to write about them. She briefly described one of the stories—one about a single grandmother taking on the task of raising her grandchildren—and asked for a quick response so she could surprise her fiancé for the holiday. She included her phone number, so the editor could easily call her with an offer and sent off the letter.

Once she'd mailed the letter, Darcy went from feeling confident to desperately foolish. At any rate, she told herself, she'd hear soon—one way or another. Telling Austin and his parents and grandfather about her success would be a dream come true. She'd met his parents once, shortly after the engagement, but there'd been little time to make a real connection before they were off traveling again.

Though it was only the 20th of December, Austin's parents

were in town to celebrate Christmas with Austin, his grandfather, and her before leading a very special group to England for the actual Christmas holiday. It seemed strange to Darcy for them not to share Christmas with their son, but Austin was used to it. In fact, he often traveled with them for the holidays. But, with her commitment to the hotel and with the start of his new job, he was staying put in Florida.

She opened the box holding the present she'd purchased for his parents and studied the small, leather-bound, double picture frame. She hoped they'd like it. After listening to them talk about their home in New York and hearing about their travels, she'd found it difficult to think of anything they might want or not already have.

She unrolled the wrapping paper and set to work dressing up the package.

Regan walked into the office. "Wrapping gifts?"

"Yes, it's already Christmas in Blakely Land," said Darcy.

"Better get used to doing things differently," Regan said, laughing.

Darcy smiled. "Actually, it's pretty exciting. Two days to celebrate instead of just one."

Regan sat in the chair near her. "I've got to find a gift for Holly. It's strange to think of her as my mother-in-law when we've been friends of sorts."

"That should make it easy," said Darcy. "Austin's mother is very nice, but a little distant. I'm not sure how to take her. His father is easy to get to know."

"Mothers and sons have special relationships," said Regan. "I'm finding that out. Holly wants me to do things for Brian exactly as she would do them. You know?"

Darcy clucked her tongue. "That can't be easy, but I guess it's all part of getting to know one another and setting up our own routines. Sheena and Rosa have worked out a nice mother-in-law relationship. We can too."

"You're right. In the meantime, what do I get Holly?"

Darcy waggled a finger at her. "That, my dear sister, is your problem, not mine."

"You're no help," Regan pouted, getting up and leaving the office.

Darcy watched her go and turned back to her wrapping. She hadn't told Regan, but she was nervous about the party that evening. As a nice gesture to her and her sisters, Austin's parents had arranged to have dinner at Gavin's before returning to his grandfather's house to open gifts.

That evening, Darcy sat with Austin and his family at a secluded corner table in Gavin's, seeing the restaurant from a guest's point of view. She thought of Sheena's worries and made a mental note to tell her how great the restaurant was.

"So, you two, have you decided on all your stops on your whirlwind wedding trip?" Austin's mother, Belinda, smiled at Darcy. A pretty woman with fine features and carefully coiffed dark hair, Belinda was a bit intimidating.

Darcy turned to Austin and waited for him to speak. "Since Darcy hasn't been to Europe before, we want to hit the high spots—Paris, London, Madrid, Rome and other major areas."

Belinda frowned. "But you won't have the chance to spend time anywhere but in big cities. Don't you want an idyllic time somewhere in the country, such as Provence or Tuscany?"

"Mom, we'll go back to Europe again and again because Darcy likes to travel. But for now, she'll get a good idea of the more popular places. Besides, it's our honeymoon. We're probably not going to spend all our time sightseeing."

Belinda's mouth formed an O, which she quickly covered with her hand. "Oh, my! Of course. Forgive me." She turned to Darcy. “As Austin says, a trip like that will give you an overview of the places you might like to visit in the future.”

Darcy took a sip of her ice water hoping to cool the heat in her cheeks caused by the mention of the honeymoon.

“I think it’s a very sensible thing to do. You guys are young and curious and don’t need to spend the whole time in one place,” said Austin’s father, Charles. Tall, gray-haired, and gentle, his manner was a nice contrast to his wife’s intensity.

Darcy gave him a smile of gratitude.

Casey came over to their table. “How is everything here?” he asked Charles.

Charles looked around the table and said, “Everything is fine. My compliments to the chef. My steak was done to perfection.”

“And the sea bass was divine,” Belinda added. “I think we could use another bottle of wine. We have much to celebrate.”

“I’ll send the wine steward right over,” Casey said, giving her a little bow.

“Nice service,” said Charles.

Darcy caught the wink Austin’s grandfather, Bill, gave her and smiled. His story was one of the first she’d written, and she still thought of him as one of her special angels.

At Bill’s house, the five of them gathered around the Christmas tree with after-dinner drinks. Darcy sipped her white crème de menthe, comfortably full from her dinner.

Bill raised his glass. “I’d like to toast Margery. She’s been gone only a few months, but it seems like forever to me. I miss her.” He turned to Austin and Darcy sitting on the couch. “She’d be happy to know Austin and Darcy are together. I wish you both the very best on this the first of many Christmases together.”

"Hear! Hear! To Mom!" said Charles, blinking back tears. "She was the best."

Belinda, Austin, and Darcy raised their glasses together.

"Okay," said Bill after they'd settled down. "Age before beauty. I get to hand out my gifts first."

He handed a small package to Darcy. "Merry Christmas from Margery and me. Go on, open it," he urged with a smile.

Her fingers trembling, Darcy unwrapped the red foil paper and lifted the cover off the box. Tears filled her eyes. A lovely pair of Mikimoto pearl earrings lay on a bed of black velvet.

Bill smiled at her. "I brought those back from Japan on my way home from 'Nam. They were a favorite of Margery's."

"Thank you so much," said Darcy, touched by the gesture. "I will treasure them always."

"Not to be outdone, we have a gift for you too, Darcy," said Belinda, handing over a small box wrapped in silver.

Darcy clapped a hand on her chest. "I'm not used to such ... shiny gifts."

Amid the chuckles that followed, Austin said softly, "Open it, darling."

Lifting the paper off, Darcy stared at the label on the lid. *Tiffany*. She opened it, and a velvet box fell out. When she lifted the lid, her breath caught. Two diamond solitaire earrings winked up at her.

"Oh, my! Now I really don't know what to say. Thank you all so much! I've never had a Christmas like this," she said honestly.

"Diamonds and sentimental gifts are the best," said Belinda kindly.

Darcy swallowed hard. Her gifts seemed so small, so insignificant.

Other gifts were opened, and then Darcy said, "I have gifts too."

She handed Belinda the picture frame. "I hope you like it."

Darcy held her breath as Belinda opened the comparatively plain package. When she lifted out the frame and saw what it was, a smile crinkled the corners of her eyes. "How nice. A perfect gift from a lovely daughter-in-law."

A sigh of relief escaped Darcy. She hoped it meant she and Austin's mother would be all right. Her former boyfriend's parents had made it clear neither she nor her family measured up to their standards.

Bill appeared to like the books she'd chosen for him, along with the gift card to Gracie's. "Lynn and the others there are anxious to see you again," said Darcy.

"Lynn? Who's that?" asked Belinda, giving her father-in-law a curious smile.

"The widow of an old friend. We talk sometimes when I go to the restaurant." Bill said. "Just someone to talk to."

"Okay, I guess my gift is the last one," said Austin. "I'll be right back."

He returned carrying a wooden carving. Placing it in front of Darcy, he grinned at her. "I can't wait until we're married and actually living together. Love you, Darcy."

As she studied the carved-wooden figure, tears once more filled her eyes. The detail was stunning—a child, sitting in the grass, holding up a hand on which a butterfly perched.

"Is it a boy or a girl?" Belinda asked, leaning forward for a closer look.

"Neither and both," Austin said. "A symbol of the children we hope to have one day."

Darcy hugged the gift to her. "It's gorgeous, Austin. I think you might be wasting your time with dentistry. This is a real artist's work."

"Hold on," said Charles. "You can't raise a family on wood carvings."

Darcy started to reply and quickly stopped. Austin's parents were practical people. Why else would they exchange a holiday at home for a lucrative business trip?

"The carving is beautiful, Austin," said Bill. "Can't wait to see the real children you and Darcy will produce."

"Yes," Belinda said, smiling at Darcy. "I wanted more children, but that didn't happen for us. Hopefully, you and Austin will give us lots of grandchildren."

Darcy exchanged smiles with Austin, but inside her stomach twisted. Would she be a good mother like she hoped? Even then, would it be good enough for Austin's family?

Austin took hold of her hand and gave it a comforting squeeze, and the fear that had gripped her faded. She knew Austin would make a great father. She'd just have to try her best.

CHAPTER EIGHT

REGAN

Regan waited at the pool gate for Brian to reach her. He was making progress on his ability to walk using a cane. His right elbow was no longer in a cast or sling. His left arm would be free of a cast in a couple of days. That was the good news. The bad news was neither arm would be able to hold a lot of weight for some time, which meant he was limited to directing his crew and doing paperwork.

"Okay, let's get on with it," grumbled Brian as he approached her.

Regan smiled. "C'mon! I'll race you to the end of the pool and back."

His lips curved. "We'll see."

On this December evening, no guests were using the pool. Regan slipped the towel off her shoulders onto a chaise lounge and eased into the heated pool water. Without waiting for Brian, she began swimming laps.

In the pool, he caught her in his arms and pulled her close enough to feel his arousal. He grinned at her. "Hey, mermaid! Haven't we met before?"

She laughed and nestled up against his strong chest. She loved that they could play games like this.

They went to work beginning the exercises Brian's doctor had given him. He did them without complaint and was able each day to do them for longer periods. His dedication, Regan knew, was driven by his frustration at not being able to work at his job as he wanted.

Still puffing from the exertion, she sat next to Brian on the pool steps. Brian wrapped an arm around her shoulder.

"Thank you." He lowered his lips to hers.

She responded to his touch, filling with desire.

His kiss deepened.

When he finally pulled away, he looked at her with such love, Regan's breath caught. There were still times she couldn't believe, of all the women he could have chosen, he'd chosen her.

"I don't want to wait to get married," Brian said. "Why don't we elope?"

Regan took hold of his hand. "I wish we *could* run away and get married. I know most women want a big, fancy wedding, but, as long as I have you, I honestly don't care about it."

His smile lit his brown eyes, and he hugged her to him. "That's my girl."

She smiled happily and then pulled away, suddenly serious. "As much as I want to elope with you, I can't do anything to destroy Darcy's wedding. If we get married before Darcy and Austin, she'll be furious at me for upstaging her."

Brian studied her and sighed. "I guess you're right. We'll have to wait. Besides, my mother would be disappointed if we eloped."

Later, lying in bed next to him, Regan thought about the conversation and wished there was a way to make a secret wedding happen without hurting anyone's feelings.

CHAPTER NINE

SHEENA

Feeling better a few days later, Sheena headed out to do some Christmas shopping. It still seemed odd to her to be doing this when the temperature was in the low 70s, and decorated trees for the holidays were palms whose trunks were wrapped with lights. But after learning Boston was struggling with an ice storm, she loved the idea of a tropical holiday.

As they did for Thanksgiving, the family was going to celebrate Christmas dinner at Gracie's. Gavin's was booked, and dining at Gracie's meant Gavin's people would be included as family. She and her sisters had decided to give each member of Gavin's group a gift bag filled with little presents, sweet treats, and a very nice gift card. Getting into the excitement of the season, Meaghan had even offered to handmake a Christmas card for each one.

It wasn't difficult to decide on what to get her family. Having hastily discarded most of their winter clothes, they needed replacements more suited to their new location. As Sheena worked her way through department stores, she decided to pick up a few things for herself—something for the Florida winter.

After seeing the clothes in stores catering to young women like Meaghan, the styles and selections Sheena looked at for herself seemed staid. She tried on several pairs of pants and wondered who would buy them. They were much too small for her, designed, no doubt, for the woman who dieted constantly. Scrutinizing herself in the mirror, Sheena vowed to cut back on Gracie's good cooking. Gavin's food was another challenge she'd have to learn to control.

By the time Sheena had found enough practical and fun stuff for her family, she was anxious to get back to the hotel. She needed to relax for a while before closing out the registration office for Regan, who was meeting Brian and Holly for dinner.

Back in her suite at the hotel, Sheena hid the packages she'd purchased and made herself a cup of coffee. Lunch had been a protein snack bar, and she needed a jolt of caffeine. Instead of giving her much-needed energy, the coffee upset her system. Sheena rubbed her stomach, wondering if she had an ulcer. No matter what it was, she vowed, she'd say nothing to anyone until after the holidays and the meeting with Archibald Wilson. Thinking of her upcoming trip to Boston, she picked up the phone and called her old doctor there for an appointment.

CHAPTER TEN

REGAN

Regan checked herself in the mirror and sighed. It had been a long day working with Mo on Kenton's house, and she was exhausted. That and a case of nerves made her wish she could postpone the dinner with Brian and his mother. Holly Harwood had always been warm and pleasant to her sisters and her, but Regan detected a certain wariness in her behavior lately. Brian told her it was nothing, but Regan wasn't so sure. Something was going on. She hoped Holly didn't have second thoughts about Brian's and her engagement.

She pinned a sparkly, gold Christmas tree onto her long-sleeved black dress and patted it with satisfaction.

At a knock on her bedroom door, Regan called out, "Coming."

She stepped out to the living room to find Darcy and Brian in quiet conversation.

"What's going on?" Regan asked, glancing at the guilty expressions on their faces.

A corner of Darcy's mouth turned up impishly. "Christmas."

"Yeah, Darcy's giving me a few gift ideas for you," said Brian, winking at her. "C'mon, let's go meet my Mom." He held out an arm, and Regan took it to give him support.

"Where are we going?" she asked as they left the suite.

"Not far." Brian's appreciative gaze warmed Regan's

cheeks. "We decided on Gavin's."

Regan gave him a lop-sided grin. "Perfect. We won't have to drive anywhere."

When they entered Gavin's, Nicole, acting as hostess, greeted them with a smile. "I believe your dinner partners are here already."

Brian and Regan glanced at one another with surprise.

"My mother brought someone?" Brian asked, his voice rising.

Nicole merely smiled and led them through the dining room to an alcove overlooking a small, private garden.

Regan stopped in surprise when she saw Blackie Gatto seated beside Holly.

"Hello, Mother, Blackie," said Brian crisply.

Holly smiled at them. "I thought I'd bring a date for such a nice occasion as this."

Blackie got to his feet, shook hands with Brian, and waited until Regan was seated before sitting down again.

He gave Brian a steady look. "Your mother and I have been seeing one another for a while, and we thought it was time to share that with you."

Regan was as surprised as Brian appeared to be.

Holly gave Blackie a smile that could only be called intimate. "Blackie has been an enormous moral support to me while you've been recovering from the accident, and the two of you have been making plans of your own."

Blackie covered one of Holly's hands with his own. "It's been nice. Really nice."

Brian sat back in his chair and let out a puff of surprise. "Guess more changes are in store, huh?"

"I know how close you and your mother are, Brian," said Blackie. "That's why I didn't want to wait any longer for you to know what's going on. You've been the man of the house, so to speak, for most of your life."

"Yes, I have," said Brian quietly.

Regan knew him well enough to understand it would take time for Brian to relinquish that role and thought Blackie was very clever to bring it up so early in the relationship. From the way Holly and Blackie were gazing at each other, this was serious.

"This calls for a celebration," Regan said, nudging Brian's leg.

He perked up. "Yes, we all have something to celebrate this year."

Blackie grinned. "I've already ordered champagne if you don't mind."

Right on cue, the wine steward approached the table with a silver ice bucket that held a dark-green bottle. A waiter brought four tulip glasses to the table and placed one at each setting.

The wine steward showed Blackie the bottle, and at his nod of approval, opened it. He poured a small bit into a glass for Blackie to taste, and then, after Blackie nodded his approval, he poured some into each guest's glass.

"Here's to a wonderful holiday for these two lovely women," said Blackie, nodding at Regan, and smiling at Holly.

"Here's to all of us," Holly quickly chimed in.

They clinked glasses together before taking sips of the bubbly liquid, and a momentary quiet settled at the table.

"So, you say you started dating in September?" Brian asked.

Regan knew by his challenging tone Brian was hurt by being left out and hastened to add, "It's so nice you're able to share the holiday together."

"Yes," said Blackie. "Holidays can be pretty lonely, even with my brother, Rocky, around."

Regan studied him, seeing him in a new way. With his dark, curly hair edged in gray, strong features, and self-assurance, she'd never thought he might be lonely. At the opening party at Gavin's, he'd been surrounded by women eager to talk to him. And as Gavin's financial manager and now theirs, he was a successful businessman.

Holly and Brian shared a lot of the same looks with sandy-brown hair and brown eyes, and each had a likable personality one couldn't ignore. Studying her surreptitiously, Regan figured Holly was not much over fifty, though she looked more like forty—a well put-together forty.

"Rocky used to scare my sister Darcy," said Regan. "But we've all learned his tough looks hide a kind heart."

Blackie laughed. "My brother likes to play the tough guy, but, as you said, he's a good man. He's a total pushover for people and animals who are suffering."

"We sometimes wish he wasn't so kind. He's the one who brought Petey to the hotel. Although guests seem to like having that peacock around when he's behaving, he can be a real nuisance."

Holly laughed. "He's even chased me a few times. How about you, Blackie?"

"What's everyone going to have to eat?" interjected Brian, looking up from his menu. "Looks like Graham's been busy with some creative items for the holiday."

"I'm thinking of apple-stuffed pork loin," said Holly, giving him a long look.

"Sorry, did I interrupt anything?" Brian asked.

Well aware of the tension between the two men, Regan took a last sip of her champagne and picked up her menu.

"I was here for dinner with a couple of clients last night," said Blackie. "The glazed sea bass with ginger-butter cream sauce was superb."

"Thank you for bringing your clients to Gavin's," said Regan. "I know you like the Key Pelican restaurant."

Blackie smiled. "Gavin's is going to give them a run for their money. Great to finally have a choice between the two."

"Guess I'll try the sea bass," said Brian, nodding an acknowledgment to Blackie.

Holly smiled, and the four of them settled down in a more comfortable atmosphere.

Later, Regan and Brian stood by while a valet brought Blackie's bottle-green Jaguar to him.

"Want me to walk you home?" Brian said to Holly.

She smiled and shook her head. "Thanks, but Blackie will drive me."

After Blackie and Holly took off, Brian turned to Regan. "Wow! It seems serious between the two of them. You'd think Blackie would have talked to me about it earlier."

Regan took his arm and gave him a teasing smile. "You're Holly's son, not her father. What in the world will you be like if we have any daughters?"

Brian laughed. "God! I guess I'm going to be awful. It's just that I would've thought Mom would have said something to me. You know how responsible I feel for her."

"Yes, I do," said Regan. "It's very sweet, but things are moving in a different direction. I guess we'd both better get used to it."

"You're right," said Brian. "Let's go practice making a daughter so I can do my fierce father thing."

Even as Regan laughed, she felt a thread of sexual excitement move through her.

But as they walked away from Gavin's, instead of heading toward the Sandpiper Suites Building, Brian led Regan to the bank of the nearby bay.

"It's such a pleasant evening; I thought we could sit for a minute."

"Are you going to propose to me again?" Regan teased. This was the spot where she thought Brian was going to break up with her. Instead, he'd gone down on one knee to ask her to marry him.

Brian burst into laughter. "Not quite. Once is nerve-wracking enough." He sat on a wooden bench they'd placed under a palm tree and patted the space next to him.

Regan sat beside him and leaned into his open arms.

The night was clear but cool. Brian slipped off his sport coat and put it over her shoulders.

Regan smiled at him and gazed out over the bay. Moonlight painted the moving water with golden light, creating an ever-changing mural. She sighed with contentment.

Brian kissed her on the cheek. "I want to talk with you about what is going to happen to us after the first of the year and the end of your challenge. Even if you win Gavin's challenge, I don't want to live here at the hotel. And I definitely don't want to go back to my apartment above the bar if Blackie is going to be hanging around."

"How would you feel about living in a guest house on a seaside estate? Kenton Standish has a beautiful cottage next to his house just down the road. By staying on the property, we'd be helping him out when he's gone, and yet we'd have all the privacy we'd want, even when he's there."

Brian gave her a thoughtful look. "We can build our own house in the same neighborhood as Tony and Sheena, but that can't happen for a while. I've put my money into buying the land. What do you think? Does that sound good?"

"I'd rather start off at Kenton's and then build a house. That will give us some good time alone. In the suites, we're all part of the family, which doesn't give us much privacy. And, Brian, we have to talk about a wedding. That will help us decide."

"I don't give a hoot about a fancy wedding, but I don't want to take anything away from you. You seem pretty excited about Darcy's wedding. Do you want one like it? Something bigger?"

Regan shook her head. "I don't want a big wedding at all. Just you and me and the preacher," she said. "I've waited a long time to find the right guy. I don't want to lose you."

"You won't," he murmured before pressing his lips to her, proving he wasn't about to go anywhere.

CHAPTER ELEVEN

SHEENA

Christmas Day was gray and rainy. But instead of disappointing her, the weather reminded Sheena it really was winter, and though it wasn't snow, the rain provided a memory of other Christmases in the past.

As was their pattern, Sheena would fix breakfast for the family before they all were to sit down beside the tree and open gifts. This year, the tree was a bit scrawny, but they didn't have room for a big one. She hoped when she got a house of her own, there'd be plenty of room for a tall, full tree.

While Meaghan and Michael slept and Tony showered, Sheena got out eggs and bacon and some English muffins. Though the hot coffee she'd fixed was unsettled in her stomach, she opted for another cup for the jolt of energy she sought.

A soft knock on the door caught her attention. She went to answer it. Regan and Darcy, still in pajamas, smiled at her. "Merry Christmas!"

She gave them each a hug. "Come on in. I've got coffee ready."

They eagerly accepted the cups of hot liquid she offered them.

"It's nice to be together so early Christmas morning. Usually I didn't get to see you until later in the day when Mom had dinner for all of us," Regan said to her."

Sheena smiled at Regan with affection.

"I like having you and Darcy around," said Regan. "And Rosa and Paul are coming to Gracie's for Christmas dinner, aren't they?"

"They can't wait!" said Sheena, smiling. "Having my in-laws living here in Florida has been very satisfying for us. What are you and Brian going to do with Holly?"

Regan gave her a sly smile. "With Holly *and* Blackie?"

Sheena couldn't help chuckling. She and her sisters were still surprised by the hot romance that had emerged between Holly and Blackie.

"Blackie has invited us to his house for lunch. Apparently, he's a good cook and wants to show off his skills. Brian is still reconciling himself to a future like this, but I think it will be fun."

Sheena and Darcy exchanged amused glances. Brian was very protective of his mother.

"Austin's grandfather is looking forward to dinner at Gracie's," said Darcy. "He and Lynn have become reacquainted. It's nothing serious, but it's a sweet friendship. He's lonely."

Tony emerged from the bedroom. "Well, if it isn't the Sullivan sisters! Merry Christmas—our first together in Florida." He kissed Sheena on the cheek, filled a cup with coffee, and turned to Darcy and Regan. "Did Santa Claus come to your suite?"

Darcy pointed to her ears. Diamonds were sparkling on her earlobes. "He came a couple of days ago. But I've got great news for all of us. Cyndi Jansen sent me a text last night. She and Tom are hosting a group of eight couples at Gavin's on New Year's Eve. They've signed up for the early dinner, and seven of the couples have made reservations for hotel rooms. If I'm not mistaken, that leaves only two rooms open for that night."

Sheena clutched her hands together. “That’s the best Christmas present ever! I wanted to be able to give Archie some proof we were growing. This helps a lot.”

“How are the other dinner reservations at Gavin’s filling up for New Year’s Eve?” asked Regan.

A smile spread across Darcy’s face. “Nicole and I had drinks together before she started her shift last night. She says reservations are slowly coming in. The ad we put in the paper is paying off. That and discounted hotel rooms as an option.”

Some of the tension that had become part of Sheena’s life ebbed away. Maybe all this worry was as foolish as she sometimes thought. They would or would not beat the challenge.

“Is it time to get the kids up?” Tony asked.

Sheena laughed. “Go ahead.” Tony was more excited about Christmas than their teenage kids, who were sleeping in.

“Guess I’d better go.” Regan gave Sheena a hug. “See you later.”

“Me too,” said Darcy. “Merry Christmas, Sheena. Enjoy the day without worrying about the hotel. You look tired.”

Sheena gave her a weak smile. “Thanks, I guess.” Though it had kept her awake at night, she hadn’t mentioned her doctor’s appointment to anyone else, not even Tony.

Later, as she sat with Tony and the kids around the Christmas tree, Sheena watched Michael and Meaghan open their gifts. Both she and Tony had explained there would be no fancy gifts; their money was tied up in the hotel and Brian and Tony’s business. Sheena and Tony had agreed not to exchange gifts, but Sheena had wrapped underwear, socks, and a couple of T-shirts for Tony just for fun.

Michael and Meaghan’s enthusiasm as they opened each

practical gift filled Sheena's heart with pride. Gone were the entitled children of Boston. Here were kids with a growing understanding of what life was about—filled with challenges, disappointments, wonders, and love.

"That about does it," said Sheena when the last gift had been opened. "It's been a nice Christmas."

"Hold on. I have something for you," said Tony. He reached behind the tree and handed her a small box.

"Tony, we promised ..." Sheena began.

"Just open it," Tony prompted. "You'll see."

Sheena tore off the wrapping paper and opened the plain white box. When she saw what was inside, she gazed up at Tony with confusion.

"What is it, Mom?" asked Meaghan.

"It's a key," Sheena said, holding it up for everyone to see.

"It's a promise," said Tony, his face flushing with emotion. "It's both a key to my heart and a promise that someday soon you'll have the house you've always wanted."

Sheena's vision blurred with tears as she reached for Tony.

He came into her arms, and they hugged each other, laughing softly.

"It's perfect," Sheena said. "Thanks so much." She turned to her children. "Soon, we'll all have the house we want."

Meaghan's eyes grew wide. "Are you winning the challenge?"

"I hope so," said Sheena.

Still later, at Gracie's, Sheena watched Michael hand out gift bags to Gavin's people. Wearing a Santa hat and a big smile, he looked adorable. The therapist Michael had seen was a big help to him. An unexpected image of him as a father playing Santa to his children came to her mind. She blinked, and the moment passed. As Sheena studied him, she thought of how close she'd come to having an unexpected grandchild. For all of them, it was both a relief and a sadness that the baby had been lost.

She searched for her daughter. Dressed in a bright-red holiday sweater and black slacks, Meaghan was playing a game of cards with Maggie, who'd received a deck of cards in her gift bag. Sheena smiled. Coming to the Salty Key Inn had, in so many ways, been about finding family. Living at the hotel, working with Gavin's people, had brought them all closer together. Observing the various conversations around the room, the smiles on faces, Sheena thought Gavin would be very pleased.

Tony came up to her and gave her a loving hug. She gasped softly at the pain where his arm had squeezed her breast.

"Sorry. Are you all right?" Tony asked her, giving her a worried look.

"Fine," she lied, hiding her fear. Her mother had died of breast cancer, which was a strong reason for Sheena's doctor's appointment. Fatigue plus sore, lumpy breasts could mean she'd inherited more than red hair from her mother, a thought so frightening she felt sick just thinking of it. She didn't want to miss out on her children's growing years, seeing Meaghan wed, welcoming grandchildren into the world.

Tony continued to stay by her side. "Mom and Dad look wonderful— tanned, healthy, happy," he said unaware of the emotions she fought to hide. "The move to Florida has been good for them."

Sheena's smile was sincere. She loved her in-laws. "Nice also to have our own space."

Tony chuckled. "To think we shared that duplex for almost eighteen years." His smile lifted the corners of his eyes. "We're coming up on our twentieth anniversary in another year or so.

That will be something to celebrate."

Sheena smiled, but inside her stomach took a dive. Would she even be around for it?

CHAPTER TWELVE

DARCY

Darcy escorted Bill Blakely into Gracie's, pleased to have him a part of their Christmas celebration. He'd always supported her relationship with Austin, and, never having had living grandparents, she felt close to him in a way she'd never experienced.

Austin caught up with them inside and handed her a small bag with several envelopes inside. "You forgot these."

Darcy smiled her thanks and took the bag from him. She'd printed up wedding invitations for Gavin's people. As part of their marriage celebration, Austin was giving away a free dental visit to each member of the group.

"What'll you have? The usual?" Austin said to her.

She shook her head. "No margarita. Just a glass of red wine. Thanks."

Austin and Bill headed toward the corner of the closed restaurant where a little bar had been set up on a table.

Darcy moved through the crowd, stopping to give each person in Gavin's group a cheery Merry Christmas hug and two envelopes. When she was through handing them out, she gave a signal to Sheena.

Sheena tapped on a glass until the sound of it stilled conversation. "Darcy, Regan, and I each want to wish everyone a Merry Christmas and a Happy New Year. We have no idea what the future may bring, but this past year has shown us how awesome family—new and old—can be."

"Yes," said Darcy. Her grin was impish as she gazed around the room. "You get family discounts at a certain dental office." Even as laughter erupted, her expression became serious. "And, as family, everyone here is invited to my wedding on Valentine's Day."

Regan stepped forward from Brian's side. "We love you all."

Darcy took hold of Sheena's hand and reached for Regan's. As applause broke out, the three of them laughed and bowed together.

Gracie was the next to speak. "Before he died, Gavin spoke to us about his hopes for you girls and asked us to cooperate. None of us was sure how it would be having you here, but I think we all agree it has been better than we could've imagined. Gavin would be proud of you, my dears."

Darcy's eyes misted over. After interviewing them, she knew more about Gavin's people than others. They'd been shunned, abused, or blamed for things they either didn't do or couldn't avoid, but her uncle had accepted them as good people. She hoped she and her sisters would be able to ensure that they'd be taken care of in the future.

On a long table, Gracie and the crew set out a large ham, a cheesy-potato casserole, a green bean and almond vegetable dish, a tossed green salad, fresh rolls, and both a pecan and an apple pie. Along with the others, Darcy helped herself to food, relishing the idea of a large family meal. The laughter and companionship that accompanied the meal was, for her, the best gift of the day.

A couple of days later, Darcy was searching through the mail, hoping to find requests for brochures, or better yet, reservations, when she came upon the envelope she'd mailed to the small publisher. She stared with dismay at the red-stamped message: *Return to sender. Person unknown.* The name of the editor had been crossed out.

She immediately checked online for the editor's name and quickly discovered he'd changed jobs. Disappointment coursed through her. In doing her research, she'd thought he was her best chance of approval for her angel book. Maybe it was time to look for an agent. She was glad now she hadn't mentioned this to anyone.

When Regan came into the office, Darcy quickly closed her laptop computer.

"What'cha doing?" Regan asked, giving her a puzzled look.

"Trying to figure something out. How are things at the registration office?"

"Sheena just relieved me, but, Darcy, I'm worried about her. She's been awfully quiet the last few days. I know this business with Michael and his old girlfriend has been difficult, but she's not herself."

"I know. She can be a worrier. I've been telling her not to think about our meeting with Archibald. He seemed pretty impressed with Gavin's."

"Are you all set for New Year's Eve? I think Casey was right about our being hostesses for the evening," said Regan. "It's a good way to build business. Besides, we'll celebrate after the restaurant closes, so it will be fun."

"As long as we can all sleep in the next morning, I'm fine with it. I want to be well-rested for our trip to Boston. As soon as we find out what's going to happen with us and the hotel, I'm coming back to Florida and moving in with Austin. I'm tired of staying here all the time."

"Me too. I'm meeting with Mo and Kenton to see about renting the cottage on Kenton's estate."

"Really? How cool," said Darcy. "Does Sheena know?"

“No,” said Regan. “And don’t tell her. She’s feeling a little out of sorts about the future and what it holds for her.”

“Now that the kids don’t need her as much, she’s still trying to figure out her role. Lord help her if we don’t win the challenge. She’ll be an emotional mess.”

CHAPTER THIRTEEN

SHEENA

Sheena adjusted the flowy top she'd selected for the evening's event, pleased it was long enough over her black slacks to cover up her typical holiday weight gain. She reminded herself a New Year's resolution was in order but quickly decided tonight she wasn't going to worry about her looks. She was feeling a little better, and that was important to her. She'd soon be in Boston for both her doctor's appointment and the meeting with Archibald Wilson, and then the worries that had dogged her for weeks would be resolved.

"Ready to celebrate?" Tony said to her.

At her nod, he approached her, placed his hands on her shoulders, and planted a kiss on her cheek. "You look beautiful, Sheena. Like my bride. No one would ever believe you're thirty-seven."

Pleased, she kissed him back. "Thanks, hon. I'm feeling every one of my years, what with the hotel challenge and the scare we had with Michael."

"Where is Mike? I thought he wasn't going out tonight."

"He isn't. He's just dropping off Meaghan and a couple of her girlfriends at the movies, and then they're coming here to the hotel for a sleepover. Last minute plans. Hope you don't mind."

He shook his head. "I don't mind at all, as long as we know what they're up to. As for you, my darling, let's celebrate. It's been one hell of a year."

Sheena laughed. "I have a feeling this next one is going to be a doozy too."

They left the Sandpiper Suites Building and walked over to Gavin's. The restaurant glowed from each window, where white, battery-lit candles flickered. Outside, small white lights woven through the hibiscus bushes that lined the foundation of the building glittered like stars. To Sheena, they signified a bright beginning to another year at the Salty Key Inn.

Casey and Nicole greeted them at the door.

"Thanks for coming and helping us out," said Casey. "The second seating at the restaurant is underway. It should be a nice evening. By the way, people love the live piano music. Great idea."

"What do you want us to do?" Tony asked, adjusting the collar of his shirt. It was rare these days for him to wear a dress shirt, tie, and blazer.

"Earlier, at the first seating, Darcy and Regan greeted people individually, making sure guests had everything they needed and were aware of our upcoming Sunday brunch specials," said Nicole.

Casey smiled at them. "Tom and Cyndi Jansen and their party just left. Arthur and Margretta Weatherman and party have arrived and are seated in the private dining room upstairs. But there are a lot of new faces, and that is good."

Tony turned to her. "Guess we have our work cut out for us. I promised Brian I'd do my share in chatting up the business."

"You look very nice," said Nicole, giving them an encouraging smile. "Have fun! See you later!" She hurried away to greet the guests who were just arriving.

"Okay, let's go," said Sheena, looping her arm through Tony's.

They started upstairs to make sure the large group in the main room were well tended to with drinks, plenty of appetizers, and good service. A small band was playing music in a corner of the room, where a temporary dance floor had been set up. The group, mostly older couples, was fairly quiet, but Sheena was delighted to see so many people dancing.

After speaking to the two organizers of the group, Sheena and Tony entered the smaller dining room where Arthur and Margretta were entertaining.

When he noticed them, Arthur stood and came over to them. "Thank you so much for taking care of all the details for us. Margretta is very pleased with what you've done, and she likes things to be perfect."

"If either of you needs anything else, just let Casey know. We're here to make sure you have a lovely evening."

Arthur smiled at her. "Well done. I'm so impressed by all of you Sullivan sisters. Good luck in the year ahead."

Sheena smiled even as a wave of nausea swept through her. She'd know in a matter of days what that year would hold.

Downstairs once more, Sheena and Tony stopped at tables to greet guests and to extend wishes for a Happy New Year. Doing so gave Sheena an opportunity to observe service and to hear comments on everything from the food to the décor. All were positive. Glowing with success, Sheena and Tony sat at the bar. "What'll you have?" said the bartender, an older man whom Casey had brought into the operation.

"Champagne?" Tony asked her.

Sheena shook her head. "How about a ginger ale and lime?"

Tony grinned. "Okay, guess we've had enough fancy food and drinks. You have the ginger ale, and I'll have a draft beer."

Sheena chuckled. That was more like Tony.

###

Two days later, Sheena sat on a plane with her sisters, facing her future in not one way, but two. The hotel challenge was something that concerned both her sisters and her. The worry about her health was hers alone. Memories of her mother's final days fighting breast cancer flooded Sheena's mind. She hadn't been able to feel any specific lumps in her breasts, but that wasn't unusual. Dense breast tissue made it difficult. She continued staring out the window, lost in dread.

Sitting next to her, Darcy bumped her elbow. "You okay? You've been so quiet recently."

Sheena forced a smile. "I just have a lot on my mind."

"We all do. As soon as we find out the results of our year in Florida, I'm heading back there to move in with Austin. What are you going to do to celebrate?"

"I hope to be able to continue working at the hotel, making it bigger, better." Sheena shifted in her seat. "I've changed my flight plans. I'm staying an extra couple of days in Boston. I thought I'd check on Dad and maybe see a friend or two."

"Oh? But I thought you'd handle the registration desk for me while I make the move," said Darcy.

Sheena felt her cheeks grow warm. A snappish retort formed in her mind, but she silenced it.

Sensing her anger, Darcy placed a hand on her arm. "Sorry. Instead, I'll ask Sally to cover for me."

"That might be best."

Darcy regarded her with a steady look. "Are you sure you're all right?"

Sheena wanted to say no, tell her sisters all her worries, but she didn't want to spoil their excitement.

Darcy shrugged. "All right, then. I know how worried you are about the meeting with Archibald."

As Darcy picked up her book, Sheena let out a soft sigh. She'd just have to wait out the verdicts.

CHAPTER FOURTEEN

DARCY

Darcy leaned over Sheena's shoulder to look out the window at Massachusetts Bay below and downtown Boston in the distance as they approached Logan Airport. In the past, seeing the familiar landscape, she'd always felt she was coming home. Now, she was certain where her home lay—with Austin in Florida. Still, the skyline was appealing, showcasing the city that drew people in with its history and charm.

After a smooth landing and taxi to the gate, Darcy stood in the aisle of the airplane with Sheena and Regan, waiting to disembark.

"I'm going to drop my suitcase off at Archibald's office before I try to meet up with an old friend," said Darcy. "I'll see you back there at 4:30 PM for our meeting."

"Okay," said Sheena. "I'm dropping my luggage off at Dad's house. I'll meet you later at the law office."

Out in the waiting area, Regan said, "You both off to do your thing until our meeting with Archibald?"

"Yes, said Darcy. "What about you?"

Regan shrugged. "I'm not sure what I'll do, but don't worry about me. I'll find something to keep me busy. Are you sure you don't mind taking my backpack for me?"

"Not at all," said Darcy. "Give it to me, and I'll be on my way." Darcy slung Regan's backpack over her shoulder, grabbed the handle of her small, rolling suitcase, and hurried on her way. She hadn't told her sisters, but she'd made an appointment to see a special friend of hers, and she didn't want to be late.

After dropping her suitcase and Regan's backpack off at Archibald's office in International Place, Darcy pulled her coat closer and hurried down High Street to the Boston Harbor Hotel. She was meeting Allison Berkhardt, a friend from college who was now a literary agent, at the Rowe's Wharf Bar for a quick lunch and, she hoped, a deal. The disappointment of having her query letter to a publisher sent back unopened still ate at her insides.

Darcy entered the bar and gazed around the room, looking for Allison. A young woman Darcy barely recognized lifted a hand and waved to her. Darcy smiled and went to join Allison, surprised to see the shy, quiet, dark-haired woman she knew had become a brassy blonde whose dark-framed eyeglasses sparkled with fake diamonds.

"Sorry, I'm a few minutes late," said Darcy sliding into a chair opposite Allison at one of the small, square tables lining the wall.

"No, problem. You look terrific! I've been sipping my wine, wondering about you. I was surprised to hear you're living in Florida. How do you like it?"

Darcy smiled. "It's become home for me. My family is there, and my fiancé."

"Fiancé? How nice for you, Darcy." Allison gave her a warm smile. "I'm curious, though, as to why you wanted to meet with me. Don't tell me you've written a book."

Darcy felt heat rush to her cheeks. "It's not a novel, but a book of short stories about angels I've met."

Allison's brow furrowed. "Angels you met? Are you talking

about science fiction?"

Darcy shook her head and quieted as a waiter approached. He handed her a menu and asked what he could get for her.

Without looking at the menu, Darcy said, "I'll have a glass of the house sauvignon blanc and the oyster stew with cornbread."

He chuckled. "You've obviously been here before."

"Not for a while, but it's a perfect, blustery day for it."

"Guess you're not used to the cold anymore." Allison smiled up at the waiter. "I'll have a bowl of the oyster stew too. Thanks."

After the waiter left, Allison gave Darcy a steady look. "You're not the crazy type, Darcy, so tell me more about this book of yours."

"First of all, let me tell you about the hotel, our challenge, and the people living there." Her lips curved happily. "Do you have plenty of time?"

Allison chuckled. "For you, yes. You were one of the few people who went out of their way to be kind to me."

By the time Darcy was through with her discourse, their meal had come and gone, and they were each sipping a cup of coffee.

"So, you started at the newspaper. That's good. It gives you some credentials. But stories about other people can be pretty boring. Tell me about a couple of them."

Darcy searched her mind for one that stood out for her, and without further ado, launched into Bebe's story. Using just the name Bertha, she told of Bebe's pain of her abuse, her search for meaning in her life, and finally, how she'd found a family with others, baking special items with love. When she finished, Darcy dabbed at her eyes with a tissue, struggling to hold back the deeper emotions she felt all over again. She looked over at Allison and saw her struggling with tears too.

"Are all the stories this emotional, this brutally honest?".

"Yes. And they cover a whole range of topics—from sexual abuse to dealing with PTSD. But at the heart of each story is a person who does her or his best to cope."

Allison's brown eyes captured Darcy's blue ones and held on. "If you don't mind my being totally honest with you, I didn't know you had this depth of sensitivity to others. Yes, you've always been nice to me, but you hung out with Alex Townsend, and the only sensitivity she has is to herself. But what you're telling me about here, Darcy, is worthy of seeking publication."

Darcy grinned and clapped her hands together with a little cry of joy.

Allison held up her hand. "Don't get carried away by my words. It's a tough business, and because I liked your one story, it doesn't mean I'll like the whole book. But I'm willing to look at it. I know of a small press that might be interested. No promises, you understand."

"Oh, but ..."

Allison stopped her. "Before we do anything else, send me the entire manuscript. I'll take a look at it and get back to you. If I still feel strongly about it, I'll send you a contract. If not, we'll part as friends. Yes?"

Darcy nodded, though her mind rebelled at the thought of rejection.

"Pretend I'm your newspaper editor and send me the cleanest, best version of what you've written. We'll go from there."

Darcy couldn't help herself. She stood, went over to Allison, and wrapped her arms around her. "Thank you! Thank you!"

Allison laughed. "We'll see how it goes. By the way, how is Alex?"

Darcy's mouth spread into a grin so wide it hurt. "I have absolutely no idea. But Nicole Coleman is working for us at Gavin's, our new upscale restaurant. Away from Alex, she's doing very well."

Allison bobbed her head. "Glad to hear it."

As they left the hotel bar together, snowflakes began to drift lazily from the gray sky above them. Darcy threw her arm around Allison. "If my sisters and I win the challenge and are still at the hotel, do you want to take a warm break from this, no strings attached?"

Allison laughed. "I just might."

CHAPTER FIFTEEN

SHEENA

Hi, Dad! I'm here!" Sheena called as she entered her old family home in Dorchester. She set down her suitcase in the front hall and waited for an answer. When none came, she sighed with relief. She had just a few minutes to grab something to eat before heading out to her doctor's appointment. She swallowed nervously. The appointment was for an initial exam. Her doctor had said if any tests were needed, she'd schedule appointments for Sheena for tomorrow.

Sheena stood a moment gazing at the surroundings that had lost their familiarity with time and with Patrick's girlfriend, Regina's, touches. *Guess you can never really go home again*, she thought sadly, missing her mother. She walked into the kitchen and found a note on the table beside a plate of cookies. "Your father and I are shopping. Be back around four."

Picking up a cookie, Sheena smiled. Her mother had never had cookies in the house. No wonder her father liked Regina O'Brien. He loved sweets.

Sheena opened the refrigerator, got out a container of milk, and poured herself a glass of it feeling like a kid coming home from school. At the kitchen table, she sat thinking of the appointments that lay ahead of her. She tried to tell herself not to worry, life had a crazy way of turning out all right, but she'd worked too hard at the hotel to be told she'd failed. And cancer? No one deserved it. She hoped, by some miracle, she'd escaped it. She'd always tried to eat well, stay healthy.

Sheena checked her watch and rose. She wanted extra time to catch the T to the Longwood Medical Area, knowing she'd have to change from the Red Line to the Green Line at Park Street.

Sheena stepped off the streetcar and walked along Longwood Avenue toward the medical building where her doctor practiced. With the bustle of traffic and people around her, she was reminded how small the town and how simple her life appeared to be in Florida. She wrapped her scarf tighter around her neck and braved the cold, onshore breeze that forewarned of even colder times ahead. Florida never seemed better.

She checked into the office, glad to have the first appointment following lunch. Hopefully, it would mean the doctor would be on time. Soon, an assistant came to the rapidly filling waiting room and called her name.

Sheena eagerly jumped to her feet and followed the assistant into a corridor leading to the exam rooms. A nurse greeted her and weighed her, then directed her to an exam room, and offered her a cloth gown.

"Doctor Romano will be with you shortly," the nurse said crisply, after taking her blood pressure, temperature, pulse, and respiration rate, and making notes for the doctor to review.

Sheena's fingers turned cold with dread. As she waited for the doctor, she studied the charts on the wall showing the various organs of the body. A horrible thought filled her mind. If it wasn't breast cancer, was it another kind? Before that thought could go any farther, the door opened, and Dr.

Romano entered the room.

Of average height, stocky, and with short gray hair that surrounded a pleasant face with bright, inquisitive eyes, Elizabeth Romano walked with sure, quick steps that indicated her self-confidence.

"Good to see you again, Sheena. You look fabulous—tanned and rested." She studied her closer. "Maybe not so rested. Want to tell me what's going on?"

At the calm voice speaking with such concern, Sheena burst into tears. "I haven't been feeling great, I've gained weight, and my breasts are sore. My mother died of breast cancer, and I think I might have that too. But I'm way too young to die, you know?"

Dr. Romano placed a steadying hand on Sheena's shoulder. "How long has this been going on? And have you located any lumps?"

Sheena sniffled. "A couple of months now, and you know how hard it is to find any lumps on me."

"Hmmm," Dr. Romano said, feeling the glands in her neck and under her arms. She checked her eyes and her throat and glanced at her with concern. "Let's do an exam and see what we're dealing with."

Sheena did as the doctor asked and stretched out atop the examination table.

Dr. Romano said, "I'm checking everything. Put your feet in the stirrups and just relax."

"Wait! Aren't you going to check my breasts?"

"Later," said Dr. Romano, studying her. "First things first."

In the awkward time while she performed an internal exam, Dr. Romano said, "So, Florida is treating you well?"

Sheena smiled. "Yes, my husband has bought into a business there, and it's great having him home on a more regular schedule." After she said the words, Sheena sat up with a start. "Oh my God! Do you think ..."

Dr. Romano beamed at her. "Yes, I do. Sheena Morelli, you're pregnant!"

Sheena shook her head so hard her auburn hair swung back and forth above her shoulders. "I can't be! My tubes were tied several years ago. The doctor promised me I'd have no more children. We didn't want more ..."

She stopped talking when Dr. Romano continued to smile at her. "It can happen. After five years following a tubal ligation, the odds become a little greater. For someone in your age group, there's a one percent chance it could happen. That sounds like a real low risk, but it happens to more women than you'd think."

Sheena hid her face in her hands. She didn't want another baby. She wanted to be free to be with Tony, work at the hotel, and, maybe, do some traveling. She lifted her head and caught the doctor staring at her.

"Give yourself time to get used to the idea. I know what a shock it is," Dr. Romano said sympathetically. "But at your age, with almost-grown children, it could be a wonderful opportunity to enjoy special time with a new baby. You're in good health, Sheena. We'll do blood tests and any others to make sure of it, but everything looks good, and your blood pressure and oxygen levels are fine."

"Every time I felt sick, every time I felt sore, I told myself it couldn't happen to me," said Sheena. "I should have known. Tony and I ... well, we won't go there."

"How's he going to take it?" Dr. Romano asked.

Sheena shook her head. "I don't know. I really don't."

Sheena left Dr. Romano's office in a quandary. She couldn't say anything to anybody until she and Tony had worked out a solution. She hadn't told the doctor the truth. Tony wouldn't like the idea of a new baby at all. He'd often told her how excited he was to have some time alone with her after Michael and Meaghan had left the house. And the kids? They'd probably hate the idea of a much younger sibling they might or might not have to babysit.

Tears sprang to her eyes. Her stomach spun in a circle of awareness. A baby growing inside her?

CHAPTER SIXTEEN

REGAN

Regan stopped and stared at the building in the distance. Her years at the Catholic high school had been disappointing, but now she saw the school in a different light. She'd managed to graduate, get a job, and survive on her own because teachers there had cared for her.

She stood outside the school, empty now with kids still on Christmas break. At the sound of footsteps behind her, Regan turned.

A woman dressed in a black outer coat and wearing a gray scarf approached her. "Is that you, Regan Sullivan?" As the woman came closer, a smile crossed her plain face. "Hello, Regan! How are you?"

Regan smiled at Sister Joan Marie, a teacher who'd been a favorite of the kids. "I've had a little accident, but I'm fine. I just wanted to look at my old school. So much has happened to me since I left here."

"Do you want to talk about it?" Sister Joan Marie said. "We can go somewhere and have coffee. If you don't mind the walk, the bakery is only a block or so away."

Regan smiled. "Yes, I'd like that. My treat."

As they walked along, Sister Joan Marie chatted about the unusually cold weather they'd been having. Listening to her, Regan realized it was Sister's ability simply to be herself with her students that made her so popular.

The warm air inside the bakery washed over Regan's cold

cheeks. She found a table by a window and waited for her teacher to join her. As a student, she would never have imagined sharing a cup of coffee with one of her teachers. Now, after meeting so many different people in her job in New York and at the Salty Key Inn, she found it an enjoyable experience.

Sister Joan Marie sat across the table from Regan and smiled at her. "It's so nice, Regan, for me to have this chance to find out more about you. I knew, of course, your mother passed, but until recently, I hadn't heard much about you Sullivan girls. Tell me, how are you? You look tanned and healthy."

A waitress came over to them. "Hello, Sister. Would you like your favorite—coffee and an egg salad sandwich?"

Sister hesitated, looked at Regan, and bobbed her head. "That would be lovely."

Regan smiled at the waitress. "And I'll have the same."

The waitress poured their coffees. "I'll be right back with the sandwiches."

While they waited for their lunches to be delivered, Regan asked quietly, "How are you, Sister? Are you still teaching English?"

"Yes," said the nun, "but it's not the same. The magic of words has been overtaken by computers, smartphones, tablets, and things that 'do' instead of making someone pause. It's a shame, but many students today don't like to read."

"I can see the attraction to action things, but I agree it's a shame. I wish I enjoyed reading more, but as you know, reading and writing have always been a bit of a struggle for me."

Sister Joan Marie gave her a tender look. "But you never stopped trying. What are you doing now?"

"My sisters and I own a hotel in Florida," Regan said with

a surge of pride.

"Yes, I heard something about that," Sister Joan Marie said. "What do you girls do there?

"I've been working with a talented interior designer decorating the guest rooms as we upgrade them. And I've discovered I'm very good at that." Regan felt tears sting her eyes and did not attempt to brush them away. "It's been a blessing finally to find something at which I excel."

Sister Joan Marie's lips spread into a wide smile that lit her blue eyes. "I remember your artwork. How nice that you've found a niche with it! God works in mysterious ways, don't you agree?"

"Yes, and in addition to my work, I've found the man of my dreams." Regan held out her left hand so Sister Joan Marie could see the sparkling diamond residing on her ring finger.

"Another reason to thank the Lord," said Sister.

Yes," agreed Regan, seeing her life in a different way. Maybe it was all part of a bigger plan. If so, she still had a lot to learn.

Their sandwiches came, and Regan ate in comfortable silence with her former teacher.

Sister Joan Marie broke into the quiet. "I'm so happy you thought to come see the school. As teachers, we live for moments like this—hearing of the success of our students and finding satisfaction in knowing we just might have contributed in some way."

"Oh, yes," Regan said earnestly. "You were one of the teachers who tried to help me. I'll always be grateful to you."

The waitress approached as they finished their meal. "Will there be anything else?"

Regan and Sister Joan Marie looked at one another and shook their heads.

"But I'll take the bill," Regan said.

“Thank you so much,” said Sister.

“My pleasure.” Regan stood, put on her heavy coat, and paid the bill at the cash register.

“I’m going to do an errand,” said Sister Joan Marie. “Thank you again for lunch and filling me in on your doings. I appreciate it so much.”

Regan hugged her. “Thank you for everything.”

As Regan walked away, she wondered if she’d ever see the nun again. Sister Joan Marie’s eyes were alert, but the wrinkles on her face and her slow movements indicated her age. Regan couldn’t stop the smile that curved her lips. Back in high school, she, like the other students, had thought of the nun as ancient. But seeing her now, Regan appreciated her more than ever. And if she never saw or heard from her again, it was enough to know they’d had this time together.

Regan checked her watch, wondering what her sisters were doing. They’d both been secretive about their time. Regan headed back into town. Soon, she’d find out their future.

CHAPTER SEVENTEEN

SHEENA

Sheena sat with her sisters in a small conference room at the Boston office of Lowell, Peabody and Wilson, feeling as if she was repeating the scene of a year ago. Then she and her two sisters had wondered why Archibald Wilson wanted to meet with them. Now they knew exactly why, and it scared her to death. If for some reason, it was decided she, Darcy, and Regan had failed to meet the challenge as their uncle wanted, Sheena and her family could very well be without a home and she without a job.

At the thought, Sheena silently shook her head. No, they would have a home; it just might not be the one she'd envisioned. And her job? Did it matter? How could she work with a newborn? She sighed. She'd been such a fool. All the symptoms had been present, but she'd ignored them, certain it couldn't happen to her. Yet, she and Tony had had more sex in the past few months than they'd had in years. Enough, apparently, to rupture the 99 percent safety net.

Sheena snapped to attention as Archibald Wilson walked into the room carrying a notebook and a manila folder in which she could see several papers.

Archibald stood a moment and gazed at each of them silently before taking a seat at the table.

Sheena glanced at her sisters. They looked as nervous as she felt.

Archibald cleared his throat. "A year can bring many

changes—some good, others not. I hope this year has done for you what Gavin Sullivan wanted for his beloved nieces. He wanted you to come together as a family, to learn to live together, and, hopefully, to like each other in a way that hadn't happened before."

"Oh, yes," said Darcy. "All of this is true for me."

"Me, too," Regan said. "I love my sisters."

Archibald looked at Sheena.

Sheena bobbed her head "And for me. If we could survive one old-fashioned bathroom together, we could learn to get along anywhere. Very clever of Uncle Gavin."

Archibald laughed. "Yes, your uncle was extremely innovative, which is why he was so successful."

"So, did we meet his goal?" asked Darcy, outspoken as always.

Archibald held up a hand. "Let's go through this step by step." He opened the notebook. "I've had one of my assistants track changes in expenses and income for the property."

Sheena swallowed hard. She knew the numbers better than her sisters, and they were a little shaky.

"In your favor, you made improvements to and were able to sell as hotel rooms twenty of the forty units in the Egret Building. The twenty rooms on the top floor are renovated and ready to receive furnishings and finishing touches. However, you've not been able to do any work on the eight suites, except what you could manage in order to live there."

The silence in the room was deafening.

"But what about the restaurant?" said Regan.

Archibald smiled. "That's very well done, and the income for the two weeks or so it has been open is very impressive. And plans for the future are creative and well thought out."

"Don't forget the waterfront area," said Sheena.

"And the pool and the registration office," Regan added.

"That's in here, too." Archibald studied Sheena. "The financials you kept for the past year and the financial projections for this new year are impressive. That work has won you a lot of points."

"Thank you," said Sheena, wondering where this was going to lead.

"I'm proud to say, according to his wishes, the three of you have met the challenge Gavin offered you."

Darcy and Regan jumped to their feet and rushed to Sheena. Pulling her up out of her chair, they danced around her.

Laughing, Sheena joined in.

When things quieted, Archibald cleared his throat. "There is one more part of the challenge I have yet to tell you. First, let me explain what winning the challenge may mean to you."

Sheena and her sisters quickly took seats.

"At this time," Archibald continued, "Gavin's estate is worth two million, eight hundred-ninety-two thousand dollars and thirty cents. Of course, the two-hundred-fifty-thousand dollars you borrowed for completing Gavin's restaurant will have to be repaid from this amount."

"Oh my Gawd!" said Darcy. "We're millionaires!"

"I can't believe it!" Regan cried. "All that money!"

Sheena watched Archibald carefully. He hadn't said it, but she heard a "but" in the statement. "And the final part of the challenge?" she asked, her mind still whirling with the idea of having so much money.

"It depends on your plans," said Archibald. "That's all I'm allowed to say." He rose. "By ten o'clock tomorrow morning, you must present me with plans for the hotel's future."

"What kind of plans?" asked Darcy, scowling.

"I've said all I can say," Archibald responded mysteriously. "I'll leave you alone. As before, help yourself to the coffee, cookies, and soft drinks we've set out for you. Good luck, ladies. I, too, am very proud of all you've accomplished."

He left the room.

"What do you think he meant, Sheena?" asked Darcy. "Does he want to know how we plan to spend our money? I don't know about the two of you, but I'm going to buy a fancy car, take a few trips, and work on writing a novel."

"I'm going to buy a house on the beach for Brian and me," said Regan. "What about you, Sheena?"

Sheena let out a long breath. "I'm not sure what the last part of the challenge means, but I'm guessing it has to do with the hotel."

"We're doing all right with it. Sure, it's slow, but it's getting better," said Darcy.

"Think about it," said Sheena. "Do you think Uncle Gavin left us this money to spend on us? I think he wanted a good part of it to go to the hotel."

"But that's not fair," protested Regan. "He shouldn't give us money just to make us spend it on the hotel."

Darcy stared at Sheena. "Everyone says you're like him, Sheena. Tell us what you think we should do? If we make a mistake now, we might not get any money at all."

"That's what I'm thinking. Let's work the numbers a bit. We need to come up with a plan. Uncle Gavin was very shrewd, but he was also very conservative. I think if we each put in 55% of the money allocated to us, it would prove our loyalty to the hotel."

"Fifty-five percent? That's a lot," said Darcy, punching numbers into her smartphone. "That's almost half a million dollars each."

"Fifty-five percent of what we would never have had on our own is more than fair," countered Sheena. "I think he'd want us to be grateful for what we have. That's why he put us in that small, inconvenient house."

"That makes sense," said Regan. "From what I've heard from Gavin's people, Uncle Gavin was generous but very careful with his money."

"Let's go over the numbers," said Sheena, feeling more confident about Gavin's intentions. "Let's say we each put in five hundred thousand dollars. That will give us each close to four hundred thousand dollars for our personal use and give us a million and a half dollars to continue upgrades and renovations at the hotel and provide good working capital."

"Wow!" said Darcy, leaning back in her chair, and staring up at the ceiling. "That would do wonders for the hotel."

"Yeah, we could complete the rooms in the Egret Building the right way and redo all the units in the Sandpiper Suites Building," said Regan. "I could make them real nice."

Sheena held up her hand. "Nice, but not too pricey. It sounds like a lot of money, but it isn't when you're doing gut renovations. Air conditioners need replacement, the roof of the main building should be redone, and there are a lot of other considerations."

"Yeah," said Regan. "We want to complete the waterfront, build a gazebo by the bay and construct a bohio-style hut for an outdoor bar by the pool."

Darcy smiled at Sheena. "Maybe we could hire Casey to work with you on managing the hotel. I know that's what you want to do, especially now that your kids are all but grown."

Sheena blinked several times, but couldn't stop the tears behind her eyelids from rolling down her cheeks.

"What's wrong," asked Regan, wide-eyed. She rushed over to Sheena and wrapped her arms around her. "We've been so worried about you. Are you sick?"

Sheena lifted a tear-streaked face. "I have been. I'm pregnant."

The shocked expressions on her sisters' faces said it all.

"Please don't mention it to anyone else," Sheena said, breaking into the stunned silence. "Tony and the kids don't know, and I'm still trying to cope with the idea."

"Oh my Gawd! I can't believe it! How could it happen? I thought you had your tubes tied," said Darcy.

"There's a one percent chance of it happening. I guess I'm one of those lucky ones." The whole idea made Sheena miserable. "The funny thing is, I was so sure it couldn't happen to me, I thought I might have breast cancer like Mom."

"And you didn't say anything to us about it? That doesn't sound like close sisters," said Regan. "We could've given you moral support or something."

Sheena lowered her head and sighed. "I didn't want to worry you. I knew how much you were counting on winning the challenge and moving on with your lives. And besides, I just got confirmation a couple of hours ago from my doctor here in Boston."

"Look at me!" said Darcy. "We're not going to abandon you. We'll stick together to make the hotel a better place, and yes, we'll need to divide the time, so one of us isn't stuck with this project all the time."

"That will give you time for the baby and allow you to do the work you love at the hotel. Even though I'll be working with Mo, I can still devote some time to the hotel," said Regan. "Brian will be busy working with Tony on their projects."

"And travel can't be my main focus. Austin can't leave his work for too long anyway. I'll help at the hotel, too," Darcy quickly added.

Sheena looked from Darcy to Regan and drew a deep breath. The Sullivan sisters would somehow come through for one another. Wasn't that Uncle Gavin's greatest lesson?

CHAPTER EIGHTEEN

DARCY

Lost in thought, Darcy sat with her sisters in the restaurant Regan had chosen in the North End for their celebration dinner. What at first had seemed a wonderful triumph had turned into another challenge she hadn't expected. Gone were the ideas of world travel, glamorous events, a fancy car. A large amount of the money she would inherit had to be set aside for the hotel's future use. She knew Sheena was right; it was the right thing to do, but still ...

Gazing across the table at Sheena, Darcy was struck by the emotional turmoil she saw on her face. Michael had been a surprise that had changed Sheena's life. How would *this* baby change her? She and Austin wanted children, but Darcy didn't like the idea of being surprised. She wanted time with Austin as husband and wife before they ventured into parenthood.

"When is the baby due?" Regan asked Sheena.

"The doctor and I guess sometime in June." Sheena sighed. "In time for the summer heat."

Darcy reached across the table and squeezed Sheena's hand. "It's not like you to be so pessimistic. That's a good time to stay inside, anyway."

Sheena agreed, but remained silent.

"On a brighter note," Darcy continued. "By then, you should be in a house of your own."

"We were going to build a nice, small house in the neighborhood where Brian and Tony are working. Guess we'll have to change plans for the house, make it bigger."

The waiter returned with their drinks—a margarita for Darcy, a glass of red wine for Regan, and bubbling water and lime for Sheena.

After placing their dinner orders with the waiter, Darcy raised her glass. "Here's to us!"

"The Sullivan sisters!" said Regan, clinking her glass against Darcy's and turning to Sheena. "And here's to the new baby! I hope it's a girl."

"Yes, so Meaghan can have a sister," added Darcy, finally bringing a smile to Sheena's face.

Regan turned serious. "I hope we've met this final challenge. I was going to speak to Mo and Kenton to see about renting the cottage on Kenton's property, but if the money is ours, Brian may want to use some of my money to build a house. That, and having a car of my own would be a dream come true for me."

Sheena gave her a long look. "It's amazing Uncle Gavin did this for us. What a kind, interesting man he was."

"Are you sure you want to stay at Dad's instead of at the Boston Harbor Hotel with us?" Darcy said.

"I'd made those plans thinking I'd have to stay on for medical tests, but now that I know I don't, it's too late to change them. He's expecting me," said Sheena. "Besides, I promised I'd go through some paperwork with him. He's thinking of selling the house, after all."

"He's moving to California?" asked Regan.

"Nooo, he wants to move to Florida."

"Wha-a-at? No way," said Darcy. "I thought he decided not to move there."

Sheena laughed. "Guess the whole dang family will end up there." She sobered. "With everyone planning to get married and raise a family, he told me he doesn't want to miss out."

"Wait until he hears about your baby," said Regan. "He'll be as surprised as we were."

Sheena gave Regan a warning look. "Remember, don't say a word to anybody else. I have to tell my family first. And I'm pretty sure they won't be as excited as the two of you."

At ten o'clock the next morning, Darcy sat with her sisters in the conference room hoping they'd done the right thing. She'd tossed and turned all night, wondering if Uncle Gavin had wanted them to put all the money back into the hotel. She was going to invest most of her money for the time when she'd be able to leave the hotel work, spend several months abroad, and write a whole series of novels. In the meantime, she hoped Allison and her literary agency could find someone interested in her short stories.

Archibald Wilson entered the room looking bright-eyed on what was another gray, snowy morning in Boston. "Good morning, ladies. I hope you had a pleasant evening," he said, taking a seat at the head of the table. "What information have you come up with for me?"

Darcy, with the others, turned to Sheena.

Sheena smiled nervously at Archibald. "We tried to think like Gavin and have come up with a plan to invest 55 percent of his estate back into the hotel project, giving us an additional one and a half million dollars to completely restore the hotel. In addition to completing the rooms, we need to take care of deferred maintenance of the buildings, including air conditioners and some electrical and plumbing work. We also want to make the living quarters of Gavin's people nicer, including construction of a private, outdoor patio and an indoor community room."

Grinning, Archibald jumped up out of his seat and waved

his fists in the air. “By God! You’ve done it! You’ve actually done it! I’m so proud of you!”

Darcy felt her jaw drop and turned to her sisters. Their mouths had formed perfect O’s.

Archibald seemed to realize what he was doing and stopped. His cheeks were bright red as he took his seat again. He gave them a sheepish look. “I’m sorry to get carried away, but when I first met the three of you, I wasn’t at all convinced you’d make decisions like this.” His eyes watered. “Gavin was betting the Sullivan genes would come through, and they have.”

“What exactly was this challenge?” said Sheena.

“After spending a year working on the property he loved, his challenge was to get a commitment from you that you’d continue to work on it, that you would see the same promise in it as he had.”

Sheena arched an eyebrow at him. “And ...?”

“And you’d see life at the hotel was good for his people.” Archibald grinned and slapped a hand on the table. “And you came through, just like he thought you would.”

“What would have happened if we hadn’t?” Darcy asked.

Archibald chuckled. “In addition to the hotel, you each would have inherited one thousand dollars. That’s all.”

Darcy gaped at her sisters. “Oh my Gawd! All that work for nothing?”

“But I thought we were to get the money regardless,” said Regan.

Archibald shook his head. “Only the opportunity to win the money. A fine line, but one that always existed. Gavin was a very interesting man.”

“That’s exactly what Sheena said last night,” said Darcy. “I wish I could really have known him.”

Archibald gave her a funny look. “But you do know him—

through his actions and the people he's helped. I understand you've interviewed everyone in his group."

"Yes, you're right. In his own way, Gavin was the biggest angel of all," Darcy said, feeling a sting of tears.

CHAPTER NINETEEN

SHEENA

Still shocked by the news she'd received in the last two days, Sheena sat aboard the plane bound for Florida. After winning and then learning the details of the final challenge of Uncle Gavin's will, they'd sat with Archibald figuring out the best way to handle the funds. They each opted to invest the bulk of their money with Blackie Gatto. He would also handle the money set aside for the hotel. They settled outstanding legal bills, signed documents, resolved the note for the money they had borrowed for Gavin's restaurant and got everything in order for the transition.

Now, the plane took off with a roar of its engines and lifted into the cold air, taking her back home and to another phase in her life.

Sheena stared out the window, observing the clouds that blocked the sun as the plane climbed through them to a higher, smoother altitude.

Above the clouds, the blue sky shimmered with sunshine. Sheena sat back in her seat. The flight from Boston to Tampa would seem extra short because she dreaded telling Tony about the baby. Last night, sleeping in her childhood home, the memories of crying and hiding in her bedroom after she'd learned she was pregnant with Michael filled her mind, making it impossible to sleep well. There was no question of her not having this new baby. She loved her children, and she'd love this little one too. But she couldn't pretend to be happy by this turn of events.

She focused her thoughts on the future. She was so very grateful to Uncle Gavin. The money she'd received from his challenge would cover Michael's and Meaghan's college educations and would replace the funds Tony had used to buy into Brian's business. And if they ran the hotel well, she and her sisters could draw a sufficient income from it to cover other expenses. Having this financial security would be a relief to Tony, who worked hard to provide for his family. At the thought of him and his reaction to her news, a nervous shiver tap-danced across her shoulders.

In the baggage claim area of the airport, Casey greeted Sheena holding a sign that read: "Sheena Morelli." Sheena laughed, remembering all their expectations of just a year ago. Life had turned out so differently for all of them, so much better.

"Tony asked me to pick you up in the hotel van," said Casey. "The kids are back in school, and he and Brian are on the job."

He helped her with her bags and led her to the van. After they got settled in their seats, Casey took off, wending his way through the airport traffic before heading toward the Salty Key Inn.

"How was your trip?" Casey asked in a conversational tone.

"Nice," Sheena said. "But it was cold. I'm glad to be back in Florida." Even sitting in the car with the windows rolled up, she was able to smell the salty tang of the air. In the warmth of the sun shining through the windows, she felt some of the tension leave her shoulders. She'd have time to unpack and walk the beach before Tony came home from work.

###

Sheena was changing into jeans and a T-shirt when Tony called her.

"How'd it go, honey?" he asked. "'Thought maybe I could come by for a late lunch before the kids come home from school. I've missed you!"

That, thought Sheena, *was why she was in the state she was in—late lunches, early morning romps.* A flare of irritation surprised her, but she held it back. "Okay, there's something I need to talk to you about."

"Something good?" he teased.

"We'll see," she answered cryptically. "See you soon. I'm going to take a walk on the beach."

Sheena disconnected the call, grabbed her flip flops, and left the suite. Outside, she hurried through the hotel grounds, across Gulf Boulevard, and onto the stretch of white sand. In the crisp January air, her flip flops made slapping sounds against the moist, compacted sand along the water's edge as she walked along.

It felt good to stretch her muscles, get lost in the regular movement, and free her mind. The breeze tossed her hair around playfully. She stopped, closed her eyes, and lifted her face to the sun, drawing in a deep breath and then slowly letting it out. She could do this—have a new baby, take care of her family, and oversee the hotel. Her thoughts flew to Rosa and Paul Morelli. Tony's parents had moved to Florida to have a new, fun lease on life. But, surely, they'd be happy about another Morelli, wouldn't they? Rosa had been an enormous help in caring for Michael and Meaghan. Would she be willing to start all over again, helping her with this new baby?

Head down, Sheena headed back to the hotel, wondering how she was going to break the news to Tony.

At the sound of her name being called, Sheena looked up. Tony was heading her way.

Sheena lifted her hand to return his wave. Her stomach fluttered nervously.

Smiling, Tony trotted toward her. "Glad you're home!"

When he reached her, he swept her up in his strong arms. "I missed you, Mrs. Morelli!"

She smiled at him. "I've been gone only three days. Everything all right?"

"Great," Tony said. "I've been working on plans for the house, and though it's small, it'll be perfect for us after the kids are gone. How did it go in Boston? You've been very quiet about things."

"We didn't know how it was going to turn out until yesterday morning. Then, we had to complete all the legal and financial details. Darcy, Regan, and I decided not to say anything to our men until we were home, and we could talk privately with you."

Tony slung an arm over her shoulder. "Yeah? So, did you get the hotel?"

Sheena gazed into his dark eyes. "And then some." She gave him the details of the financial arrangements. "And now we have enough money to set aside for Michael's and Meaghan's education and to put toward a new house."

"Great! Like I said, I've been working on the house plans the couple of nights you've been gone, and I think you're going to like them."

Sheena came to a stop. "About that. We need to talk, because three bedrooms aren't going to be enough."

Tony shook his head. "With my parents living here in their own home, we don't need a guest room, do we?"

"We do if our guest isn't going to leave for at least eighteen years," said Sheena, unable to keep her eyes from tearing up.

Tony frowned at her. "What are you trying to tell me, Sheena?"

She let out a long breath. "I'm pregnant."

Tony's eyes widened. He stared at her in shock. "Pregnant? You can't be. You took care of protection a long time ago."

"Apparently, there's a one percent chance of a woman my age getting pregnant after having her tubes tied." Sheena swiped at her eyes. "And we've been pretty active the last few months. Her voice trailed off ...

"Aw, honey," Tony said, wrapping his arms around her and bringing her close. "We'll get through it. Just like we did before."

Sheena couldn't hold back her sobs. It was exactly like the conversation they'd had over eighteen years ago.

Tony lifted her chin. "Look at me, Sheena. It's not the end of the world. With the other two kids grown, we'll have a chance to really enjoy this new one."

"Yeah? Well, you're not the one going through the pregnancy and childbirth. And you're not the one who'll get stuck with all the work of caring for it." Sheena lowered her head and covered her face with her hands. "Oh my Gawd! Listen to me! I sound awful. Simply awful."

"Sheena, honey, we'll work together on this. And Michael and Meaghan can help too."

Sheena lifted her head. Thinking back to the times when they were young, she remembered how it felt to rock a baby in her arms. A new feeling of excitement rose in her. Maybe, she thought, Tony is right, and I'll be able to enjoy this baby in a different way. She looked at him and gave him a shaky smile.

"That's my girl," said Tony, giving her a kiss on the cheek.

"You're really okay with this? I thought you'd be upset we'll lose our time alone after Michael and Meaghan are gone."

The corners of his mouth tilted into a roguish grin. "Okay with it? I think it's great. I guess the old man hasn't lost his touch, huh?"

Sheena pushed him playfully. She wouldn't be surprised if he started to crow like a rooster. Darn him anyway; she never could resist him.

"So, when is this baby due?" said Tony.

"The doctor and I guess sometime in June. I can't be sure when it happened. We were fooling around a lot."

"Yeah, it was fun," said Tony, grinning at her again.

"Next time, you can take care of the situation. After this, I'm done," she warned him, erasing the smile on his face.

As they were walking up the beach toward the hotel, Tony pulled Sheena to a stop. Gazing at her, he said, "I want you to know how much I love you, Sheena. And I always will."

"Even when I'm nine months pregnant and unable to tie my shoes?" Sheena said, giving him a dubious look.

Tony laughed. "Yes, even then."

"I wonder how the kids will take it?" Sheena asked.

Tony checked his watch. "We'll find out soon. They're due to be home from school any time now."

Michael sat on the couch as he was asked. Meaghan sat next to him, eating an apple. Every crunch of her teeth into the apple set Sheena's nerves on edge.

"What did you want to talk to us about? Did you and Darcy and Regan get the hotel, like you wanted?" asked Michael.

"Do we have lots of money for your beating the challenge?" said Meaghan. "That's what you were hoping for, right?"

"To answer both of your questions, yes," said Sheena. She explained about the finances and how much added work would be done to the hotel. "And your college educations can be taken care of. That's a big relief to Dad and me."

"Sounds good," said Michael, starting to rise.

"Hold on, son. There's more news," said Tony, giving

Sheena a look of encouragement.

Sheena gulped, feeling like a teenager telling her parents she'd kissed her first boyfriend. Or worse.

"Yeah? What is it?" prompted Meaghan.

"In June, probably early in the month, you're going to have a baby sister or a baby brother," said Sheena bluntly. She watched her children's eyes round in shock.

"You're kidding! No way," said Michael, giving her a horrified look.

"Mom and Dad ... you ... really?" Meaghan looked as if she might feel ill.

Tony stepped over to Sheena and put an arm around her. "We're all going to need to give Mom support, both before and after the baby comes."

"Okay. Can I please be excused?" asked Michael.

"Sure," said Sheena. "It'll take time for everyone to get used to the idea." Sheena realized Michael was thinking of the baby he almost had with Kaylee. Later, she'd talk to him about it.

"Do Aunt Darcy and Aunt Regan know about the baby?" asked Meaghan in a small voice.

"Yes," said Sheena. "They're pretty excited about becoming aunts again. Grandma and Grandpa Morelli don't know yet. Your dad and I will tell them a little later."

"All right. Can I go now? I want to see if Aunt Regan is home," Meaghan said, her voice quavering. At Sheena's nod, Meaghan rose and hurried out of the suite to go next door.

"So much for excitement from them," said Sheena, unable to hide her disappointment.

"Don't worry. It's just the shock of it. Over time, we'll all get used to the idea. How did your sisters take the news?"

Sheena's eyes filled. "They're going to support me all the way, so we can finish the hotel renovations and get it running well."

Tony gave her a nod of satisfaction. “Onward and upward and all of that. Good news.”

“I hope so,” said Sheena, feeling vulnerable. Her whole world had turned upside down.

CHAPTER TWENTY

REGAN

Regan was changing into a dress for dinner with Brian when Meaghan burst into the bedroom they shared.

"Mom's having a baby!"

"A big surprise, huh?" Regan smiled and turned to her.

Meaghan plopped down on the bed, looking forlorn.

Regan went over to Meaghan, sat down next to her, and wrapped an arm around her shoulder. "What's going on? Why the glum look?"

"I don't want a baby in the family. I can see it now. I'll be the babysitter stuck at home changing dirty diapers."

"Why don't you think of the positive things? You'll have a little one to hug and love. And you know very well your mother is not going to enslave you, though having you around will be a huge help to her. Think of all the nice things your mother has done and is doing for you."

"I know," sighed Meaghan. "It's really hard to think of my parents doing *it*, you know?"

Regan held back the laugh she felt bubbling inside her. "Parents are humans, you know. And yours love each other. Be happy they do, and when this baby comes, love him or her."

Meaghan's jaw dropped. "Him? Oh no! If we're having a baby, I want it to be a girl."

Regan gave her a pat on the back. "You've got a fifty-fifty chance. But I'm with you on that. I'd love it if you had a sister. Whatever it is, we'll all love that baby. Right?"

"Yeah. Guess it took me by surprise." Meaghan's eyes lit with excitement. "If it's a girl, I'll get to dress her up and everything."

Regan laughed. "She'll be the best doll you ever had."

Meaghan jumped to her feet. "I've got to go talk to Mom."

Watching Meaghan dart out of the room, Regan shook her head. *Teenagers!* She finished dressing for dinner. She and Brian were meeting Mo and Kenton at Gavin's to settle arrangements for them to rent the cottage on Kenton's property. Brian had flat-out refused to use any of Regan's money to buy a house for them. At the time, Regan had been hurt, but now she was pleased the bulk of her money could be used to go into business with Mo.

Brian knocked on the door to the suite and entered. "Ready?" His eyes took on a brightness as he advanced, continuing to stare at her. "You look beautiful, Regan." He lifted her chin and kissed her on the lips. "I missed you so much."

She gave him her crooked smile. "Not as much as I missed you and Florida. I'd forgotten how cold Boston winters are."

He chuckled. "I'll remind you of that next summer when it's hot here."

They left the Sandpiper Suites Building and walked over to Gavin's. Mid-week nights were usually not that busy, but, tonight, the parking lot was full.

Nicole greeted them when they walked in.

"What's going on?" Regan asked.

"We have a big birthday celebration for Tampa's mayor going on upstairs. His sister lives in St. Petersburg, and she's throwing him a surprise party. We were thrilled to get the business."

"Nice," said Regan. "It's important to keep the momentum going. Has Mo arrived?"

Nicole smiled and said, "They're in the small alcove toward the back of the restaurant."

"Thanks. Don't bother to seat us. We'll make our own way." Regan took hold of Brian's arm, and they made their way to the alcove overlooking a small garden. It was Regan's favorite spot in the restaurant.

Mo and Kenton were seated facing away from the main dining room. Both men stood as Regan and Brian approached. Mo, then Kenton, greeted Regan with kisses and shook hands with Brian.

"A belated Happy New Year to you," said Mo, smiling at them. "How did your trip to Boston go, Regan?"

Regan smiled. "It went well. The hotel officially belongs to my sisters and me, and we're going to be able to do more renovations to the property. Best of all, I'll be able to go into business with you, Mo."

Mo and Kenton glanced uneasily at one another.

"I'm starting a new television series in a couple of weeks," said Kenton. "In California."

"And Kenton has asked me to move in with him," Mo said, looking both happy and miserable at the same time. "I'm leaving for California in two weeks, as soon as we wrap up Arthur Weatherman's restaurant projects."

"Oh, but ..." Regan's stomach clenched with acid. "I thought ..."

Mo reached across the table and clasped her hand. "I'm sorry, but I don't want you to worry. I'm going to help you set up your own business."

"My own business? How can I do that? I don't have a degree in interior design." Regan fought the sting in her eyes.

"You can advertise as an interior decorator," said Mo. "I'll be a resource for you in California, providing support, offering suggestions. I promise you that."

"Think of what you've already done as a decorator. You're the one who brought in the business for the Weathermans' project."

"And look at what you've done with the hotel," said Brian. "Tony and I have already talked about installing you as the official decorator for the homes we're building."

Regan flopped back against her chair, her mind spinning so fast she had to grab hold of the edge of the table. *Her own business? Could she do it?*

"I hope you understand," said Kenton. "Your wanting to go into business with Mo has been a grave concern of his. But after discovering what Mo and I have together, I want to share my life with him. In the crazy existence I lead, he's the one I trust to keep me grounded." He turned to Mo. "And I love him."

"You know more than most how important this is to me," said Mo, giving her a pleading look.

"Yes, I do," said Regan softly. She rose and gave Mo a kiss on the cheek. "I'm happy for you. I really am." She turned to Kenton. "And I'm happy for you, Kenton." Still shaken by the news, she forced a smile. "I guess we've each found what we've been looking for."

Regan took her seat, and when Brian gave her hand an encouraging squeeze, she squeezed it back. Truth to tell, she was scared to pieces to have her own business. But somehow, she vowed, she'd make her dream come true.

A couple of days later, Regan met Mo at Kenton's house. They'd already agreed on the decorating changes they wanted to make to the house—changes Regan would now oversee.

"This will be another project you can use as a reference for your future clients," said Mo, indicating the kitchen with a sweep of his arm. "For the next week or so, I'll introduce you to suppliers, manufacturing reps, and others. I'll give you all my sample books and do anything else I can to get you off to a good start. But, Regan, you're a natural at this decorating business. You're not going to have any problems being on your own, except for one thing."

"What?" Regan held her breath.

"You're going to be so busy you're going to need to find help to handle the office. I know of someone who might be willing to work for you. She and I were in school together."

"Okay, before you leave for California, give me her name," said Regan. She placed a hand on Mo's arm. "I'm so relieved you're not abandoning me, that you'll guide me by phone and the internet until I feel comfortable."

"Of course," said Mo. "And you know I'll be back to see you and the family. My grandmother will see to that. She had a hard time accepting Kenton and me together, but she's over that."

Regan laughed. She loved Mo's family. His grandmother, Carlotta Beecher, oversaw the group like a queen and her court. And his cousin, Bernice, had opened her own cleaning business to handle the housekeeping department at the hotel.

"Now, let's do a walk-through of the cottage," said Mo. "Kenton wants me to make sure you and Brian will be comfortable there. You're moving in this week?"

"We can't wait to move out of the Sandpiper. Renovations are going to start there soon, so we'll all have to be out. Darcy's already moved into Austin's condo, and Tony and Sheena are buying a house in the development he and Brian are building. They were going to build their own smaller house, but with the baby coming, they decided to buy one already built, one that is bigger and more convenient."

"Where are you going to set up your office? At the hotel?"

"No," said Regan. "Because I'll be working at the development, Brian and Tony are setting up a design office in the model house there."

Mo shook his head. "Funny how everything is working out. I never thought I'd be happy living in California, but I'm excited about it. Of course, it has everything to do with Kenton."

"I don't want you to miss my wedding," said Regan. "I was going to ask you to be my man of honor."

"Well, that's not a problem, if you can do it within the next two weeks."

Regan clasped a hand over her heart. "Darcy would kill me if I got married before she did."

"But? I hear a big 'but' ..." prompted Mo.

"It would make things a whole lot easier to set up my business in my married name." Regan shook her head. "But I could never hurt Darcy by upstaging her wedding. We'll have to plan mine for another time when you and Kenton can be here."

"Deal," said Mo.

"Let's see the cottage," said Regan, full of excitement. Wedding or not, she and Brian would be sharing the cottage for the foreseeable future. When things settled down at the housing development, they'd build the house of their dreams. Brian had already reserved a building lot for them.

Later, Regan followed Mo out of the cottage, thrilled with the whole arrangement. It was a perfect size for Brian and her and was fully furnished with top-of-the-line furnishings. The building consisted of three bedrooms, two-and-a-half baths, a nice kitchen, an open living area, and a gorgeous, screened-in patio with an outdoor kitchen. It still surprised Regan the lovely house was called a cottage. It was as lovely a home as any she could imagine for herself.

While they stood outside talking, Kenton drove up in his red Corvette.

Regan nudged Mo with her elbow. "You get to ride in that?"

He grinned. "It's a whole different world for me, but I love it."

Kenton got out of the car and came over to them. "You all set on renting from me?" he asked Regan.

She clasped her hands together. "It's perfect for us. I can't wait to move in."

"If you need anything else at all, you let me know. It's a huge relief to me that you and Brian will stay here and keep an eye on things while we're away." Kenton put his arm around Mo and grinned. "I'm so glad Mo introduced me to you. You're a good friend."

Regan returned his smile. "Thanks, but I'm the lucky one." She knew she spoke the truth. Mo had opened up her world in a way no one else could. She'd always be grateful to him.

CHAPTER TWENTY-ONE

DARCY

Darcy awoke in bed, rolled over, and peered at the man she was going to marry. Austin was asleep on his back, his hands thrown up near his head. His broad shoulders and muscular chest were a turn-on, even at this early-morning time before the alarm went off. But rather than disturb him, Darcy rose out of bed, grabbed her robe, and padded into the kitchen.

After fixing herself a cup of coffee, Darcy carried it out to the patio. The cool morning air felt chilly on her skin, but she didn't mind. After the trip to Boston, she reveled in the weather in Florida. Soon, she and Austin would be on their honeymoon trip to Europe. In anticipation of the much cooler weather there, she'd shopped online for warm clothing. She'd even picked up a couple of things in Boston.

Darcy pulled her feet up on top of her chair and wrapped her robe around her legs. Taking a sip of the steaming coffee, she gazed at her surroundings. The condo was a townhouse complete with patio and private lawn area. The Australian pines, hibiscus, bougainvillea, and oleander around the older buildings were lush and green and added a softness to the appealing landscape.

The interior of the condo was comfortable with high ceilings and open spaces. Austin had built several bookcases for the den, upgraded the kitchen and bathroom cabinets, and added a few other features to make it even more attractive and livable with better convenience and storage.

Darcy had offered the use of some of her money to buy a house, but she and Austin had decided there was no need to buy something bigger until they had children. Sitting outside, enjoying the peace and quiet, Darcy was happy they'd agreed on that.

Austin slid open the sliding glass door and stepped out onto the patio. "I missed you in our bed." He bent over and kissed her on the lips. "Good morning, Almost Mrs. Blakely."

Darcy laughed and drew him closer for another kiss. It sometimes seemed a dream she'd found him—someone who understood her sass and respected her dreams.

"I go for the final fitting of my wedding dress later today. And then Sheena and I are going shopping for a dress for her. The one she'd picked out earlier is too small for her. It's hard to believe another surprise pregnancy has happened to her, but she's pretty excited about it now."

"How about the kids?"

Darcy chuckled. "Now that Meaghan is used to the idea, she's thrilled about it. Of course, she, like Regan and me, wants a girl."

Austin smiled and lowered himself into a chair beside her. "I can't wait until we start a family. Being an only child, I want lots of kids."

"Down, boy," said Darcy. "We're starting with one or two. Right?"

"At least two," Austin said. He gave her a sly grin. "We'd better start practicing. I've got a little extra time before my first appointment today."

Darcy's lips curved with satisfaction at the way Austin's eyes burned with desire. She loved that she could make him so happy. She got to her feet. "I don't think we should waste that extra time."

Austin jumped to his feet and threw an arm around her. "I love you, Darcy."

Later, Darcy stretched like a cat in warm sunshine, feeling a deep sense of satisfaction. Making love with Austin was as much an emotional journey as one filled with sensual sensations. She could hardly wait to begin life officially as his wife.

She'd once thought upon her return from her honeymoon she'd begin writing the novel that hovered in her head. But that idea had been put on hold after she promised Sheena she'd help oversee the hotel's renovations. It would take the work of all three sisters to see the job was done quickly and well while they were trying to build their business.

Hearing Austin singing in the shower, Darcy hurried out of bed. As she'd told him, she didn't like to waste time, and she knew how good Austin was at soaping her body.

CHAPTER TWENTY-TWO

SHEENA

With Regan covering the registration desk, Sheena felt comfortable accompanying Darcy to the fitting of her wedding dress, and she hoped to find a dress of her own for the ceremony. The simple, white sheath she'd chosen several months ago was a little too small for comfort now.

Sheena stood outside the Sandpiper Suites Building waiting for Darcy to pick her up in her new car. As she gazed at her surroundings, excitement filled her. With the money they'd dedicated to the hotel, they'd be able to make it a very special place. She hoped they could do the upgrades while still allowing guests a pleasant stay. It was all a numbers game.

When Darcy's silver Mercedes convertible pulled into the lot, the corners of Sheena's mouth turned up. The sassy car was so Darcy. It was the one extravagance Darcy had allowed herself. Per an agreement between her and Austin, Darcy was investing the bulk of her money for future use.

"Ready for a spin?" Darcy said, resettling her white baseball cap on her red curls. She handed Sheena a scarf.

Laughing, Sheena wrapped the scarf around her head and settled into the passenger seat. The air was cold, but the sun was warm as they pulled out of the parking lot.

"Thanks so much for coming with me to my fitting," said Darcy, turning to her with a smile. "At times like this, I really miss Mom. She'd be so pleased with the whole idea of my marrying Austin. He's such a good guy."

"And don't forget Regan. She'd like Brian too," said Sheena. Her mother had been disappointed by Sheena's rushed wedding but had grown very fond of Tony.

"I wonder when Regan and Brian are going to get married? Regan hasn't said much about it." Darcy glanced at Sheena. "Maybe they're waiting until Brian is completely healed."

"Could be. But, in this family, who knows? It's been one surprise after another."

"Speaking of that, how are you feeling? You're looking a lot better."

Sheena patted her stomach. "I think things are finally settling down with me. My family is rolling with the idea too. Now, we just have to move to the new house. It should be ready for us in another couple of weeks, right before your wedding. The kids can hardly wait to have their own swimming pool."

"Does it seem strange to be living at the hotel with Regan and me gone?" Darcy asked.

"Honestly, it'll be hard to leave. I'm going to miss the activity and the convenience of being close by. But I agree with Tony; we need to come together as a family away from the hotel."

Darcy pulled into a parking spot in front of the bridal shop, and they went inside.

The owner, Georgia Hiller, greeted them with a smile. "Hello, and thank you for being prompt, Darcy. This is a busy time for us, and the seamstress is swamped." She turned to her. "And this is Sheena, right?"

"Yes, Sheena Morelli, Darcy's sister," Sheena reminded her.

"Are you here to oversee the fitting?" Georgia said, giving her a speculative look.

Sheena shook her head. "Actually, I'm here to find a dress

for me for the wedding. Something very simple in white."

Darcy grinned at Georgia. "The others have their dresses. But Sheena needs to find a new one for a special reason."

"I've just found out I'm pregnant, but I'd already put on a little extra weight and need to feel comfortable in something with a little more room."

Georgia studied her. "All right, I can do that. Please help yourself to water, coffee, or tea in the waiting area, and I'll bring some dresses to you I'm sure you'll like. Considering Darcy's dress, I imagine you want something in a light fabric, not too dressy. Right?"

"That would be perfect," said Sheena. She followed Darcy into the waiting area. Plush loveseats in pale pink and overstuffed chairs in floral prints sat atop a soft, ivory carpet. To one side, a white tea cart held the beverage offerings.

"See you later," said Darcy. She followed a tiny, gray-haired woman out of the room.

Sheena poured herself some ice water and sat on one of the couches. This whole scene was so different from the hurried, almost-too-casual wedding she'd had. She was happy Darcy had the chance to enjoy planning and preparing for hers.

As she waited for Georgia to appear, Sheena thought of the changes ahead for her and her family. Meaghan was now thrilled with the idea of a baby. Michael was another story. Sheena suspected he was dealing with guilt over being happy he was off the hook of becoming a co-parent with Kaylee. He now detested her.

"Here we are," said Georgia, breaking into Sheena's thoughts. She bustled into the room carrying several dresses over her arm. She carefully placed them over the back of one of the couches and then lifted them up, one by one.

Sheena easily dismissed several of them. The last two, however, intrigued her. One was a simple, sleeveless linen sundress with an eyelet hem that added enough of a decorative touch to be attractive, yet nicely understated. The other dress had an empire waist, from which silky fabric flowed neatly, without excess bulk.

"Try them on and let's see how they look," Georgia urged her. "With your coloring and stature, both are going to look stunning."

Sheena took them into a dressing room. As she removed her clothes, she studied the body that had betrayed her. Her stomach had a new curve, and her breasts were definitely bigger.

She tried on the empire-waisted dress first because she already liked the other one better. This dress reminded her of the clothing she'd be forced to wear in the coming months as she grew bigger. She took it off.

She changed into the sundress and sighed. It was perfect. Or would be for the few weeks between now and the wedding. And after her body recovered from the delivery, she might be able to use it.

"Well?" said Georgia, as Sheena stepped out of the dressing room in the sundress.

"This is the one. I love it."

"It looks lovely on you." She studied Sheena carefully. "And I don't think it needs any adjustments."

"Good. I'll take it." Sheena was tickled by the idea she wasn't worried about the cost of the dress. For the first time in her life, she had a little extra money to spend.

Darcy approached her. "Find a dress?"

Sheena twirled in front of her.

"Oh, Sheena! It's perfect!" Darcy's eyes gleamed with satisfaction. "And I'm happy with mine. It's everything I dreamed it would be. Now, it's time to find some sandals. Are you game?"

"Sure," Sheena said. "As long as I can get some food. I've gone from feeling sick to wanting to eat all the time."

"Let's have an early lunch, and then we'll get back to the hotel to relieve Regan. She's meeting with Mo late this afternoon to go over the finishing details of the Weathermans' project."

They left the bridal store and drove to the International Plaza and Bay Street in Northwest Tampa. There, they grabbed a quick chicken sandwich and went into Nordstrom's. Sheena couldn't remember when she'd had time like this to browse in a store without the feeling of guilt for looking for herself. After Darcy found the sandals she wanted, they raced to the sales racks to see what Darcy could find for her trip to Europe.

A couple of hours later, they made their way to Darcy's car with armfuls of bargains. Sheena had even found a couple of maternity tops that would be cute when she needed them.

They stowed their packages in the backseat, settled in their seats, and took off.

Darcy turned to Sheena with a smile. "Thanks for sharing this day with me."

"You don't mind that I wouldn't let you buy that outrageous pair of boots?"

Darcy laughed. "Regan and I know you're the bossy one. But, yeah, you were right. They were ridiculously expensive. Even on sale."

As they made their way back home, Sheena thought about her sisters. Growing up, their mother had often been ill in bed, leaving the care of her two younger sisters to her. Sheena hadn't liked it, but she didn't resent the responsibility of babysitting as much as Darcy had when she'd been forced to watch Regan. Living and working together during the last year, they'd finally come to understand one another.

###

Sheena entered the registration office and stopped in surprise. Two couples were waiting to be checked in.

"Where's Regan?" Sheena asked Sally, one of Gavin's people they'd hired to help them out.

"Taking guests to their rooms," Sally answered, giving her an apologetic look. "Everyone arrived at once."

Sheena turned to the couple with a smile. "Hello, I'm Sheena. We're so glad you're here. Sorry for the delay. Who's next?"

Sheena slid behind the registration and took over for Sally. After quickly registering the two couples, Sheena offered to walk them to their rooms.

Before she could do so, Regan appeared. "Hi! Everyone ready to go to their rooms? I'll take you. I'm Regan."

After the two couples left with Regan, Sheena checked the reservations list. Fourteen of the twenty rooms were sold. Their numbers were slowly coming up.

"Thank goodness you appeared. This last half-hour, Regan and I were swamped," said Sally. "Funny how everyone arrives at the same time."

"I'm glad you were here to help Regan. It's getting busier and busier." Thinking of the twenty rooms they were about to complete, along with the eight suites, Sheena thought they might have to hire an additional, part-time employee to handle the afternoon rush. It was something she'd discuss with her sisters. In the meantime, she needed to make sure Sally was comfortable in the office alone because she and Michael had agreed to talk.

When Regan came back, Sheena took her aside and explained the situation. "Okay if Sally stays here for a while longer? I'll be back to close up, but I need some private time with Michael before Meaghan gets home from cheerleading."

"Sure, Sally's knows the routine. But remember, Sheena, I won't be available at all tomorrow. I'm working with Mo to get my office set up at the development."

"No problem," Sheena said. She left and hurried to her suite.

Michael was in the kitchen eating a snack when she walked into the room. He looked up at her with a weak smile.

Sheena sat down opposite Michael and studied him. He appeared tired. And troubled.

"What's going on? You said you wanted to talk to me."

"I don't think I want to go to college. My baseball coach thinks I have a good chance of being drafted by a major league baseball team for one of their minor league teams."

Sheena's mouth grew dry. "I thought you were excited about going to Florida State or the University of Miami for a college education and to play baseball. What happened? You've already been told you have a good chance of getting a scholarship to either school."

"Maybe college is a waste of time," Michael said, giving her a questioning look.

"Does this have to do with the situation with Kaylee? Because, if it does, I wouldn't even go there. Someday you'll have a family of your own—a good one. And then it will be necessary to be able to support them. In the meantime, learn all you can so you have choices on how you're going to do that, not only for the immediate future but for the long term."

Michael let out a long sigh. "I've been thinking about you and Dad and the baby. I see how happy and proud Dad is, and it makes me feel bad about what happened with Kaylee."

Sheena rose and gave him a hug. "Oh, honey, you're such a good guy, and someday you're going to be a fantastic father. But what has happened is over. Time to move on. Isn't that what your counselor has suggested?"

"Yeah," said Michael. He looked up at her. "Are you excited about the baby?"

"You know what? I really am," said Sheena, surprising herself.

CHAPTER TWENTY-THREE

REGAN

Regan hurried to the development Brian and Tony were building. Ventura Village would one day consist of forty-eight homes. Twelve were underway and four completed. The location, about a mile inland outside St. Petersburg, was in a nice, secluded pocket of homes between two golf courses.

She drove through the entrance admiring the decorative stone walls and plantings on either side and pulled into the driveway of an attractive, two-story home. This model—The Palms—had a master suite on the first floor, as well as an office, an open floor plan with a gourmet kitchen, a dining area, and a large family room. Outside, a huge, screened lanai looked out to a swimming pool landscaped with a waterfall and a spa. Upstairs, four bedrooms and two baths offered plenty of space. Regan loved it. She was excited about helping other families choose colors, fabrics, and finishing touches for the homes of their choice.

As Regan was getting out of the hotel van she'd borrowed, Mo drove up in his white 300ZX. She went over to him and gave him a quick hug. "Glad you could make it."

He grinned. "Sure. It'll be good to put together the final billing for Arthur. Tomorrow, I'll help you set up your office, go over the contact list with you, and then, sweetie, you'll be in business!"

"I have to admit I'm scared."

He gave her an encouraging smile. "Remember, I'll be only

a phone call away. Any questions that come up can be referred to me until you're comfortable. And before I leave for California, as I mentioned several days ago, I'll connect you with an old classmate of mine, if you'd like. She's been working in real estate, but she's looking to get back into the decorating business. I've told her about you, and she's pleased to meet with you."

Regan's eyes stung with unshed tears. "Nobody can take your place, Mo. Our friendship was perfect from the beginning."

They went inside the house and to the office, where furniture of their choosing had recently been delivered. Furniture for the rest of the house was being delivered that week. Then, just before he left for California, Mo would help her with the finishing touches. Regan was both excited and saddened by the prospect.

Shelving had been placed along one wall of the office to hold sample books of fabrics, carpets, flooring, plumbing accessories, and other decorating items Regan would need to have available to show clients in the development.

They sat at a desk to work on a presentation book for the Weathermans' projects. They included the preliminary drawings for each of the six restaurants, photographs of the final results, and, in a separate area in the back of the book, they presented the financial data for each project and included all invoices from suppliers and sub-contractors. Putting the book together like this was extra work, but both Regan and Mo had decided it would be time worth spending, hoping it would provide an incentive for a client like Arthur to work with them again.

A couple of hours later, the book and the financials were completed. Regan couldn't help worrying about the final bill they were about to present for the work on all six restaurants.

It was a big number.

Mo got to his feet. "We'll meet with Arthur tomorrow morning and then work here in the office. Sound good?"

"Sounds great. Thank you," said Regan. "You're going into Orlando tonight?"

Mo nodded and smiled. "Kenton needs to meet with someone for PR on the new show. We'll stay at the Ritz Carlton, and come home tomorrow. Have fun at Kenton's place in your cozy little cottage."

Regan smiled. She couldn't wait to have some time alone with Brian.

Regan left the development eager to get to the cottage. She and Brian had moved in a couple of nights ago, but this would be the first evening she'd greet him with a home-cooked meal, and the first time they'd have complete privacy in Kenton's luxurious pool.

Because her mother had been ill, Regan hadn't been taught how to cook any more than the basics. But after eating Gracie's good home cooking and tasting the meals at Gavin's, Regan was interested in learning how to cook more exciting things. She'd bought the old, standard, Betty Crocker cookbook and was planning a simple, baked chicken dish and a tossed green salad with fresh, sliced tomatoes and avocados.

Regan pulled up to the cottage and hurried inside. She'd watched how easily Sheena prepared dinner for her family and wanted to have everything organized when Brian walked through the door. He would, she now knew, want a moment to have a beer or a glass of wine before dinner. She'd found it a nice way to start their evening and to build communication between them.

As she was setting the table, Regan studied the simple

white dishes that came with the cottage. Darcy and Austin had picked out china and flatware for the condo together. Regan realized she had no idea what Brian would like. They hadn't talked about such things. He'd told her when the time came, he would like her input on the house she wanted, but that's as far as it had gone.

She sat down in a kitchen chair suddenly aware though she loved Brian and knew his body very well, she needed to know more about him if they were going to make a home together. The cottage was a good beginning, but everything had been provided for them.

At the sound of Brian's truck pulling into the driveway, Regan jumped to her feet to greet him.

When he walked through the door and saw her, a huge grin lit his face. "Ahhh, so nice to come home to you." He wrapped his arms around her and drew her close.

Regan leaned against his strong chest and sighed with satisfaction. Who cared what the house looked like as long as Brian lived there with her.

Brian lifted her chin and planted his lips on hers. As they embraced, his tender kiss changed, became more demanding.

Regan's heartbeat raced. She could never seem to get enough of him.

When they broke apart, Brian smiled down at her. "Miss me that much, huh?"

She laughed. "I've been looking forward to this evening all day."

He gave her a gentle hug. "I knew we'd be good together."

"Let's sit for a few minutes while the chicken cooks," said Regan. "There's a cold beer in the refrigerator, unless you'd prefer a glass of wine."

"Beer sounds good," said Brian before going to the kitchen sink and washing up.

As Brian splashed water on his face, Regan observed the way his chest muscles rippled. The consistent exercises he did each day had kept those muscles strong.

Regan slid the chicken into the oven and followed Brian outside to the patio. They had a few minutes before sundown. Like every tourist to the area, Regan delighted in watching the sun disappear behind the horizon, spreading rosy hues in the sky that seemed to her like a heavenly benediction. She stared at the sun, hoping for a glimpse of the green flash—a phenomenon that arose when the right conditions in the atmosphere coincided with the exact moment the sun slipped from view. Though she had yet to see it, she never tired of looking for it.

Sitting in a chair beside her, Brian reached over and took hold of her hand. "You're beautiful, you know."

Regan turned to him with a smile. At one time that had been important to her. Now, she knew how little it mattered. After the accident, comments of her looking like Liz Taylor had ended, yet, she felt more confident than ever.

"How was your day?" Regan asked him.

Brian shook his head. "Frustrating as usual. I can handle the paperwork, do a lot of promo for the company, and even oversee the work, but I still can't handle a hammer or a saw the way I want. I know I'm getting stronger, but I still have to be careful."

Regan squeezed the hand that was still in hers. "I'm sorry, hon."

"Me, too. How about your day? Getting settled in the office? I saw you brought some stuff in."

"Tomorrow, Mo and I are going to get everything organized and go through his contact list. He's told me of someone who could possibly help me out, but I want to see how I do on my own."

"No need to rush into anything," Brian said. "You can handle the work at the development just fine."

"But I have a lot more to do than that," Regan said. "I'm overseeing the renovation of the hotel. We're about to start completing the top-floor rooms in the Egret Building, and as soon as Sheena and Tony move into their house, we'll begin completely redoing the eight suites. And we're doing work on the spaces for Gavin's people, and ..."

Brian's eyebrows shot up. "That's an awful lot of work. Are you sure you want to tackle it alone?"

Worried about it herself, Regan frowned. "You don't think I can do it?"

"I didn't say that," said Brian, shaking his head.

Regan slumped in her chair. "I'm sorry for snapping at you. I thought I was over being upset about Mo leaving, but I'm obviously not."

"It'll all work out. You're better than you think you are," said Brian.

Regan got to her feet and leaned over to kiss him. "Thanks for being here for me. It means so much to have your support."

When their lips met, Regan felt her earlier tension disappear. She'd do the best she could, and maybe, as Brian said, she was better than she thought.

After dinner, Regan unpacked a few more of her things in their bedroom and then turned to Brian. "Ready for a swim?"

"Mo and Kenton are gone for the night?" Brian asked, arching his eyebrows at her.

Regan grinned. "We have the pool to ourselves."

"Great. I'll grab the towels." He took off his shirt, jeans, and undershorts and grabbed his bathing suit.

Regan watched Brian walk naked into the adjoining

bathroom. The scars on his hip and his arms were less noticeable now. His hip seemed normal though they were still careful of it. An image of how he'd looked right after the accident flashed through her mind, and she thought, as she had before, how lucky they both were.

Brian returned with the towels. "Well?"

Regan changed out of her clothes into a bikini, and wrapping a towel around her, followed him out the door.

The moon was rising in the sky, shedding enough light to add a glow to the scenery around her, forming swaying shapes of the palm trees among shadows. The dimly-lit, heated pool sat in the darkness, luring her on. After working with him in the hotel pool, Regan was delighted Brian now shared her love of swimming.

He was already in the water when she lowered her towel onto a chair and dove in. She rose to the surface gasping at the water's coolness. She began swimming laps, her muscles lengthening with the exercise. Brian soon caught up with her, and a spontaneous race broke out.

Well aware of Brian's competitiveness, Regan sprang forward to reach the far end first.

Brian swam up to her and, laughing, wrapped his arms around her. "You little mermaid! Someday, I'll beat you."

She turned to him and lifted her face to his. Their lips met, warm among the skin that was chilling in the onshore breeze.

As Brian's kiss deepened, Regan clasped her legs around his waist and hugged him tightly. She loved him so much words were not enough.

He caressed her back and shifted her, so she felt his excitement.

"Race you back to the house," she whispered in his ear.

He laughed. "Looking for a little playtime?"

"Could be," she murmured, giving him a playful smile.

He'd taught her what fun, how wonderful, making love could be.

They hurried out of the pool, grabbed their towels, and ran to the cottage.

Still shivering, Regan hurried inside and heard Brian's cell ringing.

Behind her, Brian shut the door, picked up his phone, and studied it.

She waited while he punched in a number. He said, "Hi, Mom! You called?"

Regan gave him a questioning look. Holly's calls usually meant she wanted something.

Brian shrugged.

Disappointed the sexy moment was gone, Regan went into the bedroom, towel-dried her body, and slipped on her pajamas. She still hadn't come to terms with Brian's devotion to his mother. She liked Holly, even loved her, but Holly sometimes demanded a lot of attention.

Brian walked into the bedroom. "Strange call from Mom. She's asked us to come to Blackie's house on Friday for dinner. And she told me to dress nicely, that it's a special occasion."

"Is it her birthday?"

Brian shook his head. "Not until next week."

"Want to watch T.V. or something?" Regan asked.

Brian grinned at her. "Or something."

She patted the bed beside her.

Brian dropped his towel and joined her.

"Better than T.V. any day," he said, putting his arms around her and nuzzling her neck.

CHAPTER TWENTY-FOUR

DARCY

Darcy sat with her sisters at the kitchen table in Sheena's suite going over plans for the further renovation of the hotel. Sheena had been dealing with Blackie's business partner and lawyer, Greg Ryan, to set up Salty Key Enterprises as a Limited Liability Corporation or LLC. With their funds under the control of the LLC, they could draw upon them as needed and, more importantly, as agreed upon and budgeted.

"I've drawn up a list of projects in our budget and allocated funds to each," Sheena said, handing them each a spreadsheet. She turned to Regan. "We need you to approve these numbers and then keep the costs down."

"Nicole and I have worked on advertising for weddings," said Darcy. "We've taken photos of the small, private room upstairs in Gavin's as a place for changing and pre-wedding celebrations for the bride and her bridal party. However, we need to complete the Bridal Suite in the Egret Building right away so we can show that as well. Can you do that, Regan?"

Regan gave her a big smile. "Yes. Remember, we have a couple of extra couches we'll move into the sitting area. I've got photographs to show you of the chairs I want to add to the room, along with end tables, lamps, and a special, three-way, full-length mirror. The bridal party will want to be able to check themselves out. And we've already discussed the king-sized bed I've ordered for the suite."

"Sounds good," said Sheena. "Let's look at the pictures."

Darcy pointed out the items she liked, and, surprisingly, Sheena quietly went along with her choices.

"As you can see, any of the selections go well with the simple beach theme we have in the décor. But they dress up the room quite a bit," said Regan. "I'd like to add high-end bedding and towels not only to that room, but to all the rooms on both floors."

Sheena frowned and looked at the spreadsheet she'd handed them. "How much do you estimate for doing that? I know it seems as if we have a lot of money, and we do, but it will go fast as we work on completing the renovations."

Darcy and Regan exchanged knowing looks. This was more like the Sheena they knew.

"I'll get back to you on that. In the meantime, do I have your permission to go ahead and order the items we liked for the Bridal Suite?" said Regan.

Darcy looked at Sheena and nodded her assent. Though the room would retain a casual look, it would have an upscale feeling to it that wasn't there before. She knew from putting together things for Austin's condo how important nice bedding was, and she wanted that for their guests.

Sheena sat back in her chair. "Any questions on the spreadsheet?"

"What does the timetable look like?" Darcy said. "I'm sorry I'll be away for three weeks while some of this is still going on."

"Go ahead and enjoy your honeymoon," said Sheena. "We'll do what we can as fast as we can."

"Yes, don't worry about us. We're so excited for you," Regan said, beaming at her.

The breath Darcy had been holding escaped her in a sigh of relief. They were under pressure to get things done, and she didn't want to be considered a slacker.

As if hearing Darcy's thoughts, Sheena said, "Our goal is to have everything done by June 1st before my baby comes, but you're doing your share, Darcy. I'll be working with Tony and Brian to get crews in here at the appropriate times."

"I saw someone working on the gazebo this morning," said Darcy. "That will be great for weddings—both for the ceremony and for photographs."

"I agree," said Sheena. "As soon as that's done, they're going to work on the main building to convert a large, ground-floor storage room into a sitting and recreation area with a private, outdoor patio for Gavin's people." She checked her watch. "What do you say we get a cup of coffee or something at Gracie's before it closes?"

Darcy shook her head. "I think I'll head back to the condo. I'm working on an idea for signage for the hotel grounds."

"No!" said Regan. "I mean, let's take advantage of some time together while we can. Right?"

Darcy paused at the way Sheena and Regan were staring at her. She lifted her shoulders and let them drop. "Okay, I guess I can take a few extra minutes with you."

They walked across the hotel grounds to Gracie's, stopping to talk about the bohio hut they were going to build near the pool—a place where people could get refreshments during the day.

"We can ask Gracie about providing some food for it," said Darcy. "Better now than never."

Neither Sheena nor Regan responded, but kept on walking.

Darcy ran to catch up to them. "What's up with you two?"

"I'm ready for a break," said Regan. "That's all."

Darcy followed her sisters to the restaurant.

Sheena held the door, and Darcy walked inside.

"Surprise!"

Darcy rocked back on her heels.

"Go on, Darcy," prompted Regan, giving her a gentle push.

In shock, Darcy blinked as Gracie, Bebe, Sally, Maggie, Lynn, and Clyde smiled at her. Beside them, Meaghan, Holly, and Nicole greeted her with more smiles. Sam and Rocky stood aside and bobbed their heads at her in greeting.

"It's a surprise," said Clyde proudly. "It's for you. See?"

A cake sat on a nearby table, surrounded by gaily covered packages.

"Thank you," said Darcy, fighting tears. "I certainly didn't expect anything like this."

"A family wedding is something to celebrate," said Sheena, giving her a hug.

As Darcy looked around the room, that's all she saw. Family.

CHAPTER TWENTY-FIVE

REGAN

Friday evening, Brian drove Regan's new, white Jeep Summit into the front circle of Blackie's luxurious home and parked behind a BMW convertible.

The tan-stucco, one-story home overlooked the bay and had been used as a show house for a charitable group when it was built four years ago. It was still awe inspiring, thought Regan, as Brian helped her out of the Jeep. Standing a moment, she studied every detail she could, including the stunning pots beside the front entrance and the lush landscaping.

Blackie opened the front door to them. "Welcome. We're so glad you're here." He kissed Regan's cheek and shook hands with Brian. "Come on in. We've been waiting for you."

Regan checked her watch. "We're not late, are we?"

"No," said Blackie, giving her a mysterious smile. "You're right on time."

Regan followed him inside. The tall ceiling in the marble-tiled entrance made the space seem enormous. Her gaze shifted to the large living room ahead of her. A grand piano sat in a corner of the room. Two Oriental carpets lay atop the soft-gold marble tile, softening the sound of conversation between Holly and a man Regan didn't know. Greg Ryan stood by with a woman Regan assumed was his wife.

Blackie led them over to Holly. "Our special guests are here, sweetheart."

Holly smiled at Regan, kissed her, and threw her arms around Brian. "So glad you're here. I want you to meet Father Joe. Father, this is my son Brian and his fiancée, Regan Sullivan."

Father Joe bobbed his head, smiled at Regan, and shook hands with Brian. "So nice you could join us."

Regan and Brian exchanged looks of confusion.

Blackie put his arm around Holly's shoulder and turned to them. "Rather than simply elope, like we talked about, Holly and I wanted to share this moment with you."

"Elope?" said Brian, his eyes widening. "You're kidding!"

"No, we're not," said Holly. "With Darcy's wedding coming up and your engagement, we decided to make our wedding as simple as possible, so it wouldn't take away from anything you might plan."

"I would've asked for your blessing," said Blackie, "but that would've given our plans away."

"I see," said Brian.

Regan slipped her hand into his and gave it an encouraging squeeze. "Thanks for including us. I'm so happy for the two of you."

"Yes," said Brian, nodding. "Me too. You sure you want to do this, Mom?"

She let out a girlish chuckle and sent an adoring look to Blackie. "I never dreamed I could be so happy. I love this man of mine."

Blackie's tan cheeks turned pink. "I love her, son. More than she'll ever know."

"Well, then, let's get going," said Brian, kissing his mother on the cheek.

"Thank you, Brian," she said, blinking back tears.

Greg Ryan joined them. "Brian, Regan, I want you to meet my wife, Beth."

A pretty woman with sparkling, hazel eyes, Beth shook hands with both of them. "Such a nice occasion. I've never seen Blackie so happy. All because of Holly."

"By the way," said Greg to Brian. "After things settle down, I'll need to meet with you. Holly is turning the bar over to you."

Brian turned to his mother. "You're giving me the bar?"

She laughed. "Yes, I am. It's yours to do with what you want. Blackie wants me available for travel and whatever else we decide."

Regan observed the way Blackie smiled at Holly and felt a thread of happiness weave through her. Every woman deserved to be treated the way Blackie was treating Holly, the way Brian treated her.

Standing on tiptoes, she kissed Brian. "Let's go to a wedding."

He grinned. "Guess we already are."

The wedding ceremony was simple, quick, and meaningful. Holly's eyes filled with tears of joy as she recited the words that bound her to Blackie. And Blackie, tough-talking businessman he sometimes was, couldn't stop tears of his own as he vowed to honor and protect her.

Beside her, Regan could sense emotion well inside Brian. She squeezed his arm and watched as Blackie and Holly shared an embrace as man and wife.

After the short ceremony, Blackie announced, "Thank you for attending our special moment. My wife has ordered a celebration dinner. Please join us."

Holly led the way into the dining room. Dim lighting from two chandeliers spread a warm glow below. A long, glass and metal table was set with seven places—seven islands of seafoam green matching colors in what Regan knew was a handwoven rug below. Place cards indicated where they were to sit. Regan sat opposite Holly and next to Blackie, who sat at the head of the table.

Blackie stood and removed a bottle of champagne from a silver ice bucket that had been placed near him. He removed the foil cover, loosened and pulled off the wire cage and slid the cork out of the bottle with a soft, satisfying hiss. Then he poured a tiny bit of the wine into a tulip glass and tasted it.

"Good enough to share," he said with a smile. He filled the other glasses and then his own. Raising his glass, he said, "To my lovely wife, Holly. Thank you for marrying me. I'm the luckiest man alive."

"No, sir," said Brian. "I am. Here's to Regan." He gazed at her with such love, the sip of champagne Regan had started to swallow stayed bubbling in her mouth. Trying desperately not to cough, Regan braced herself and swallowed.

"Are you all right?" Brian asked her.

She nodded and took a sip of water. "Lots of bubbles."

They all laughed.

Later, lying in bed beside Brian, she turned to him. "Are you okay? You've been awfully quiet."

He faced her and traced a finger down her face. "I'm fine. I'm just surprised by all that's happened. What in the hell am I going to do with a bar? I'm busy working with Tony on our development."

"It's a great gift, really. I'm sure your mother wanted you to have some options, in case you could never work on construction as you wanted."

"No matter what, I'm not giving up on my construction company. I'll have to find someone to run the bar."

"How about Casey? He's busy with Gavin's at night, but he could hire a manager and oversee it for you. He knows the business."

Brian grinned. "Anyone ever tell you how smart you are?"

His words were as sweet as the wedding cake she'd shared with him.

The next morning, Regan joined Darcy and Sheena for coffee at Gracie's and filled them in with the details of Holly and Blackie's surprise wedding.

"How did Brian take it?" said Sheena. "He's very protective of his mother."

"He was as surprised as I, but he's happy for them. Holly is giving him The Key Hole bar, and he's not sure what to do about it. I suggested having Casey oversee it for him. Casey can hire a manager and keep tabs on it."

"Whoa! Would he ever consider making it part of the hotel?" said Sheena. "We were planning on sharing the waterfront with The Key Hole. Now, maybe we can work out a deal to pull it all together by making it some kind of affiliate, so it appears to be seamless to guests."

Darcy sat quietly, but Regan could see her mind working.

"Do you mean making it part of Salty Key Enterprises?" Darcy asked.

"Yes," said Sheena. "We'd have to have Greg Ryan work things out, so Brian maintains ownership of the bar itself, but by managing it, we could provide purchasing power and share in the profits with it. We could also set up a separate waterfront operation under our corporate umbrella."

"Wow, Sheena, you sound like you've been thinking about this for a while," Regan said, impressed by her sister's business sense.

Sheena laughed. "Greg Ryan and I discussed several scenarios for the hotel. It may turn out to be even bigger than Uncle Gavin ever imagined."

"I like the idea, as long as we can afford to have good outside expertise on many different levels," Darcy said. "Sheena, you've told us you intend to keep overseeing the hotel. Are you going to be willing to see this through? With a baby coming, it could be difficult."

"The bulk of the remaining renovations work is scheduled to be done before the baby," said Sheena a little sharply. "And afterward, I will be thrilled to have the opportunity to work on hotel stuff while I'm caring for a baby."

"I was just asking," Regan quickly said, aware Sheena didn't want to lose herself again to raising a new baby with little outside stimulation.

Darcy gave them a thumbs-up. "Okay then. Big deal stuff, here we come!"

CHAPTER TWENTY-SIX

SHEENA

Later that day, Sheena sat alone in her kitchen reviewing their plans. Just as Regan needed a boost of confidence now and then, so did she. Darcy was right to question her ability to work on hotel issues and still mother a baby, but it felt so wrong to be thought incapable of doing both. That feeling of needing to find herself is what had encouraged her to take their uncle's challenge and come to Florida in the first place. None of them had imagined where it would lead.

She patted her stomach. "You and I are going to do just fine."

Laughing at herself for talking to the baby like this, Sheena went back to her spreadsheet. She'd review numbers and give Greg Ryan a call so they could talk to Brian sensibly.

Meaghan came into the room and plopped down into a kitchen chair with a loud, long sigh.

"What's up?" Sheena asked.

"I'm tired of taking the bus home. Can't you pick me up at school?"

"No-o-o," said Sheena cautiously. She wasn't about to be roped into a schedule like that. Besides, she knew where this was leading. "And, no, you're not getting a car."

"But Trish got one," said Meaghan. "And we have money now."

"We're working hard to finish the hotel and keep it running," said Sheena. "All funds are going there except for college educations for you and Mike."

"I know," said Meaghan, nodding glumly. "It's just that I'm disappointed Rob doesn't take the bus anymore. His father bought him a car. And then I had to tell him I couldn't go to his Valentine party because of Aunt Darcy's wedding. Now, he thinks I don't like him."

Sheena gave her a hug. "Things will work out. You'll see."

"Can we go look at the house? I want to check to see if my room is painted and if the pool is done."

"Sure," said Sheena, understanding Meaghan's disappointment.

Sheena drove through the entrance to Ventura Village with a sense of pride. It was, she thought, a handsome development. There were several floor plans to choose from, and each choice had different exterior elevations, so the houses didn't look the same.

Sheena drove into the driveway of one of the larger homes—a two-story with a pool. After living side by side with Tony's parents for all her marriage, Sheena was pleased by the space between their house and the neighbors on either side.

As she got out of the car, Sheena noticed the blue Cadillac convertible sitting in the driveway and wondered who was there. She followed Meaghan into the house, and hearing voices on the second story, she climbed the stairs and followed the sound of the voices into the guest bathroom.

At the sight before her, she stopped in surprise.

"Hello, what are you doing?" she asked with dismay.

Tony had his arm around a tall, leggy, red-headed woman who was teetering on high heels.

Turning to her with a sheepish look, Tony all but jumped away from the woman. "Hi, Sheena! Taylor twisted her ankle.

I'm helping her get to a place where she can sit down."

He held the woman's arm as she hobbled to the edge of the tub and sat down.

Tony straightened. "Sheena, this is Taylor Hutchison. She's looking to buy a house here. I was showing her what we're doing for the guest suite that we're using for Meaghan's bedroom."

"Hello, Taylor," said Sheena forcing a pleasantness into her voice that she didn't feel. She recognized the look of desire the woman was bestowing upon her husband. Sheena gazed at Tony, waiting for him to say something as he continued to stand next to Taylor.

Tony cleared his throat. "Taylor, this is my wife, Sheena."

Meaghan burst into in the room. "Wait until you see ..." She stopped, and seeing Taylor, frowned and blurted out, "Hi, Daddy! Who's this?"

Though Tony's cheeks colored, he spoke calmly. "Taylor Hutchison is looking at houses. She likes what we're doing to your suite."

"Yeah, it's really cool having my own bathroom." Sensing the tension in the room, she looked from Sheena to Tony. "Can I show you something, Daddy?"

"Sure, sweetheart." He turned to Taylor. "Maybe Sheena can show you out. Let Brian or me know which house you decide on, so we can put it on the schedule."

"Thanks, Tony. It was so sweet of you to take so much time out of your day to spend with me," gushed Taylor in a breathy way that made Sheena want to slap her.

"No worries," said Tony, glancing at Sheena before following Meaghan out of the room.

"Would you like me to help you down the stairs?" Sheena asked Taylor.

She smiled. "I'm much better now. But, thanks."

Sheena walked behind Taylor to make sure she didn't stumble, but, inside, she was fuming. Didn't Tony realize what was up with Taylor? The woman, who wore no wedding ring, now seemed able to do a ten-mile race.

After seeing Taylor off, Sheena returned to the house.

Outside, behind the house, Meaghan and Tony were talking while sitting on the wall surrounding the spa.

"Why don't you go check on your room?" Sheena said to Meaghan. "I want to talk to Daddy."

"Okay," said Meaghan. "Is that Taylor woman gone? I don't like her, Mom."

"It's nothing for you to worry about. She's just looking at houses," said Sheena, surprised by Meaghan's intuition.

Meaghan left, and Sheena lowered herself onto the wall next to Tony.

"What's all the fuss about?" asked Tony. "I hope you're not mad because I spent time with Taylor."

"I'm a little uncomfortable with it, but I'm not mad, Tony. Her interest in you was so obvious it was almost alarming. Do you get many prospective customers like that?"

Tony shook his head. "Brian's been handling prospective clients. He's busy with something else, so I offered to show her around. That's all. Regan will be onsite soon, and then she or someone she hires will talk to people interested in the development, show them around."

"I thought Regan was going to do the interior decorating for customers," said Sheena, concerned with the idea of Regan being gone so much of the time when they were involved in the renovations for the hotel.

"She is. We were thinking of maybe hiring Nicole for the marketing. Then she can choose a salesperson and give Regan more time for the hotel. We're still trying to work out the details." Tony slipped his hand into Sheena's. "You're not really worried about me and other women, are you?"

Sheena studied his face, saw the love in his eyes, and shook her head. "No, but it bothers me when someone like Taylor goes after men they know are married." She tapped the gold wedding ring on his hand.

Looking inordinately pleased, Tony smiled. "I like when you get jealous."

Sheena laughed. "I guess I am. Especially now that I'm pregnant and feeling a little fat."

"You're beautiful, Sheena. Believe it," said Tony, giving her a kiss so passionate they didn't hear Meaghan approach.

"Ugh," said Meaghan. "You two are so mushy."

Satisfaction filled Sheena. Someday, Meaghan would understand the importance of keeping it that way.

Sheena fixed cups of coffee for her sisters and sat down at the kitchen table with them. "Time to talk logistics," she said and explained the situation at the development. "If Brian and Tony hire Nicole to run their sales and marketing program, will that leave her enough time to do our marketing?"

"Don't forget she works at Gavin's at night," said Regan. "And we wanted her to run marketing for The Key Hole."

"Why don't you let me talk to her," said Darcy. "I'll be working on marketing for the hotel with her, but it's a big responsibility for Nicole to be in charge of all three projects. Can we offer her enough money to entice her to do all three of them?"

"What if we offer great incentives for all three—Ventura, the hotel, including Gavin's, Gracie's, and The Key Hole?" said Sheena. "Working with those three would make it a full-time job with time for little else."

"I like the idea," said Regan. "I can't do more at Ventura

than the interior decorating and still oversee hotel renovations. Sales will be picking up at the development, and we still have a lot to do here."

"Okay, I want to get this settled before the wedding. Dad and Regina will be here before we know it, and then none of us will get much work done as we prepare for the celebrations." Darcy fluttered her hands in an uncharacteristic way. "I'm starting to get a little nervous about it."

"It's going to be lovely," said Sheena. "A nice, small, sweet ceremony."

"It'll be a good way to test our facilities before our first official wedding," said Regan. "I hope Mo and I have thought of everything."

Darcy gave Sheena and Regan worried looks. "You'll be fine without me, won't you? Three weeks is a long time for me to be away."

"We'll be fine," said Sheena. *They would, wouldn't they?*

CHAPTER TWENTY-SEVEN

DARCY

As Darcy was going through the morning mail, her heart stopped at the sight of an envelope from New York City. She lifted it to her lips, kissed it for good luck, and opened it. Glancing at the cold, impersonal rejection letter from the publisher, she crumpled it up and threw it down to the floor. This was the fourth response of its kind. As much as she hated those letters, she'd read she would be lucky to get any response at all. Allison Berkhardt hadn't had any luck with her contacts in the industry and had informed Darcy she'd done all she could.

This business sucks!

Darcy pounded her desk in frustration. She'd hoped to be able to surprise Austin with publishing success as a special wedding gift. With just one more response to come in—or not—she was out of options for the time being. Even as she vowed not to give up, she knew she owed it to her sisters to keep her focus on hotel business. Sheena said they'd be fine without her, but too much was going on in her sisters' personal lives for her not to worry.

She picked up the phone to call Nicole. They hadn't been able to meet yesterday. Today, she hoped, would be better.

Nicole answered with a cheery, "Hi, there! Sorry I missed your call yesterday. I was in Miami for a couple of days."

"Hope it was for something fun," said Darcy. "Can we meet for lunch? I need to talk over something with you."

"That would be great," said Nicole. "I've got some exciting news to share with you."

"You didn't find another job, did you?" Darcy blurted out.

"Nooo, why do you ask?"

"We'll talk at lunch. Meet me at Gracie's at noon."

"See you then," said Nicole.

As she waited for Nicole to show up for lunch, Darcy studied the work being done on the patio for Gavin's people. A waterfall was being constructed as part of the small spa pool. When she and her sisters had asked for suggestions for the space, both Gracie and Bebe had thought the sound of water would be a soothing feature after working long hours in a chaotic kitchen.

"Hi, Darcy!"

Darcy swiveled around to face Nicole. "Hey! You look great! How are you doing?"

"For a woman in love, I'm doing very well," said Nicole, beaming at her.

"You and Graham? How wonderful!" Darcy threw an arm around Nicole.

Nicole shook her head. "Not Graham. It's Casey and me. After working together almost every night for the last couple of months, we found we really enjoyed one another. Graham's a nice guy, but there wasn't the same kind of magic between us that I share with Casey. I want someone sexy whom I not only like, but who gives me goose pimples. You know?"

Darcy grinned. "Oh, yes, I know exactly what you mean. Like Austin and me."

Nicole's eyes sparkled. "We've talked for hours and hours about what we want out of life and agree on almost everything."

"How does he feel about your working?" Darcy asked, taking Nicole's arm and leading her inside Gracie's.

"He likes that I've become interested in the hotel business. Why?" said Nicole, giving her a quizzical look.

Darcy led Nicole to the family table in the corner. "Let's enjoy lunch, and then let me tell you what my sisters and I have in mind."

Nicole smiled. "Going to be a big tease, are you?"

"Oh, heck! I'll tell you now." Darcy laid out the plan and waited to see Nicole's reaction.

"Really?" said Nicole, her eyes wide. "You would trust me to handle all the locations? It's a big job."

"I have an appointment for you at Ventura. After lunch, if you're willing, I'll drive you there. Brian will meet with you.

"That would be terrific!" said Nicole. "Casey told me he's going to manage the bar for Brian. We can work together on the advertising portfolio I'm putting together for it and coordinate it with the work I'm already doing for the hotel."

Maggie approached their table. "Ready to order?"

Darcy smiled. "Thanks."

She and Nicole ordered lunch, and while they ate, they discussed the finer details of such an arrangement. By the time they were ready to leave the restaurant, Darcy was pretty certain Nicole would be amenable to their plan. The one difficulty would be finding a reliable broker and realtors to handle Ventura. Nicole could guide them, but she did not have a realtor's license.

Darcy arranged to meet Brian at the show home in Ventura Village so she could fill him in on her earlier conversation with Nicole. More than that, she wanted to have some time alone with him to discuss the future. It bothered her that Regan wasn't talking about a wedding anytime soon when Darcy knew how much Regan wanted to be married.

Brian was already in the office looking through different house plans when she arrived.

"Hey there!" he said pleasantly.

"Hi. Brian. Can we talk privately?"

"About Nicole? Sure."

"No, about you and Regan," she said, hoping she wasn't crossing over any lines. But family was family, and she loved her sister. "Why isn't Regan talking about any plans to get married? Is something wrong between you?"

Brian chuckled. "Not at all. In fact, we already have our marriage license. We're just waiting for you and Austin to get married. Regan didn't want to do anything to upstage you on your special day. So, as soon as she gives the word, we're going to take the leap. Nothing fancy. In fact, we'll probably elope."

"Oh, but the family will be so disappointed not to share in the fun."

"We'll see," said Brian. "Now let's talk about Nicole."

A few minutes later, Nicole walked into the room.

Darcy sat in on the meeting between Brian and Nicole, impressed by the enthusiasm for the project Brian easily made Nicole feel. When they began talking salary, Darcy excused herself, giving them the privacy they deserved.

On a whim, she decided to check on the progress of Tony and Sheena's house. As she walked toward it, a red-headed woman got into a blue Cadillac convertible and drove away.

As Darcy reached for the front door, Tony opened it. "Hi, Darcy. What are you doing here?"

"I brought Nicole Coleman over for an interview with Brian about the sales manager position. What are you doing here at the house?"

Tony raked his fingers through his dark curls. "I honestly

don't know. Taylor Hutchison claims she's interested in buying a house from us, but we can't pin her down on which one."

Darcy's eyebrows shot up. "Taylor Hutchison? The same woman Sheena told me about?"

"Yeah. Do me a favor, will you? Don't mention this to Sheena. She won't like the idea of my meeting with Taylor."

Darcy's concern for her sister rose in a scowl. "Why can't Brian meet with her instead of you?"

"He's meeting with Nicole, remember?" Tony snapped at her. His expression softened. "I'm sorry. I'm just trying to do my share and make a sale. Brian makes it seem so easy, but I can't seem to close what should be a simple deal. I'm more of a construction guy, anyway."

Darcy gave him a steady look. "All right, I won't say anything to Sheena, but if you hurt my sister, I'll never forgive you."

Tony raised a hand in defense. "Believe me; I have no intention of doing so. C'mon, I'll walk you back to the office."

As they strolled along the new sidewalk, Tony turned to her. "Getting excited about the wedding?"

Darcy smiled. "For that and the honeymoon. I can't wait to travel with Austin. He's going to show me some of his favorite places."

"I'd hoped to do some traveling with Sheena, but I guess that's out of the picture now with a new baby coming."

Darcy turned to him. "Are you disappointed?"

"Funny," he said. "I'm not. I thought I would be after a day or two of excitement, but that's not how I feel. We're much more financially secure, and that will make a difference to both of us, I hope."

Darcy stopped and gave him a pat on the back. "You're a good man, Tony."

"Thanks. You won't tell Sheena about Taylor. Right?"
She shook her head. *Men!*

Two days later, after all agreements had been completed with Nicole and Casey for their new roles, Darcy sat with them, Sheena and Tony, Regan and Brian, and Austin in the small, private dining room on the second floor of Gavin's.

Sheena lifted her glass of bubbly water in a toast. Here's to the two new members of our group—Nicole and Casey. We welcome you to Salty Key Enterprises."

"Hear! Hear!" came the response.

Brian stood. "And, Nicole, we welcome you to the staff of Ventura Village. We hope it leads to many sales."

Nicole laughed. "I hope so too!"

Darcy looked around the room and sighed with satisfaction at the sight of the people gathered together. They represented a growing family to her. Her father would be here soon, and while she was caught up in preparations for her wedding, he would look for a new home. Marriage would expand her family even more. She already loved Austin's grandfather, Bill Blakely, and in time, she'd get to know Austin's parents better. With him, they'd given her the best gift imaginable.

CHAPTER TWENTY-EIGHT

REGAN

Several days later, Regan hid her discomfort as she always did when she faced the camera to do one of her ads for Arthur Weatherman's restaurants. The red light signaling she was "on camera" flashed before her, and then everything around her seemed to disappear as she focused on her words. She'd learned if she memorized the script carefully, the words could carry her through the uncomfortable time before the camera. Being in the spotlight like this hadn't become easier over time. Even when her face was so-called "perfect," she hadn't wanted attention centered on it. Now that her scars were apparent, and her lip still drooped at one corner, it was harder still.

Regan smiled as she had been directed and spoke the words she'd been given, pleased the money she was earning for being spokesperson for the restaurant chain was something she intended to put to good use by supporting a variety of charities. Her first project would be to help Cyndi Jansen raise funds for children of war veterans to get scholarships to college. Cyndi and her husband, Tom, a disabled war vet, had been among their first guests at the hotel using a special military discount she and her sisters had offered. They'd remained loyal customers and had encouraged others to come to the hotel. Because Regan had never been able to get into college, she was especially anxious to help Cyndi in this way.

"That's a wrap," said the cameraman. "Mr. Weatherman is going to be pleased with this special Florida visitor campaign. Good job, Regan!"

"Thanks," she said, feeling the tension in her cheek muscles ebb. There was only so much smiling one could do. It was easier when she was sharing the camera with a child or an animal. But Emily had decided she didn't like being in front of the camera, either.

Regan left the studio and headed back home. She loved sharing the cottage on Kenton's property with Brian, but it bothered her that she was doing exactly what her mother had warned her against—living with a man before marriage. They were engaged, but still ...

At the cottage, she changed her clothes into something more suitable for work at Ventura Village. She and Mo had set up her office there, and she was meeting with a new client that afternoon. First, she was going to check on progress at the hotel.

She drove into the entrance to the Salty Key Inn and stopped to admire the plantings recently installed in well-designed groupings to accent the property's view corridors and to provide some privacy for guests seated at the pool and on their patios or balconies. The new hibiscus, oleander, bougainvillea, and sabal and queen palm trees gave a distinctly tropical look to the grounds that hadn't been present before.

By habit, she pulled into the parking area behind the building containing the eight suites they had yet to renovate. The space was empty now except for the hotel van and cars belonging to Sheena's family. At night, the patrons of Gavin's would fill the lot.

Regan got out of her Jeep and studied the building. The sign Austin had carved of a Sandpiper had been mounted earlier that year indicating the building was officially called the Sandpiper Suites Building. She hoped Brian's crew could start on the demolition and re-configuration of the interiors of the building as soon as Sheena's family moved out shortly before Darcy's wedding.

One of the last things Mo had helped her with before heading to California was a re-design of the space inside each suite. Her sisters had agreed with Mo and her that the suites should be comfortable and convenient for long-term stays, which was how many smaller hotels and resorts in the area did well in the winter months. Each suite would contain a full-size refrigerator, stove, dishwasher, plenty of cupboards and drawers in the kitchen, and larger-than-normal closets for clothes and storage.

Crossing the lawn to the Egret Building, Regan paused to lift a beautiful pink hibiscus blossom to her nose. She loved the bright colors of tropical flora. More aware of color and tones now that she worked with them every day, she marveled at nature's beauty.

The pounding of a hammer brought her head up. She smiled at the sight of carpenters building the framing for a bohio-style, outdoor casual bar near the swimming pool. Open-aired, and with a palm-thatched roof, it would be a small operation providing a place where guests could relax with a drink and light snacks.

She waved at Sheena, who was working in the office, and then hurried across to the Egret Building. For the upstairs rooms, she and Mo had chosen a slightly different color scheme from the ground-floor rooms. Soft-yellow walls, sand-colored carpets, and the blue on the hand-painted furniture were still in place. But instead of the blues, yellows, and oranges of the soft goods on the ground floor, green was the predominant color, reflecting the color of the palm trees and other tropical foliage outside.

The main renovation project for the second-floor rooms was in the bathrooms. Sinks had been torn out earlier and re-installed in the downstairs rooms. Because they now had enough money, they were replacing the vanities with twin-basin units and also ripping out the tubs and installing walk-in showers with large, soothing shower heads. Similar shower fixtures had already replaced those in the downstairs rooms.

In each room, a new, overstuffed chair complemented the small settee Regan had purchased when she'd first met Mo.

Regan found a couple of workmen in one of the bathrooms finishing grout work in the shower. "Good afternoon! How are you doing?"

"Coming along," the older of the two replied in a voice that warned against too much talk.

"Are we still on schedule?"

"Yep," the man replied. "All the showers should be done in about ten days or less."

"Good," said Regan, happy the noisy part of ripping out the old fixtures was over. The new cabinetry holding the sinks was installed in most of the bathrooms. Once the showers were in, flooring could be installed, and then the new toilets would be placed and connected to water supply and sewer lines.

Regan hated losing the opportunity to open these rooms before March, but the result would be well worth it.

Downstairs, she checked an empty room. The new air conditioners they'd had installed were quieter and more efficient. The upholstered chairs for these rooms, recently purchased at their favorite discount furniture store, helped to fill the space nicely with a sense of comfort.

Satisfied things were moving along at an acceptable pace, Regan left the building and went to talk to Sheena.

Sheena was on the phone looking distressed when Regan

entered the office. Regan stood aside, listening.

"No, of course you didn't know about her. It will be fine. I simply ask you to keep a careful eye on her. I don't trust her for a lot of reasons. Yes, okay. I understand. Good luck, Nicole."

"What was that all about?" Regan said.

"Nicole has hired Taylor Hutchison to work in the sales office at Ventura Village. She's worked in real estate before, and Bett Ryder, the real estate broker Nicole hired yesterday, approved of her, as did Brian. She's been showing a lot of interest in the project."

"But?"

Sheena sighed. "I caught her with Tony in a bit of a compromising situation. She pretended to have an ankle injury, but, not so strangely enough, when Tony was out of the picture, she had a miraculous cure."

Regan's jaw loosened with surprise. "Tony? No way. What does this Taylor woman look like?"

"She's very attractive—tall, slim, red-hair. I trust Tony not to start anything, but this woman is a bit like ... maybe like Darcy's old roommate, Alex Townsend. You know—arrogant, self-confident, eager to get her own way. That was my initial impression of Taylor."

"Hmmm. Can't Nicole tell her there's been a mistake?"

"I guess not. She's already started on the job. She's in the office now."

"I'm headed there for an appointment later this afternoon. I'll check her out."

As Regan pulled into the development Brian and Tony were creating, her excitement grew at the prospect of helping clients make a house their home. Anyone would be grateful to have one of the upscale, beautiful homes to begin with, but Regan hoped, with her help, the buyers would be even more thrilled with their new home and its decor.

She pulled up to the model home that contained her office and the sales office, wondering about the woman who'd been flirting with Tony. It wasn't like Sheena to be alarmed about something like that. Maybe it was pregnancy hormones at work. Even so, Regan was determined to make sure Tony wasn't distracted by someone named Taylor Hutchison. He was a good-looking man.

Inside the house, in the front office, an older woman with blond hair cut into a smart, swinging, above-the-shoulder style smiled at her while continuing a conversation on the phone. Regan waved to her and went on back through the house to her office in what would ordinarily be the family room. Sample books for wallpaper, fabrics, carpeting, and flooring lined the shelves on one side of the fireplace. Kitchen and bathroom hardware choices, as well as sample cabinetry, rested on shelves on the other side of the fireplace. Two long tables sat along another wall to be used for looking through the books. Folding chairs stood stacked against the wall. Regan's desk sat in the middle of the room, giving visitors plenty of space to make their way through sliding glass doors to the lanai and swimming pool.

Regan paused and studied the scene, thrilled to be in business for herself. As a high school student, she'd dreamed of going to RISD, the Rhode Island School of Design. But with her inability to test well, that dream had been taken away from her. Mo was the one who had presented another opportunity to fulfill her dream.

Regan settled behind her desk and checked for phone messages. Her client had called to reconfirm the time. Regan quickly called her back, and because she was free, told her to come ahead of their appointed time. Regan couldn't wait to begin working on the project.

As she hung up the phone, a young woman with red hair approached her. "You're Regan Sullivan?"

Regan stood. "Yes, and you are?"

The woman held out her hand. "Taylor Hutchison. I'm the new sales manager here at Ventura Village."

As she shook Taylor's hand, Regan blinked in surprise. "Sales manager? I thought Nicole Coleman was the new sales manager."

"Oh, well, but I'm the one handling the office," said Taylor with enough self-confidence Regan almost believed her.

"Right, handling the office for Nicole and Bett Ryder, who's in charge of the real estate sales," Regan said, giving Taylor a steady look.

"Well, yes," said Taylor. "But I intend to be the best person they've ever hired. I'm even hoping to move here myself after I sell my home. But you know how it is after a divorce. Everything takes time for you to get resettled and meet a new man."

Overcome with distaste, Regan remained silent. This was definitely a woman on the prowl.

"Bett and I have worked together on other projects, so I'm sure it's going to be great. Anyway, nice to meet you, Regan. I hope we can work well together. I understand you're handling the interior decorating end of things."

"Yes," said Regan. "I'm excited to get going. Leslie Tanner is arriving shortly for her first appointment. I'll try to keep you updated on my schedule."

"Please do," said Taylor. "Update your calendar and give me access. That should do it."

Taylor turned and walked away, dismissing Regan as effectively as a principal might dismiss a dim-witted student.

Regan went into the front office. When the older woman saw her, she rushed to her feet.

"Hi, you must be Regan. I'm Bett Ryder. I'm glad to meet you. I've heard such good things about you and your work. In fact, I'm coming to the Salty Key Inn to go to dinner with Nicole at Gavin's later this week."

"Great! You'll love it! The food is terrific!"

"Where's this?" said Taylor swinging into the room on high heels.

"Gavin's restaurant at the Salty Key Inn is supposed to have fabulous food," Bett said. "You'll want to keep that in mind when clients ask where they can go to dinner."

"Oh, Brian mentioned that to me. He said he hoped I'd try it out. He was sure I'd like it." She checked her watch. "Maybe I can catch him before he leaves. He said he'd help me with a project at my house. I'm trying to sell it, you know, and everything has to be perfect."

As Taylor left the office, Regan lowered herself into a chair, her knees so wobbly she couldn't stand. *Brian was helping Taylor with a special project at her home?* From the gleam in her eyes, Regan could well imagine what Taylor had in mind.

Unaware of the sick feeling that had washed over Regan, Bett smiled at her. "Your Brian is such a nice guy. He and Tony are doing a great job with the development. I'm excited to head the sales team."

"Taylor told me she was the sales manager," Regan said.

Bett laughed. "That woman has delusions of grandeur. She's a good people-person though, and in this business, it counts for a lot. She has a way of getting people to buy into whatever she says."

"I see," said Regan, wondering if that's what happened with Brian. She swallowed bile. All her old fears about Brian and other women played a rough game of tag in her mind.

CHAPTER TWENTY-NINE

DARCY

Darcy slipped on a simple, long-sleeved, aqua-blue dress and studied herself in the mirror. Not bad. The dress was well-tailored and fit her perfectly. Hooking a silver band around her neck, she gave it, too, a silent nod of approval. Since becoming engaged and starting to build a wardrobe for travel, Darcy had learned simple and quality go together nicely. At Christmas, she'd studied Austin's mother, carefully observing how she dressed, talked, and acted.

"Ready, honey?" Austin stepped into their bedroom and let out a low whistle. "You look great, Darcy!"

Darcy turned around to face him. "Thanks. I want to look nice for your parents."

"Don't worry about it. They don't care," said Austin. "They love you because I do."

Darcy smiled, but she wasn't so sure. Whereas her family sometimes seemed smothering, Austin's family seemed detached. Of course, his parents spent most of their time traveling for their business. Traveling that included weekends and, sometimes, holidays.

Darcy wrapped a light shawl around her shoulders, and they left the condo. A cold front had come down from the Midwest, bringing a chill to the air Darcy hoped would not hang around for her wedding. "I can't wait to have dinner at the Don," said Darcy. "My sisters and I drove up to the front of the hotel when we first moved here. We'd heard about the

Don CeSar, but until we saw the big, pink building, we didn't understand how elegant it was."

"It's a beautifully maintained property," agreed Austin.

They drove from the condo to St. Pete Beach on the coast and pulled up to the front circle of the hotel. A uniformed young man rushed to open the car door for Darcy. She stepped out onto the drive and waited for Austin to come around the car and take her arm. When she walked inside and into the lobby, her glance took in the marble flooring, pillars, and sparkling chandeliers, and a shiver of nerves shook her shoulders. She knew she shouldn't feel anxious about meeting his parents for dinner, but she was. With her own mother deceased, she yearned for a close relationship with Austin's mother. Though they'd been pleasant to her, she still needed to be reassured they wouldn't turn on her like her old boyfriend's parents had.

After receiving directions, Darcy and Austin walked into the grill-type restaurant. Charles waved to them from a booth in front of a salt-water fish tank and rose to his feet. Beside him, Austin's mother, Belinda, smiled and waved.

Darcy took a deep breath and smiled, focusing on Charles, who had his arms out to her.

They exchanged quick hugs, and Darcy slid into the booth, so she was sitting opposite Belinda.

"How are you, dear?" Belinda asked. "Just a few days until the wedding."

"I'm excited and nervous at the same time. It's such a special day."

"Oh, yes! I'm so pleased you've made my Austin happy. He just beams when he looks at you."

Darcy felt some of the tension leave her.

"What'll you have? We've already ordered drinks. What can we get for you?" Charles signaled a waiter, who came right over to them.

Austin ordered a vodka and tonic, and Darcy ordered a Texas margarita, her favorite.

After their drinks came, along with menus, Charles lifted his glass. "Here's to the two of you. Best wishes and many happy years together."

Conversation was light as they caught up with each other. During a lull, Belinda said, "We have a very unusual wedding present for you. Something I hope you will accept." She and Charles exchanged enigmatic glances.

"What's up?" Austin said with a note of suspicion that surprised Darcy.

Belinda leaned forward. "We'd like to give you our travel company. Dad and I are getting a little tired, and we've made enough money to retire. However, the business is too profitable to simply hand over to strangers. We know Darcy wants to travel, and this would be a good way for you to earn a good living together."

Austin's brow creased with worry. "What about my dental practice? I worked hard to get my degree in dentistry."

Charles spoke up. "It's an admirable profession and one you will always have. If you decide not to continue in the travel business, you can always find a job in dentistry."

"What about my family's hotel?" said Darcy. "I owe it to my sisters to keep a hand in that."

Belinda raised a hand to stop their objections. "All we ask is for you to think about it. We've arranged a lovely trip for your honeymoon. That will give you an opportunity to decide if it's something you want to do."

"There aren't many businesses like ours—very high-end, very satisfying when the job is done right," said Charles.

"And you'll be experiencing so many different things together," added Belinda.

Darcy sat back, feeling as if she'd been punched in the stomach. She and Austin had their lives planned out. Now, other possibilities shredded those plans. All this less than a week before her wedding.

"Let's not worry about that now," said Charles. "You have plenty of time to decide. We'll talk again, after your honeymoon. Right now, let's order some food. The menu looks very interesting."

Darcy took a good look at the menu, searching for new ideas for Gavin's. She loved seeing unusual combinations of ingredients, and Graham was always open to suggestions. She opted for the prime filet tartare as an appetizer and the snapper with Meyer lemon risotto for the main course. Austin and Charles went for the lamb rack for their main courses, while Belinda chose a chicken dish with mushrooms and asparagus.

Conversation continued on a lighter note as they ate their meal—mostly talk of Austin's parents' activities and their latest group of travelers. With her mind spinning, Darcy kept glancing at the fish darting about in the aquarium, feeling as trapped as they.

Later, after they'd said goodbye to Austin's parents, Darcy and Austin headed home. The silence inside her car pulsed in Darcy's ear. Finally, Austin spoke up. "Wow! I didn't see that coming!"

"Neither did I," said Darcy. "What do you think?"

"I'm totally unsure about taking over my parents' business. You and I have talked about having a family. I don't want to leave children like they left me."

Darcy nodded her understanding. "It sounds like a good opportunity, but I have my doubts, too."

Austin reached over and gave her a squeeze. “Let’s try not to think about it and simply enjoy our wedding. The honeymoon sounds even better.”

“Apparently, it’s going to be first-class all the way.”

With a grin, Austin arched his eyebrows at her. “I can keep to those standards.”

Darcy laughed. “It’s a challenge I’m looking forward to meeting.”

CHAPTER THIRTY

REGAN

Regan waited at the cottage for Brian to appear. He'd sent her a text telling her he'd be late, that he had some business to tend to. As she read the words, she wondered if he was aware she knew the business, no doubt, included a certain Taylor Hutchison.

She glanced at the ring shining on her finger, remembered the unforgettable moment Brian had proposed to her and sighed. She knew he was a good person, and she shouldn't be worried about him, but her old fears were playing games in her mind. As anxious as she was to be reassured, she decided to say nothing to him about her concerns, to give him a chance to bring up the situation himself. It seemed the fair thing to do.

When Brian finally appeared, she went outside to greet him. "Hi, honey! Busy day?"

"Yeah, as usual. What's for dinner? I'm starving!" As he bent down to kiss her, the distinct aroma of perfume hit her nose.

"Whew! Where have you been?"

He frowned. "Why?"

"You smell of perfume," she said, willing her voice to stay steady.

"Ah, it must be from Taylor. I helped her with a lock on her front door, and she hugged me."

"What is it with you and Taylor? I met her this afternoon,

and she made it sound as if you two were real buddies."

Brian's eyebrows shot up with surprise. "Me? I thought she was after Tony. He spoke to me about it this morning. Neither one of us likes it, but as long as she does a good job for us, we'll let her stay. It's hard to find someone who's willing to work evening hours."

He threw his arm around her. "Give me time to grab a beer, and let's eat. It's been a long day. I'm glad to be home."

Regan let out a sigh of relief. She didn't need to worry about Brian, though she still didn't trust Taylor.

After dinner, Regan and Brian sat watching television. Curled up on the couch with him, Regan was well into the mystery show when Brian straightened. Lifting her chin, he gazed into her eyes. "I love you, Regan. Let's go to bed."

"You don't want to see the end of the show?" she asked, surprised.

Giving her a sexy grin, he said, "No, I want to see you."

She clicked off the television and rose. What an excellent idea.

Later, lying beside him in bed, Regan traced the scars on Brian's arms.

He grimaced and studied her. "I don't know what I would've done if you hadn't been so supportive of me in the hospital. A lot of times when I did those damn exercises, I was showing off for you."

She chuckled. "I knew it, and so did the physical therapist. That's why he kept asking me to watch."

"Ah, Regan, always stay this way."

She pulled away from him and studied his face. "Bri? Let's get married as soon as possible. I can't help thinking of my mother, and I know how much better I'll feel when we're not just living together. It may sound silly to you, but it matters to me."

"I'm ready tomorrow if you are," he said.

"But, I can't ruin Darcy's wedding," said Regan.

"Who says she has to know? We could quietly do our thing and wait until after the wedding to announce it. I think it isn't the ceremony that's important. It's the vows you make to each other every day."

Tears sprang to Regan's eyes. "That's so sweet! And I agree with you. We don't need a fancy ceremony. Just friends and family to celebrate with us. Let's talk about some ideas later, after Darcy is married. It's not that far away."

"Okay," said Brian. "Sounds like a plan. I'll come up with some options for you. Trust me?"

"Of course," said Regan, sighing with happiness. She reached for him, and he drew her up next to him. She lay in his arms, inhaling the sexy aroma that was his alone and closed her eyes. She loved this man.

Regan sat with her sisters in Sheena's suite among boxes stacked in the living area. Now that Darcy's wedding was getting closer and Sheena was packing for her move to her new house, they were trying to get together for short meetings on a regular basis. Because Casey was taking on management of The Key Hole as well as Gavin's, his role helping them to oversee the hotel was still being determined. Sheena wanted to run the hotel with only guidance from Casey, but both Regan and Darcy were concerned Sheena might not have time enough to do that after the baby came. Still, they'd secretly agreed to let Sheena see if she could do it. She'd come to Florida for the freedom to be herself, and they weren't about to take that away from her.

"Tomorrow, I'll help you settle the kitchen in your new house," Darcy said to Sheena. "Has Tony already moved the boxes you stored in Paul and Rosa's garage?"

Sheena smiled and nodded. "My in-laws helped him do it. Rosa said she'd help me too." Sheena laughed. "She had to schedule the time in between golf games and bridge groups."

"What about the furniture you bought?" said Regan. "I can help you place that."

"Thanks, that would be great," said Sheena. "You've got delivery scheduled for tomorrow, right?"

"Yes. The store was able to move up the delivery date from the day after Darcy's wedding to tomorrow."

Sheena let out a sigh. "Moving is never easy, but I love the house and the location. I just wish a certain someone wasn't handling the sales office there."

Regan shot Sheena a look of surprise. "Are you talking about Taylor Hutchison? You know about her and Tony?"

Sheena's eyes rounded in shock. "What do you mean Taylor and Tony? Is there something you need to tell me?"

"Last night, I was concerned Brian was going to be late getting home because he was doing a 'project' at Taylor's house. Apparently, the lock on her front door needed attention. When I told him I was concerned about Taylor going after him, Brian said he thought she was going after Tony. That's all. Tony talked to him about it, and they've decided to keep her on at the sales office because it's hard to find someone willing to work some evenings."

Darcy snorted. "Evening work? I bet she does."

"Hold on," said Sheena. "Tony spoke to Brian about it?"

"Yes. Why?""

"Okay, then, I'm not worried," Sheena said. "But it sounds to me like she's a disaster just waiting to happen. Have you spoken to Nicole about her?"

"No, but I spoke to Bett Ryder. She's worked with her before, and apparently, Taylor is very good at her job. Taylor told me she was the sales manager, but I put her in her place by making it clear Nicole is the sales manager, and Bett is in charge of actual sales."

"We'll all have to try to keep tabs on her," said Darcy. "I'm going to speak to Nicole myself. She and I have a meeting this afternoon on a spring marketing campaign. We will have all forty rooms in the Egret Building completed by March 1st, won't we?"

"I would think so. But the suites won't be finished until probably April 1st if we can get the contractors lined up."

"And if they show up," grumbled Sheena. "The work on the patio for Gavin's people has come to a stop. But after nagging them before you two got here, I got a promise they will appear tomorrow."

"The gazebo is done," Regan said. "You can advertise that as a venue for a small wedding. The plantings around it should be pretty well established by now. The bohio bar is ready too. How is the open house for wedding planners coming along?"

"Fine," said Sheena. "I've talked to Bebe about making a few cakes for the occasion, and we've started a notebook of different designs. I'm putting together a letter to send out to interested parties, and Nicole is going to help me with ads and an invitation to wedding planners here in Florida and neighboring states."

"Great," said Darcy. "I was worried about leaving on my honeymoon, but it sounds as if things will be fine until I get back." She paused. "When I return, I want to sit down and discuss long-range plans for the hotel."

"Is everything all right?" Regan asked.

"I'm not sure," said Darcy.

"You aren't pregnant, are you?" Regan said, wondering at

the worry written on Darcy's face.

"Why? Would that be a problem?" Sheena asked with an edge to her voice.

"No, no, it wouldn't," said Regan. "At least not exactly. But we're going to need all the help we can get to complete the hotel and manage it properly."

"Then why don't you give up your interior decorating business?" snapped Darcy.

Shocked by Darcy's reaction, Regan opened her mouth to speak.

"I'm sorry," said Darcy. "I didn't mean to say it that way. I guess I'm more upset about personal things than I'd thought."

"Do you want to talk about it?" Sheena asked calmly.

"No, thanks. I have a few things to work out for myself."

"Don't we all," Regan said, looking at her sisters.

Any residual tension between them was heightened by the effort of helping Sheena move into her new house. The sound of crinkling paper, the heat that came through the open doorway so furniture could be delivered, and miscommunications between them made for some tense moments.

Rosa stayed for as long as she could, then left to fix dinner for Sheena's family.

The three of them had just come back inside from taking a bunch of boxes out to the garage to be broken down, when Sheena said, "I'm beat. Let's take a break."

She pulled cold bottles of water out of the refrigerator, and each of them sat down on one of the new bar stools in the kitchen.

They were resting, sipping their drinks when the doorbell rang.

"I'll get it," said Regan, waving Sheena back to her seat. "I know how tired you are." Sheena's face was flushed, her hair damp beneath a headband, her T-shirt dirty and sweaty.

Regan opened the door to find Taylor standing there. A bouquet of red roses in a glass vase was in her hands. "Hi, Regan. I have a delivery for Sheena Morelli. May I come in?"

Regan stepped aside as Taylor breezed by, leaving behind a waft of perfume Regan recognized. Striding across the hallway to the kitchen in a short skirt that exposed her long legs, and dressed in a low-cut blouse that almost covered her perfect bust, Taylor looked calm and cool.

Hurrying behind her, Regan entered the kitchen as Taylor announced, "We in the office are all wishing you happiness in your new home. I wanted to give these roses to Tony, but he asked me to bring them along to you."

"Thank you. That was sweet of him, and I appreciate your bringing them here. Sorry, I can't offer you any refreshments. As you can see, we're in the midst of getting settled."

"Oh, yes, of course, I understand," Taylor said, studying Sheena. She looked around with curiosity. "Everything is so pretty. I'd love to live in a house like this." She smiled. "And with someone as nice as Tony."

"Really?" Sheena remarked in icy tones.

At the uncharacteristic gleam of anger in Sheena's hazel eyes, Regan hurried to Taylor's side. "Why don't I walk you out?"

When Regan returned alone to the kitchen, Sheena said to her, "Thanks. I know I may sound like one of Meaghan's petty classmates, but I can't help it. I think I hate that woman."

CHAPTER THIRTY-ONE

SHEENA

Sheena sat on the king-size bed willing herself not to lie down. She and her sisters had put sheets and light blankets on the beds in each of the bedrooms. Spreads and decorative pillows would follow after they'd ordered their final choices. Looking around at the furniture, inhaling the smell of newness everywhere, Sheena felt her body battle excitement against fatigue. Regan had done an amazing job of helping Sheena pick out furniture that would enhance the setting. The house was attractive and comfortable. The architect who worked with Tony and Brian was a woman, which showed in the little nooks and crannies for decorative items, the many storage spaces, and the big, beautiful kitchen designed by someone who obviously enjoyed cooking.

At the sound of a car pulling into the driveway, Sheena got to her feet with a smile. She'd recognize Michael's car anywhere. As she entered the kitchen, Michael and Meaghan burst through the doorway.

"We all moved in?" Michael asked.

"Is my room ready?" said Meaghan, her eyes aglow with excitement.

"The basics are done. We'll add final touches in the next couple of days. After you have a snack, I want you to work together in the garage breaking down boxes and bagging up the packing materials."

"Okay," said Michael. "What do we have for snacks? And

what's for supper?"

Smiling, Sheena shook her head. Michael was still a growing boy. "Look in the refrigerator for drinks. Cookies, crackers, and cheese are out on the counter. Grandma Rosa is making dinner for us tonight."

Meaghan came to her and gave her a quick hug. "Are you all right? You look tired. Okay if I check out my room first?"

Sheena wrapped an arm around Meaghan, touched by her concern. "Sure. Maybe later we can talk about the bedspread you wanted. And then you can unpack the boxes you sent from Boston. They're in your new bedroom."

Meaghan sprinted out of the room toward the stairs. Watching her, Sheena smiled, happy Meaghan was so excited about their new house.

Sheena was sitting in the kitchen with Rosa when Tony came into the room. "Hi, Mom!" He glanced around. "Wow, Sheena! You all did a great job of settling the house."

She accepted Tony's kiss. "We've just done enough to be able to function. The finishing touches are another matter. That will take more time."

"Sheena's worked like a champ all day," said Rosa, getting to her feet. "I suggest you and the kids handle serving the meal and cleaning up."

Tony gave his mother a mock salute. "Will do. Thanks for bringing dinner." His eyes sparkled. "Do I smell the family recipe for chicken piccata?"

Rosa chuckled. "Maybe." She gave both of them quick hugs. "'Gotta go. Paul and I are meeting friends for dinner."

Watching her leave, Sheena and Tony exchanged amused glances. Ever since moving to Florida, his parents had been on a social whirl.

"Let me grab a beer, and we can talk," said Tony, going to the refrigerator.

Sheena took another sip of her water. "Taylor dropped off the roses. The office is doing that for all the people moving in?"

"Yeah, it's a nice idea. Nicole thought of it."

"I haven't mentioned it to anyone else, but I thought maybe we could also present new home buyers with a package of gifts from Gracie's, Gavin's, and the Salty Key Inn. Maybe even The Key Hole."

"Good idea. I'll tell Taylor about it."

"No," Sheena declared. "I'll talk to my sisters, and then I'll talk to Nicole. I don't want Taylor to have any input into or interaction with our business."

Tony studied her. "You really don't like her, do you?"

"Not at all."

Tony sat down at the kitchen table opposite her. "I talked to Brian about the way she behaves sometimes. He doesn't want to get rid of her, and neither do I. But, I promise to keep our private business and your hotel business away from her."

"Thank you," said Sheena. "It doesn't happen to me often. But sometimes I get bad vibes about people. And with her, they're really bad."

Tony's gaze bore into her. "I respect you, Sheena. You were right about one of my clients in the past."

"Who knew Hank Walker would end up killing someone?" At the memory of a horrific murder in their Massachusetts town, a shiver raced across Sheena's shoulders.

"Do you want me to insist to Brian she be fired?" Tony said quietly.

"No. If he's comfortable, and Regan's comfortable, I don't want to ruin a good situation for you. But be careful, Tony. She's up to no good."

###

The next day, Regan worked with Sheena to hang pictures, place silk plants throughout the house, and shop for the bedding the kids liked. Meaghan's theme for her bedroom had gone from pink to purple to a soft green with pink accents. Michael had kept to navy-blue and white like the Tampa Bay Rays baseball team.

Standing amid the bedding in the store, Sheena gazed at the baby quilts in darling patterns and wondered what her baby would look like and whether the new addition would be easy like Michael or difficult like Meaghan.

"Ready to go?" said Regan. "We have another stop to make. You wanted decorative pillows, and I have a cute idea for the lanai. That furniture should be delivered within the week."

"Okay, and then let's have an afternoon snack. I want to sit down and relax for a minute." Sheena hesitated. "And I need to talk to you about something."

Regan gave her a questioning look. "Is everything all right?"

"I hope so. I'll tell you about it when we have the privacy to talk."

"I can't wait. Let's go have a snack right now," said Regan.

Laughing, Sheena followed Regan out of the store. Regan was so bad about secrets. As a child she'd been terrible at Christmas—wanting to open her gifts early and telling people what she'd bought for them.

Seated at a round table outside a café, Sheena sipped her strawberry lemonade and wondered where to begin. She didn't want to seem petty or mean.

"Okay, spill," said Regan, squeezing the juice from a wedge

of lime into her diet drink.

"Tony and I talked last night ... about Taylor Hutchison. I need to tell you to be careful around her."

"Is this about the fact she's got a crush thing going with Tony?"

Sheena shook her head. "After I saw her yesterday, I wondered why my reaction to her is so bad, and I remembered feeling this way only once before. That was with Hank Walker."

"Oh my Gawd! The guy who killed his girlfriend?" gasped Regan. "Didn't you have some conflict with him?"

Sheena related the story of how, as a client of Tony's, Hank Walker had had some verbal run-ins with her about paying his bill. The conversations became alarming when he'd threatened to kill her. "I don't think Taylor Hutchison is going to murder anyone, but I have bad vibes about her, and I don't want her to have any access to our business."

"Oka-a-ay. Why would she?"

"I have an idea to promote all of our hotel operations at Ventura Village. Instead of receiving only roses when people move in, they'd also get a whole package of discounted offers from us. But I want all of our material to go through Nicole. Not anyone else."

"Having control of that stuff makes a lot of sense," said Regan. "It's worth money to us."

"I was going to let it go," Sheena said, "but I had a dream about her last night that upset me. I had to tell you how I feel and warn you not to trust her."

Regan's violet-eyed gaze stayed on her. "You're not a foolish person, Sheena. Thanks for sharing that with me. We'll have to be sure to inform Darcy."

"Yes, I think it would be wise. But maybe we should wait until after her wedding. I don't want anything to disturb her happy time."

"I agree," said Regan, sliding her gaze away from her.

Sheena frowned. Was Regan trying to hide something?

CHAPTER THIRTY-TWO

DARCY

Darcy stood inside the Tampa airport trying in vain to steady her nerves. Her father and Regina's arrival signaled the beginning of the celebrations for her wedding. Tonight, she would share dinner with only her immediate family, and then tomorrow, Austin's parents were entertaining everyone for the rehearsal dinner at the Don CeSar.

Beside her, Sheena and Regan seemed as pent-up with nervous energy as she. They hadn't talked about it much, but each of them, she knew, had reservations about their father's moving to Florida. After a couple of beers, Patrick could become loud and obnoxious. Sheena didn't want him to do something to tarnish the growing reputation of the Salty Key Inn as a small, quiet, charming place. Regan had admitted to them her father's presence took her back to the days of being the dumb beauty. As for herself, Darcy didn't want her father to embarrass her or her family in front of Austin's parents. It had taken a surprisingly short time for her old boyfriend Sean to change his mind about getting engaged after his parents decided her family was nothing special in their eyes. That had crushed her heart and her pride.

"It's going to seem funny to have Dad and Regina here permanently," said Sheena. "We'll have to remember to reach out to them. Especially Regina."

Darcy nudged Regan. "There's Dad!"

The three of them rushed forward to embrace him.

Pat Sullivan gave them each a hug, stepped back, and beamed at them with admiration. “Ah, my beautiful daughters. It’s so good to see you.”

“Where’s Regina?” Darcy asked.

Pat’s face fell. “Regina and I had a long talk a couple of weeks ago. I’ve gone ahead and bought a small house in The Villages, about two hours away from the Salty Key Inn. She doesn’t want a life with me there playing golf. She wants a quiet life near her daughter. I tried to explain to her there are a lot of fun activities for her at The Villages, but I don’t think either one of us was ready to get married again. I certainly don’t want to live in California. Not when my three girls are all in Florida.”

“Oh, Dad, I’m sorry,” said Sheena. “Are you all right?”

He gave them a tentative smile. “Sure. Nothing can keep Pat Sullivan from having a little fun with the short time he’s got left.”

“You’re not sick, are you?” asked Regan.

“No, just getting old like every other guy my age,” he said, patting her shoulder. He turned to Darcy with a smile. “But not too old to get some pleasure out of giving my daughter away.”

Darcy felt an unexpected sting of tears. Her father looked older than he had just a few months ago. Grateful now for his presence, a surge of love filled her heart.

“C’mon,” said Sheena. “Let’s get your luggage, and we’ll get you settled at the hotel. Are you sure you won’t mind staying there alone?”

“No, no, it’ll be fine.” He described his luggage and handed Darcy his baggage claim tickets.

As Darcy and Regan hurried away, Sheena took hold of her father’s arm and walked with him toward the baggage claim area. "When are you going to move to Florida?"

"As soon as the house in Boston sells. It won't be long. There are three people interested already. I bought the Florida house furnished, so I don't need much to make it mine."

"You can always ask Regan for suggestions," said Sheena.

"Suggestions for what?" Regan said, approaching them, dragging a rolling suitcase behind her.

"I bought the house in Florida furnished, but I'll need you to help me with all the fancy gee-gaws you women like."

Regan laughed. "I'll help you make it nice. Nothing too fancy."

Darcy met them rolling a large suitcase behind her. "Just the two suitcases, right, Dad?"

He nodded and smiled at them. "Got me some new clothes to wear for all the festivities. Figured I'd need some better clothes for my new life here." Darcy exchanged secret smiles with her sisters. If it was anything like his usual, flamboyant style, heaven knew what he'd chosen.

At the hotel, Darcy worked with her sisters to get her father unpacked and settled in his hotel room. She hid a smile at some of the Hawaiian-style shirts her father had chosen. Yet, she knew, he'd somehow make them look fine on him. His tall, heavy-set figure and his outgoing manner easily caught the attention of others. She studied him, standing on the patio outside his room, sipping a can of beer.

His shoulders were slightly stooped, his gray hair as thick as it had always been. But his stance was that of the tough fireman he'd been for most of his adult life, feet planted firmly on the ground. He was sometimes difficult, loud, and too stubborn to listen to others, but he could also be sweet and gentle.

Darcy wondered if she should remind him how important it was to be nice to Austin's parents and told herself to forget it. She wouldn't play the old game of trying to make others respect her or her family. They were good, kind people.

Sheena came up beside her. "What do you think? Dad doesn't seem sad to lose Regina."

"I think he's going to have a lot of fun. I never liked the idea of his marrying her."

"The ladies will love him there. He's handsome and independent."

"Yeah, but he's difficult and temperamental," Darcy blurted out.

Sheena laughed. "That, too."

Pat came inside. "Guess I'll go to Gracie's for lunch. I can charge that to the room, right?"

"Yes, and now, you can also charge meals at The Key Hole to your room," said Sheena.

"But, Dad," said Regan. "You're not going to be paying for your room. We insist you're our guest."

"Just thought it was a nice gesture," he grumbled. "For you and for that brother of mine. To show you I respect what he did for you."

Darcy, Sheena, and Regan encircled him with hugs.

"That's so thoughtful!" said Regan.

"I'm glad you understand," Sheena said. "It's important to me."

"And to me," said Darcy. "Without Uncle Gavin's doing this for us, so many things would never have happened. Good things. Like my marrying Austin."

"Spoken like a true bride," said Pat, giving her a smile. "Well, family is family. Some good. Some not so good. You three girls are the best."

Darcy noticed she wasn't the only one with a grateful smile.

###

Darcy looked around at her family gathered at Tony and Sheena's new house for a pot-luck dinner. The house, with Regan's noticeable touches, had quickly and nicely come together. Darcy was pleased because, before they'd won Uncle Gavin's challenge, there had been some doubt about when, where, and how Sheena would finally get the house she'd always wanted.

Outside, the men in the group were drinking beer, watching Tony and his father, Paul, grill some steaks. Meaghan and Michael were racing each other in the pool.

Inside, the women congregated in the kitchen, sipping wine, and helping each other prepare the buffet. As the honored guest, Darcy hadn't been asked to bring anything, but she and Austin had gone ahead and brought two bottles of expensive red wine to have with the meal.

"Getting excited?" Rosa, Tony's mother, asked her.

"More like nervous. The reception is going to be at Gavin's, but there are lots of details to take care of before then."

Rosa smiled. "You'll do fine. And, Darcy, you're going to be a beautiful bride."

"Thanks," said Darcy, wishing Austin's parents were as warm and wonderful as Sheena's in-laws. Then she felt bad for thinking such a thing. It wasn't anyone's fault she hadn't had time to form a friendship with them. And their offer to have Austin and her take over the travel business was a very generous one.

"Penny for your thoughts," said Regan, coming up to her and wrapping an arm around her.

"Just thinking about family," Darcy said. She and Austin weren't mentioning his parents' offer to anyone until they'd reached a decision.

"Dad seems really happy," said Regan. "I think he made a good decision not to marry Regina. She was nice enough, but they didn't have much in common. I heard him talking to Paul. They're going to play some golf together."

"Good," said Darcy, smiling as Austin approached her.

He gave her a quick kiss. "Well, bride-to-be, are you still going through with the wedding?" he teased. "Your time to escape is running out."

"Not a chance I'll miss it," she said, her heart full.

"Time to eat, everyone," Sheena called out, and the party continued.

They made it an early evening.

As Darcy and Austin drove out of the Ventura Village development, she noticed Taylor Hutchison's blue Cadillac convertible sitting in the driveway of the model home. "Guess Taylor is working late. Let's hope she's typing up a sales agreement. I'd like to see Tony and Brian have a lot of success with this development."

"Me, too," said Austin. "They're good guys. I really like your family, Darcy."

"That's good because now they're yours too."

"All of them?" Austin teased.

They shared a laugh. As Pat said, families were families, and Austin was about to get them all for better or for worse.

CHAPTER THIRTY-THREE

REGAN

As Brian and Regan followed Rosa and Paul out of the Ventura Village complex, Regan noticed Taylor's car in the driveway of the model home.

"What is Taylor doing here so late?"

"Probably typing up something for Bett," said Brian. "I wouldn't worry about it. Let's get home." He grinned at her. "With all the talk of Austin and Darcy's honeymoon, I'm ready to have a practice one at the cottage."

Regan laughed and shook her head. She loved that Brian enjoyed making love with her so much.

Brian reached over and took hold of her hand. "Are you still willing to do a quickie wedding? I have an idea about something, but I need to know if you're serious about it."

"I am, but what is this idea?"

"I can't say. Not yet. I'll let you know when the time comes."

Regan frowned. "You can't tell me earlier?"

"I don't know," said Brian. "That's all I'm going to say about it right now."

Regan both loved and hated surprises. Sometimes they were wonderful; other times, not so great. She started to warn him about that and decided to let it go. They'd have to get through Darcy's wedding before anything could happen. She'd talk it over with him then.

###

After making love with Brian, who was now sleeping peacefully, Regan slipped on an over-sized T-shirt, wrapped a fuzzy blanket around herself, and quietly tiptoed to the patio facing the water.

Settling in a chair, Regan gazed up at the moon and admired the sparkling stars in the ebony sky. A sense of peace seeped into her. She'd been surprised by her father's break-up with Regina. She wondered if he'd loved her mother more than she'd thought. The idea pleased her.

Her thoughts flew to Darcy. She'd looked so pretty tonight, her cheeks flushed with anticipation of her big day. Regan was happy for her sister, but she realized she, herself, didn't care about a big wedding. The motorcycle accident had changed so many things for her. There'd been days when she'd feared for Brian's recovery. His health and happiness were what counted now. Tomorrow, she'd tell Brian he could plan whatever he had in mind. After their lovemaking tonight, she just wanted to be his wife with no muss, no fuss.

The moonlight edged the tips of the waves moving onto shore and away again, shimmering like gold before her, reminding her of the real riches she possessed. Never before had she felt so fulfilled as a person, so recognized for who she really was—not the beauty she'd always been called, but the sentimental person who'd learned what true love is.

She went back into the house and climbed into bed beside Brian. Wrapping her arms around him, she spooned beside him, shifting her body, so it matched the curves of his. Content to simply let the future unfold, she closed her eyes.

The next day, Regan had no time to worry about the future. She went to Sheena's in the early morning to oversee delivery of the patio furniture she'd helped Sheena select. Then, they hung windchimes and an outdoor chandelier with battery-run candles.

"Too bad all this wasn't delivered yesterday," said Sheena.

"It'll be perfect for the morning-after breakfast you're putting together before Austin and Darcy leave on their honeymoon."

"Hard to believe she's going to be gone for three whole weeks. It'll seem so ... so ... quiet while she's away."

Regan laughed. "She's a bundle of energy, all right. But I'm happy she has this opportunity. She's always wanted to travel."

"Yes, I'm happy too. But I'm going to miss her."

They stood back and admired the furnishings and decorations.

"Looks good," said Regan. "See you later. The drapes are being hung in the upstairs rooms at the Egret Building. I need to make sure they're done right."

"What about the bedspreads?" Sheena said. "Are they here?"

"Not yet. You'd think it would be an easy thing, but it's not. Especially with custom orders."

"Okay, see you later. We're meeting at the Don for the rehearsal dinner at six o'clock. Right?"

"That's what the invitations said. See you then."

Regan left Sheena's in a rush. But as she passed the model home at the front of the development, she noticed Taylor's blue convertible and another car at the model house. She checked her watch. Twenty minutes before ten. No wonder Brian and Tony had decided to keep Taylor. She was a hard worker. The office didn't officially open until ten.

At the hotel, Regan took time to go to Gracie's for a hot cup of coffee.

Maggie met her at the door. "You just missed Darcy. She's

so excited about the wedding, and I can't wait to see her dressed like a bride. It should be a lovely ceremony. Bebe is already at work perfecting a new cake design for her."

"Yes, it should be a fun wedding. So glad you all are going to be part of it."

"You here for this?" Sally said, approaching them with a smile and a mug of steaming coffee.

Regan beamed with gratitude. "Thanks. Gotta run. Drapes go in today."

Sally put a hand on her arm to stop her. "Before you leave, I want to thank you and your sisters. The private pool patio is turning out to be so beautiful. We just love it!"

"I'm glad. Hopefully, it will be done soon," Regan responded. "When it is, we'll have to have a grand opening party!"

Maggie, who'd overheard, gave Regan a thumbs-up sign. "Any excuse for some fun."

Regan left the restaurant pleased by her interaction with them. When Sheena, Darcy, and she had first arrived at the hotel over a year ago, Gavin's people had been very unsure of them and their motives. Now, it was clear Regan and her sisters wanted to do as their uncle wished.

Carrying her coffee, Regan headed into the Egret Building and up to the second floor. Though the colors in the bedspreads they'd ordered and accent pillows were different from the first-floor rooms, the drapes in all of them would be the same neutral beige compatible with the carpet, allowing for future changes of color schemes.

Working with Mo, Regan had learned to be present for these installations— a quiet observer demanding a good job.

It was near closing time in Gracie's when Regan had a

chance to catch some lunch. A half sandwich and a glass of iced tea later, she was back at the Egret Building to oversee the last of the drape installations.

After the workmen had cleaned up and left, Regan left a note for Mo's cousin, Bernice, to have her staff vacuum the rooms. Then she went to check on her father before going home to change for the rehearsal dinner.

Regan knocked on his door.

"Hold on!" came Patrick's voice.

A couple of minutes later, Pat came to the door, his hair messed, his eyes still showing signs of sleep.

"How are you doing, Dad?" Regan asked, shocked at his appearance. He looked old, drawn, and unhappy.

"Okay. Just a little tired, that's all. Come on in."

Regan stepped into the room and saw the mussed bedding. "You took a nap?"

"Yeah, a longer one than I'd intended. What time are you picking me up for the party tonight?"

"In about an hour. Are you going to be ready?"

"Sure. Thanks for stopping by, Regan."

"If you need me for anything, I'm here," she responded, attempting to hide her worry. He looked and acted depressed.

"Thanks, it means a lot. Guess I'm finding it hard to think of being on my own." He winked at her. "But I'll make it."

She gave him a hug. "Sure you will. See you soon."

As she drove to the cottage, Regan wondered if it was a good idea for their father to move away from his daughters. The Villages wasn't far, but it wasn't as close as he could be.

At the cottage, she took a shower. Luxuriating in the feel of the warm water on her skin, she closed her eyes.

"I hoped I'd find you here," said Brian, startling her.

She jumped and turned around to face him.

He laughed and kissed her. "Always love taking a shower with you." It was late when they finally exited the shower.

Regan hurriedly dried her hair and got dressed.

Brian was knotting his tie when Regan emerged from the bathroom after putting on her makeup.

"Beautiful, honey," he said, stooping to give her a kiss on her cheek.

"You look pretty handsome yourself," she replied, noting the healthy glow of satisfaction on his face. He was getting stronger each day, more and more like himself as he took on additional physical work on the project.

As they pulled into the parking lot close to the garden room Patrick was staying in at the hotel, Regan spied her father on the patio. Looking like an ad for an older version of GQ men, her father was wearing a bright lavender shirt beneath a navy blazer. His gray slacks looked brand new. His shoes were shiny. With his sturdy body and thick gray hair, he looked ... well ... good-looking, and very pleased with himself.

He saw them and came right over to the Jeep. "How do I look? Ready for a classy evening?"

Regan grinned. "You look very handsome. You're going to have all the waitresses wanting to serve you."

"Good," he said, sliding into the back seat of the car. "We're going to the big, fancy, pink hotel. Right?"

"Yes, Austin's parents like the place. It should be a very pleasant evening."

"Let's hope they aren't stuffy. I don't do stuffy very well," said Patrick, and Regan realized he'd already had a couple of beers.

CHAPTER THIRTY-FOUR

DARCY

Darcy waited for her family to show up for dinner. She and Austin had met his parents and grandfather at the hotel ahead of time to share some lovely, quiet moments, and now she was eager to see her sisters. From a special private area that had been blocked off for them in one of the restaurants, she checked the entrance once more.

Sitting beside her, Austin placed an arm around her. "Don't worry," he murmured. "They'll be here soon."

Sheena and Tony appeared and followed the hostess to the table.

Austin's father and grandfather stood to greet Sheena and shake hands with Tony.

"So sorry we're a little late," Sheena explained to Austin's mother as she took a seat opposite her. "Life with teenagers isn't always predictable."

Belinda smiled. "And now you're having a baby. I'm so pleased for you."

Sheena's cheeks turned a pretty pink. "A bit of a surprise, but we're happy about it."

Darcy relaxed. Sheena and Tony were always good company. She looked up as Regan, Brian, and her father entered the room. Noting Regan's stress and the red-cheeked grin on her father's face, Darcy tensed. *Oh, Gawd! Has my father already had a couple of beers? If so, even though he isn't drunk, he'll be loud and talkative.*

While the men exchanged greetings, Regan slipped in beside Darcy. "I'm sorry, I shouldn't have left Dad alone. I'm afraid he's already had a couple of beers."

"It's not your fault," said Darcy, wishing she could cry. Impressing Austin's parents was, no doubt, not about to happen.

After everyone had been seated at the table, a waiter came to take their drink orders. Darcy cringed when her father announced, "A beer for me, and none of that fancy, imported stuff. Just good, old-fashioned, horse-drawn American beer, if you get my drift." He looked at Darcy and winked.

Darcy held her tongue, but she wanted to lash out at him, insist he order black coffee.

The drinks arrived promptly and were quietly served.

Austin's father, Charles, rose and lifted his glass in a toast. "We're glad to have you all here to celebrate the upcoming marriage of Darcy and Austin. It's marvelous when two young people in love choose to live their lives together. I hope you, Darcy and Austin, are as happy as Belinda and I have been. Here's to both of you!"

"Hear! Hear!" said Tony, and a chorus followed him.

"Austin's damn lucky to get her," said Patrick. His eyes filled with tears. "My daughters are all fabulous women." He signaled the waiter. "How about another beer?"

Darcy stiffened with mortification.

"Okay, then, anybody else want another round of drinks before dinner and wine?" Charles asked.

No one else took him up on the offer.

"Sheesh! I'm sorry. Guess I shouldn't have ordered for myself, huh?" said Patrick. "Oh, what the hell. This is a big celebration."

As soon as they'd ordered their meals, Darcy slipped into the ladies' room. Standing in front of the sink, Darcy dabbed at her eyes, willing herself not to let tears overflow and ruin her makeup.

She heard the sound of someone entering the room and saw Belinda in the mirror heading right for her. Tensing, Darcy turned to her.

"Hey, sweetie, I just wanted to make sure you're all right," said Belinda, giving her a sympathetic smile.

Darcy nodded glumly. "It's my father ..."

Belinda put her arm around Darcy. "Oh, honey, he's fine. Don't worry about him. And if you take over the travel business, you'll have to deal with lots of people who've had too much to drink. Patrick is charming. Besides, we're not about to judge you for it. We love you, Darcy. We really do."

This time, Darcy couldn't hold back tears. And when Belinda's arms came around her, Darcy nestled into them. She knew as long as she lived, she'd remember this tender moment.

Belinda stepped away. "Okay, now pull yourself together, and let's celebrate."

Darcy's smile came from her heart. "Okay, let's go!"

Her sisters gave her curious looks when Darcy and Belinda returned to the table together, but Darcy reassured them with a smile.

Charles half-rose from his chair. "Ah, the lovely ladies return."

"Just in time," said Patrick. "Chow's here."

Austin patted Darcy's knee. "Everything okay?" he murmured.

"Fine, thanks. Your mother and I got it all straightened out."

Austin's eyes lit with pleasure.

Patrick quieted down after eating a lot of good food and switching to coffee, and the rest of the evening passed in pleasant conversation. Now that Darcy realized she didn't have to be worried about him, she enjoyed the celebration.

She looked around at her family. With the early symptoms of pregnancy over, Sheena had developed a glow about her, making her even more attractive. Tony and Brian had become like brothers, kidding each other, but obviously fond of one another.

Brian caught her eye and winked at her. Darcy smiled back at him.

Beside her, Regan laughed at their interplay.

Darcy wondered if Regan understood how perfect Brian was for her.

At the end of the meal, Darcy thanked Charles and Belinda for a wonderful evening and kissed Austin goodbye.

"I know it seems silly, but I think Sheena's idea of my spending the night before our wedding with her is sweet. That will give us time to spend together, to get our hair and nails done, and be ready for the ceremony."

"I'll miss you," Austin whispered in her ear, sending a shiver of longing through her.

CHAPTER THIRTY-FIVE

SHEENA

In the car on the way home, Sheena stared out the window thinking of her father. The evening had been an emotional seesaw ride with him. He could be irritating at times with his boisterousness, but then say the nicest things. She knew how important it was for Darcy to be accepted by Austin's family and hoped she'd have the chance to talk privately to Patrick about his drinking before the wedding tomorrow.

"Guess you didn't realize you'd use your guestroom so quickly," Darcy said to her from the backseat.

Sheena turned around and grinned at her. "You're just lucky the bed was delivered this afternoon, and Meaghan and I had a chance to make it."

"It's really sweet of you guys to have me for the night. It's a good idea, sort of builds up the excitement before the actual ceremony, though I'm already dealing with a lot more suspense than you know."

"Well then, good job in holding it together," said Sheena. "Austin's parents seem so pleasant. I'm glad you and Belinda appear to get along nicely."

"She's much easier to be with than I'd thought at first. When I get back from my honeymoon, there's something I want to discuss with you and Regan."

"Anything we should talk about before you leave?"

Darcy shook her head. "No. I need to go on my honeymoon first."

"From what Austin said, it sounds as if you have quite a trip coming up," said Tony.

"Yes. That's what I might need to talk to you about."

Conversation stopped as Tony pulled into the driveway to their house, though Sheena was left to wonder what exactly was going on with Darcy.

In the master bedroom downstairs, Sheena snuggled up to Tony in bed. She'd missed out on a lot of traditional wedding activities for herself and was pleased Darcy had agreed to spend the night. Her own mother had made sure Sheena did the same thing before her marriage to Tony—a short ceremony a priest performed in his office as a favor to her mother.

"What'cha thinkin'?" Tony said.

"Just remembering our wedding. It was so simple."

Tony rose up on his elbow and studied her. "Some couples get married for the second time. Is that what you want, Sheena?"

"No, once was enough. We don't need to make our vows again. But I do want to make it a memorable time for Darcy and Regan, too. That's why I'm treating all the women to the pre-wedding preparations. Meaghan, as well."

He smiled. "Did anyone ever tell you what a nice person you are, Sheena?" He caressed her stomach. "And you're a great mom."

She cupped his cheek with her hand and gazed into his expressive brown eyes. "I love you, Tony."

His lips met hers. As their kiss deepened, Sheena knew exactly why she'd fallen for him.

###

Sheena awoke to the sounds of Tony in the shower and rolled over. On this Saturday morning, she didn't need to get the kids up and off to school.

Tony came into their bedroom in his undershorts and stood by the bed. "Hey, Valentine. Time to get up. Your sister is getting married today, I have to leave for work, and you asked me to make sure you were awake."

Sheena gave him a stink-eye and got to her feet. She'd secretly planned a pre-wedding breakfast for Darcy, Regan, and Meaghan, and needed to get to work. From the time Darcy was a little girl, she'd loved blueberry muffins.

Later, Sheena was taking the muffins out of the oven when Regan arrived. She kissed Sheena and asked, "Where's the bride?"

"Out for a walk. She said she's too wired to sit still."

"I'm happy she's so excited about everything. It makes it fun," said Regan.

Sheena looked at her. "What about you? When are we going to do this for you and Brian?"

Regan shook her head. "Who knows? I don't want anything fancy." She sat in a chair at the kitchen table. "But it does bother me to be living with Brian. You know how Mom felt about such things. She made it seem as if it was a horrible sin ..." Regan's voice trailed off.

Sheena waved her hand in dismissal. "Don't worry about it. You and Brian are engaged, making it clear to everyone you're committed to one another."

Darcy walked into the room wearing shorts, a T-shirt, and sneakers. She beamed at them. "It's a beautiful day! I think I'll get married."

Regan and Sheena laughed.

"Too late to back out now," said Regan.

"For you too," Darcy said.

Sheena gave her a sharp look.

"I mean, you both are part of my wedding. You can't back out now."

Sheena smiled. "I wouldn't miss it for the world. Let's get Meaghan up and start the day with a special breakfast. I even have the fixings for mimosas, though Meaghan and I have to take ours plain."

"Let me wake her up," said Regan. She left the room.

Darcy gave her a worried look. "Sheena, I hope at the end of the day you're not going to be upset with me."

"What? Why would I be upset with you? What's going on?"

Darcy shrugged. "I guess I'm just worried it won't be perfect."

Sheena put her arm around Darcy. "Let's not let anything ruin your wedding day, okay?"

"Okay. Thanks."

Sheena didn't have any more time to think about Darcy's worries. With the appearance of Meaghan, their day began in earnest. Excited about each little thing, Meaghan exclaimed over the mani-pedis they each got and was ecstatic with the work of the hair stylist who worked on them all. Observing her, Sheena could well imagine the day when Meaghan would be the bride and not a bridesmaid. And when she saw Meaghan's auburn hair styled in curls at the back of her head, and observed her hazel eyes, the Sullivan features, and her father's darker skin tone, Sheena realized that time would come all too soon.

Sheena helped Darcy pack her dress and personal belongings for the trip to the private room upstairs at Gavin's, where the women would change into their wedding clothes. Regan had gone home to get her dress and would meet them there. Sheena and Meaghan would come later after Sheena made sure Tony, Michael, and her father were ready. Tony had agreed to meet Patrick for lunch.

Driving to the hotel with Darcy, Sheena couldn't help thinking of all that had happened to them in a little over a year. Darcy's marrying Austin was one of the best things. And, in time, Regan would marry Brian, adding to their family.

Sheena parked the car at Gavin's, and following Darcy inside, stopped to talk to Nicole. "Is everything all set for the reception?" Sheena asked her.

Nicole's eyes sparkled. "Oh, yes. Casey and I have made sure of it."

Upstairs, Sheena stepped into the section of the ballroom that had been set up for Darcy's wedding reception. She gasped with pleasure. Crisp, white tablecloths covered the rounds of eight—all four of them. Gray napkins, almost a silver color, flanked the table settings, offsetting crystal glasses and sparkling silverware. In the middle of each round table sat a gray vase holding Oriental white lilies edged in pale pink. The effect was stunning, not plain at all, as Sheena had once feared.

"It's gorgeous," said Darcy, coming to stand beside her. "I knew with Regan's help, it would be."

"Yes, it's beautiful. Let's relax. We have less than an hour before you walk onto the beach for your wedding."

"I hope the wind dies down," Darcy said, giving her a worried look. "It was supposed to be calm all day."

"It'll be fine," Sheena said, hoping she was right. Weather-wise, this time of year was tricky.

Sheena stood on the sandy beach in bare feet, lined up next to Regan and Meaghan, waiting for Darcy to appear. Austin stood off to the side, looking both excited and nervous.

"When is she coming?" whispered Meaghan in a voice that

others could hear, causing a few titters of laughter.

Sheena glanced at the assembled crowd, feeling a rush of love for the people gathered there. Beside her, Regan and Meaghan resembled angels in their white dresses. Tony, Michael, and Brian stood together, dressed alike in gray slacks and crisp, open-necked white shirts. Paul and Rosa stood behind them. Gavin's people, dressed in varying colors, clustered together. Holly and Blackie, sharing newlywed smiles and kisses, stood behind Brian. Austin's parents and his grandfather stood alongside Austin. Belinda looked lovely in her white dress, and Charles and Bill wore the required gray slacks and white shirt to match Austin's outfit. Behind them, a group of six friends of the Blakely family had gathered.

A minister, wearing a clerical collar over a short-sleeved, black shirt and wearing black slacks, stood by a small, portable altar that had been anchored in the sand. Sheena smiled at the sight, realizing this man, a friend of Austin's family, was no stranger to beach weddings.

The weather had cooperated by calming the wind and clearing the skies for a delightful sunset. Streaks of oranges, reds, and purples spread across the horizon adding their blessing to the occasion.

Nicole and Casey, busy with preparations at Gavin's, hurried to join the assembled group.

Then, it was time for Darcy and her father to appear.

Feeling more like a mother than a sister, Sheena held her breath.

At the sight of her father in gray slacks and a pressed white shirt leading Darcy toward them, Sheena choked up. It was so nice to have her father a part of the ceremony. He served as a reminder of her mother and his brother Gavin.

Next to him, holding his arm, Darcy appeared to float toward them in a simple, white strapless dress with a beaded top and a skirt made of layers of organza that lifted and billowed around her in the soft breeze. A thin strip of gray silk bound the waist. In her hands, she carried a bouquet of white lilies edged in pale pink. At the top of her red curls, a small lily was the only decoration.

Sheena watched Austin's eyes fill at the sight of Darcy and smiled. It was a good match.

Darcy's eyes shone with love as she walked to Austin's side. While they stood gazing at one another, Patrick kissed Darcy's cheek and stepped back to join Tony and the other men.

"Dear family and friends, we are gathered here today to celebrate the marriage of Darcy Elizabeth Sullivan and Austin William Blakely..." began the minister.

During the ceremony, Sheena's thoughts wandered until Darcy began to speak in a trembling voice as she faced Austin.

"I searched for the way to best put into words my love for you. I waded into the warm water at the beach and thought, yes, love is as constant as the waves rolling into shore and back again. I looked up at the sky and thought, yes, love is as bright as the sun that helps things to grow. I sifted the sand through my fingers and thought, yes, love is as infinite as the grains of sand beneath my feet. And when I thought of true love, your face was all I could see. My love for you is as constant, as bright and beautiful, as limitless as the magic around us—the magic you make me feel when I am with you. You've given me the courage to be a better self, one worthy of you. I promise to be there for you, to support you in whatever we decide to do with our lives and to show you in every way I know how to make you as happy, as full of love as you've made me. I promise this to you forever."

By the time Darcy was through speaking, Sheena wasn't the only one dabbing at her eyes with a tissue.

Austin thumbed the tears off Darcy's cheeks and began to

speak. His words, so similar in meaning were just as sweet and heartfelt, making both his parents tearful.

Patrick had, of course, been weeping from the start of the service.

When the words "You may now kiss your bride" were spoken, a huge sigh of satisfaction came from the group. It was, Sheena decided, one of the sweetest weddings ever.

"Well done! Well done!" Patrick said. "Now, let's go celebrate!"

Darcy and Austin led the group into Gavin's and to the upstairs room. As people entered, they had a chance to kiss the bride and congratulate the groom.

An open bar was set up at one end of the room, dining tables sat in the middle, and at the other end of the room, a small dance floor had been put in place. Soft, romantic music flowed from speakers a DJ was controlling.

As guests enjoyed pre-dinner drinks, Sheena mingled with the crowd, meeting the Blakelys' friends, talking to Gavin's people. She was as surprised as everyone else when Mo and Kenton appeared.

Smiling, Darcy rushed over to them and ushered them into the room.

"Hi! What a surprise!" Regan said, hurrying over to them.

Sheena approached as Regan was giving each of them a hug.

"I didn't know you were coming," said Regan. "I thought you were in Hawaii."

"Sorry, we're late. We just flew in," said Mo. "Thankfully, Brian arranged for us to be picked up."

Sheena was as confused as Regan. *Brian? What was going on?*

CHAPTER THIRTY-SIX

REGAN

Beaming, Brian approached Mo and Kenton. "Hi, guys! Glad you could make it. Help yourselves to something at the bar. Sheena will introduce you to her father and others."

Sheena gave him a puzzled look, but said agreeably, "Sure, but before you meet Patrick, you'd better get your drink."

Kenton chuckled. "Sounds good to me.

Brian took Regan's elbow. "Come with me. We have to talk."

"We can't leave the party!" Regan said, wondering at his strange behavior.

Brian kept walking across the hall, leading her to the private room opposite the ballroom. He pulled her inside and closed the door. Inside, he faced her, looking a bit uncertain. "You know I love you more than anything, right?"

"Ye-s-s-s."

"And you wanted to get married as quickly and simply as we could. Right?"

Regan's knees suddenly went weak. "Wait! Are you thinking we should get married right now in front of our family and friends?' Her stomach fluttered with excitement. "But we can't! This is Darcy's wedding, not mine."

"But this whole idea is Darcy's. She wants to share the occasion with you. When she and Austin found out we were holding back on eloping because of their wedding, Darcy came up with this suggestion. Both Darcy and Austin think it would be a great addition to their day. They both wanted to announce it beforehand, but I didn't want them to do anything to take away from their wedding, and I had to make sure this is what you really want. I'm okay with the idea of a short, simple ceremony like you wanted in front of the people gathered here and celebrating all together. What do you think?"

Regan wrapped her arms around him, so excited about the idea she could hardly think. Then she smiled. "It's a great idea, but I need to talk to Darcy first, to make sure this is truly what she and Austin want. Does Sheena know?"

Brian shook his head.

"Please ask Darcy and Sheena to come here, and then I'll decide."

"I love you, Regan. I'll do anything you want on this. I just want you to be mine." Brian lowered his lips to hers.

A sense of peace washed over her. Both Brian and Darcy knew her well enough to know she'd been serious about nothing fancy for herself.

"Okay, what's going on?" Sheena demanded in her big sister voice as she hurried into the room. "Are you okay? Why are Mo and Kenton here? I thought they were in Hawaii."

Regan looked at Darcy. "Do you want to explain?"

Darcy wrapped her arm around Regan and turned to face Sheena. "One evening, when Brian caught up to Austin and me at The Key Hole, I asked him when he and Regan were going to get married. He explained they wanted to elope, but they didn't want to do anything to spoil my wedding. That's when I got this idea."

"What idea?" Sheena asked.

"For them to get married during the reception of my

wedding. That way, friends and family could at least see them married."

Sheena narrowed her eyes at Regan. "You'd go ahead and get married without us?"

Regan gave them a sheepish look. "I just wanted to get married quietly, no muss, no fuss. I didn't think you'd mind."

"We would have been hurt by that," said Darcy.

"We're all sisters, remember?" Sheena said sternly.

"So, do you want Brian and me to go ahead with this? Do you really?"

Darcy grinned at her. "Yes."

"How are we going to do this?" said Regan, her head spinning.

"It's simple," said Darcy. "We'll ask for everyone's attention. The minister already has agreed to do the ceremony, Brian has the rings, and your family and friends will all be your witnesses." She grinned. "Mo's already changing into gray slacks and a white shirt."

Regan covered her mouth with her hands, realizing how much work had already gone into making this happen. "Oh, this is all so sweet, so sensational! Be sure Meaghan is standing with Mo too. I promised her she'd be in my wedding." A nervous giggle escaped Regan. "My Gawd! I knew Brian loved me, but this? Oh, my!"

"Well?" said Brian, poking his head into the room.

"Let's do it," said Regan.

"You're sure this is how you all want to proceed?" Sheena asked her sisters.

Regan and Darcy exchanged looks of determination and nodded.

Regan turned to Brian. "You're ready for this?"

Brian grinned. "I've been ready for marrying you my whole lifetime."

"Okay, Brian," said Darcy. "Tell Austin it's a go, and wait for our signal."

Regan looked at Sheena and Darcy. "Is this okay for a wedding dress?"

Both of her sisters smiled. "It's perfect."

"Let's add a circle of flowers to your hair or do something bride-like for you," said Sheena.

Darcy grinned. "You can use my bouquet. And I've already ordered a circlet of flowers to wear on your head. They're in the refrigerator." She walked over to the small refrigerator, lifted out a box, and handed it to Regan. "When I asked you about flowers for my wedding, you once mentioned freesia. So, I had this made in a variety of soft colors."

Regan lifted out the fresh floral headpiece and gasped, "It's gorgeous. Totally gorgeous. Thank you!"

Sheena took it from her and placed it on her head. "Perfect."

Regan felt her eyes fill with tears. "Thank you so much."

"Okay, you and Sheena wait here. I'll alert Austin and the minister, and get Dad. He can walk you into the room," said Darcy. She turned to them with a smile. "I'm so happy it's working out this way."

A few minutes later, Darcy returned to the room with Patrick in tow.

"What's this, Regan? My baby girl is getting married now?"

"Yes, Daddy. Brian and I want to be married, and Darcy and Austin have offered to have us use this time to get married here and now." She couldn't help the smile she felt spreading across her face. "Pretty different, huh?"

"I'll say," Patrick said, "but you kids today have all kinds of ideas."

"I'll leave you two alone and go check on things out there," said Sheena.

She left with Darcy, and Regan faced her father. "I'm doing this, in part, to please Mom. She wouldn't like the idea of my living with Brian. He and I both want to make it official."

"Your mother, God bless her, had a whole lot of ideas about things. I think she'd be pleased to know how much you girls love each other. There was a time when you were younger she worried about it." He took her arm. "Okay, let's go. We're to wait in the hallway until Darcy gives us the signal."

Standing in the corridor outside the ballroom, Regan strained to hear Austin speak.

"My wife, Darcy, and I are very excited to share a special moment with all of you. With our blessing, her sister, Regan, and Regan's fiancé, Brian, have decided to exchange wedding vows in front of you now. I'll turn the program over to Reverend Davis, and join Brian on the podium we've set up."

Murmurs of surprise broke out, and then excited clapping began.

Knowing there was no turning back, Regan's mouth became dry.

CHAPTER THIRTY-SEVEN

DARCY

Remembering how nervous she'd felt on the beach walking toward Austin, Darcy was surprised by how calm Regan appeared as she entered the room on their father's arm. Dressed in a midi, white eyelet sundress, and wearing the crown of flowers on her shoulder-length dark hair, Regan's violet eyes glowed with happiness. She looked like an ad for perfume or diamond rings. She was that stunning. Sheena slid into the chair beside Darcy and took hold of her hand. Together they watched their sister walk across the room to where Austin and Brian were waiting. Standing opposite them, Mo and Meaghan beamed at Regan.

The minister spoke quietly, but loud enough for everyone to hear in the hush that filled the room. Hearing the words spoken to her just a short while ago, Darcy listened with a sense of renewed wonder. The words, the promise to love and hold dear, meant even more to her. She gazed at Austin standing to one side and smiled when he mouthed the words, "Love you."

When the announcement came for the groom to kiss his bride, everyone in the room stood and clapped. It was, Darcy thought, a magical moment. Not one wedding, but two had given the Sullivan sisters a very special day.

Holly rushed over to Brian and Regan. "Oh, my dears! I'm so happy for you."

And then everyone gathered around them.

Austin came over to Darcy and kissed her cheek. "It worked out well, don't you think?"

Darcy smiled at him. "Everyone thought it would ruin our wedding. I think it made it even better because of what I've learned."

He smiled. "And what might that be?"

"That if you have enough love, it's easy to share it."

He laughed. "Guess that will end up in one of your books one day, huh?"

"If only," she said, wishing she hadn't received another rejection letter. She'd heard all kinds of horror stories about breaking into the book business, but she wasn't about to give up.

As dinner was served, happy conversation filled the room. It was as if not one, but two weddings were cause for even more celebration.

Darcy gazed at the diners, happy to see everyone, even shy Bebe and quiet Sally, was happily conversing with other guests.

Her father was enjoying the celebration most of all, repeating the story of how Darcy and Regan had fought as children but now had shown real love for each other and Sheena.

It became a comedy of sorts as first one person and then another stood to give a toast. When Blackie stood, Darcy held her breath.

"I can't remember an occasion other than my marriage to Holly," he stopped to smile at her, "that gives me more reason to celebrate than this. I hope to hell Gavin has a good spot in heaven and is celebrating too. What he dreamed of for Sheena, Darcy, and Regan has become a reality both personally and professionally. He was a good man whose proof of that is your presence today. Cheers to the brides and grooms!"

Darcy studied her father's solemn expression and prayed he wouldn't object.

When he stood, Darcy glanced at Sheena and saw the worry she felt.

"Gavin was my brother, and though we didn't always get along, deep down I ... I ... loved him," said Patrick. "And I'll always be grateful to him for what he's done for my girls."

"Hear! Hear!" Sheena cried.

The others joined in, and Tony jumped to his feet, forcing Patrick to sit down. "I wish to offer a toast to Darcy and Regan." He raised his glass and bobbed his head to Darcy, then Regan. "I wish you all the happiness in the world. Austin and Brian are lucky to be married to one of the Sullivan sisters. Here's wishing the four of you all the happiness I've had with my bride. Cheers!"

After taking a sip of wine, Tony continued. "And here's to Sheena. We've been married a long time, but seeing her here like this, looking like a bride herself, I'm reminded as always how lucky my children and I are."

"The baby too," said Meaghan.

Amid the laughter that followed, Darcy caught Sheena's eye and blew her a kiss.

After the main course was cleared, a waiter rolled in a cart holding a wedding cake, plates, and silverware. He brought it to the table where Darcy and Austin sat.

Darcy waved Regan and Brian over to join them.

The three-tiered cake was iced in white and accented on top by a cluster of white and pale-pink roses that spilled down the sides.

"It's gorgeous!" Darcy stood. "Bebe, please stand up. This dear friend is an artist when it comes to baking."

Her cheeks bright red, Bebe got to her feet and shyly bobbed her head in response to the loud applause.

Wait staff served the cake, along with coffee, tea, and after-dinner wine.

After dinner had been cleared away, Austin stood. "Please join Darcy and me and Regan and Brian on the dance floor."

To a romantic oldie Darcy had chosen with Austin's grandfather, Bill, she swayed in Austin's arms. The closeness, the realization he was truly hers sent a wave of desire rolling through her.

Austin smiled at her. "We won't stay late. We'll go to the Don as soon as we can."

She laughed and nestled closer.

Someone tapped Austin on the shoulder.

Darcy looked up into her father's watering eyes. "Okay if I dance with my little girl?" he said to Austin.

Austin stepped away, then left to find his mother.

"You sure are a beautiful bride," said Patrick smiling down at her with fresh tears. "Can't believe my girls are all grown up and on their own."

"We've all been away from home for a while, Dad," said Darcy.

"Yeah, but this is different. You now have families of your own." Patrick glanced around the room. "Damn good ones too."

"You won't be alone. You'll still have us."

He gazed across the room. "I've been talking to Lynn. She seems real nice."

Darcy recalled Lynn's story of how her husband, Benny, had gone searching for gold with Gavin and how Gavin had paid their medical bills after Benny had died following a long, torturous battle with cancer. Glancing at her now, dressed up and laughing at something Bill said, Darcy realized how attractive Lynn was and why both her father and Bill seemed smitten with her.

"All of Gavin's people are very special. Treat them with a great deal of respect."

"Of course," her father said. "If Gavin had them for friends, they'd have to be special."

Darcy looked up at Patrick. "I'm glad you've come to understand Gavin. He was a fun, loving, kind, and generous man. You're a lot alike, you know."

"I am?" A smile spread across Patrick's handsome face. "Lynn thought so too. Sheena asked Rocky to take us to see Duncan in the next day or two, and I agreed to do it. I want to meet my nephew."

"If you can get past your first impressions, you'll see he's a Sullivan all right."

Sadness filled her father's eyes. "Wish I'd known a lot of things earlier. Now it's too late."

"It's never too late, Dad," Darcy said softly, thinking of all the things she'd had to learn about herself and others already. Her thoughts flew to Nick Howard, her mentor from the newspaper. God! She missed him.

Brian tapped Patrick's shoulder. "Okay, if I cut in? My bride is waiting for her father/daughter dance."

"Oh yes," said Patrick. He kissed Darcy on the cheek and left.

Brian took hold of Darcy's hand and wrapped an arm around her waist. "Thanks for everything, Darcy. You've made Regan and me very happy."

Darcy beamed at him. "Guess we planned a good surprise for Regan. But, seriously, it turned out well. I had my moment, and she had hers. And now we all get to share it with friends and family. It's perfect."

Brian kissed her on the cheek. "I've always thought you

were pretty special."

"Even after what I did, propositioning you?"

He laughed. "Well, maybe not that special. But as a sister, you're the best."

He stepped away as Austin's father approached.

"May I have this dance with my new daughter?" he asked, his light brown eyes sparkling.

Darcy did a little curtsy. "Of course."

Charles took her hand and then moved her gracefully across the floor. "I really like your family, Darcy, and am so glad you're now part of ours."

"Thank you," Darcy said, pleased the evening had gone so well.

"Have you thought any more about Belinda's and my offer?" he asked.

Darcy shook her head. "Austin and I agreed to discuss it after the honeymoon. For now, we just want to enjoy our time together."

"Good thinking. If you two decide to take on the business, I'm sure you'll do very well. It's a lot of hard work, but worth it."

Darcy glanced around at her family. If she and Austin accepted his offer, she wouldn't see much of them. Pushing away those worrying thoughts, she moved with Charles across the floor.

As soon as possible after the first guests left, Darcy responded to Austin's questioning look with a smile and stood.

"Austin and I are heading to the hotel. See everyone in the morning."

"Or not," said Austin to a round of laughter.

"Come when you can. Your flight to London isn't until evening, and you're welcome anytime," said Sheena.

Austin took Darcy's arm and led her to her car. His old Volvo had been traded in for a new one, but for evenings, they liked to use Darcy's Mercedes.

As Austin pulled out of the parking spot, they heard a racket behind them, and Austin stopped the car.

Wide-eyed, they faced each other.

Then Darcy began to laugh. "Michael told me he'd do something to help us celebrate." She got out of the car and looked behind it. Several empty tin cans were tied to the back of the car.

Austin chuckled. "I'll have to get him for this." He pulled a small pocket knife out of his pants and held it up. "My good luck piece should take care of it." He cut the strings from around the bumper.

"Quick, let's tie them to Regan's Jeep," said Darcy, laughing giddily.

After taking care of it, they pulled out of the parking lot, ready to celebrate in a very different way.

CHAPTER THIRTY-EIGHT

REGAN

Regan and Brian said goodbye to Holly and Blackie and the others and went outside.

"As a surprise, I've arranged for us to go away for a couple of nights," said Brian. "I told Sheena and Tony about it at dinner, and they'll cover for us."

"Oh, Brian, that's so sweet! Where are we going?"

"I'll tell you in the car after we pick up our things at the cottage on Kenton's property."

Mo and Kenton joined them. "This is the new ride?" Mo said, his dark eyes shining as he stared at the white Jeep. He wrapped an arm around Regan. "Nothing's too good for our bride."

Brian laughed. "Get in. We'll drop you off at the house, get our things, and be on our way."

As Brian pulled out of the parking spot, a rattle behind the car made him stop. He got out of the car, took a look, and began laughing.

Regan, Mo, and Kenton joined him. When they saw the tin cans, Regan said, "I'm betting on Michael doing this."

Grinning, Michael approached. "What? Me? Meaghan and I tied them onto Darcy's car, and they must have transferred them to yours."

"Love you, Michael," Regan teased, giving him a quick hug, pleased by his participation in the day.

While Brian untied the cans, Regan turned to Mo and

Kenton. "Thank you both for making the trip to Florida. It wouldn't be our special day if the two of you weren't part of it."

"Our pleasure," said Kenton. "We're happy we could be here."

"I won't forget it," said Regan, giving each of them a kiss on the cheek.

"Well," said Kenton, "maybe you can do the same for us when the time comes."

Regan glanced at the happy expression on Mo's face and felt her eyes well with tears. It seemed they'd found love, too.

When Regan stepped out of the house with her suitcase, she was surprised to see a white stretch limo parked in the driveway. She turned to Brian. "What's this?"

"Our carriage awaits," said Brian, giving her a broad smile.

The driver held the door as they climbed inside. In the dim interior, twinkling lights hung from the ceiling like tiny stars in a dark sky. A bottle of champagne sat in an ice-filled well built into a backlit bar on one side of the passenger cabin. Two tulip glasses were in a rack on the shelf alongside it. A small TV screen glowed in the wall behind the bar. Soft, romantic music filled the cabin.

The driver closed the door and climbed in behind the wheel. "I'll close the partition now. Knock on the window if you need anything."

"Thank you," said Brian. As the car got underway, he turned to Regan. "I've arranged for us to stay at the Ritz Carlton down the coast in Naples for a couple of nights. A little later in the year, I hope to take you to Naples, Italy, for a real honeymoon."

"Really? Oh, Brian, that would be a dream come true!"

Suddenly, she was crying.

"What's the matter?" Brian asked, looking crestfallen. "Are you disappointed in all the arrangements that were made? We could have waited. I just wanted to make you happy."

Just as suddenly, Regan began laughing. "Oh, Brian! You have no idea how much I love you. You, this day, everything has been wonderful."

"Whew! You had me worried for a while." Brian lifted the bottle of champagne from the ice well. "Let's celebrate."

He easily slid the cork out of the bottle and poured champagne into the two glasses. Clicking his glass against hers, he said, "Here's to you, Regan Harwood, my beautiful bride."

"And to you, Brian Harwood."

The bubbles tickled her nose as she sipped the liquid. She laughed with the pure joy of it, her new husband, and the entire day.

As she lay in bed naked beside Brian, sated from their lovemaking, Regan couldn't help thinking of her mother. Without the nagging thought of her mother's disapproval of living with Brian before marriage, she'd experienced a new sense of abandonment making love with him.

Brian reached for her. "Mmm, Mrs. Harwood, you make me glad we decided not to wait to get married." He tugged her close, spooning them together.

When Brian's breathing deepened into sleep, Regan got out of bed, slipped on a robe, and tiptoed onto the balcony. She wanted time alone to savor her day, to think of her family and the future. Never in a million years would she have imagined her wedding day as it had happened. Darcy's generosity meant the world to her. They'd fought as kids and then pretty much ignored one another until they'd been forced to live together in Florida.

Her thoughts flew to Sheena and Tony. She was grateful to them for giving Brian and her a few days off to celebrate. It meant added work for each of them, but both Sheena and Tony had seemed genuinely happy to do it. Her father had surprised her by rallying to the occasion. His participation had added meaning to both weddings.

Staring up at the night sky, a playground for light and shadow, she thanked the stars for all she'd been given. Not only for her family but for Brian's. Holly and Blackie had made it clear how happy they were to have her now be a part of it.

The steady movement of the waves below her slowed her breathing and calmed her mind. Sighing happily, Regan went inside and crawled back into bed with her husband.

CHAPTER THIRTY-NINE

SHEENA

After the wedding celebrations, Sheena left Gavin's with her father and walked with him to his hotel room.

"What a lovely time," she murmured. "Two weddings in one day? Who would've thought it?"

"I bet other men would wish it would happen in their own families. One way to get rid of two daughters at once."

Sheena smiled. His gruff words belied the fact his eyes were tearing up with emotion.

"I wonder what Mom would have thought about it."

"She would've come around, though she might not have liked the idea. But Regan told me why she wanted to get married right away, and that would've pleased your mother."

"Poor Regan had a lot of pressure on her to do the right thing. Probably because of me," Sheena said ruefully.

Her father stopped walking and studied her. "Of all her children, you were your mother's favorite. Of course, she was upset when you missed out on college, but she loved Tony and adored your kids. No apologies needed. Hear?"

Sheena asked herself if she dared to ask the question that had haunted her for some time. She fumbled in her mind for the right way to say it and finally spoke. "Dad, you were excited about Mom having your baby when I was born. Right?" She waited, thinking his answer would help her sort out if he was her father, not Gavin.

"Oh yes! When your mother told me that you were on the

way, I cried like a baby, I did," Patrick said. "We'd been trying for some time. There was some trouble along the way, and when your blood was tested, we discovered you have my blood type. We're the only two in my family with Type B. Guess that made it seem extra special. Of course, with my being in the service, there was a gap between you and your sisters, but we welcomed them too."

"And Gavin was a special uncle to me, like she said?"

Patrick studied her thoughtfully. "Gavin had his heart broken when your mother decided to marry me instead of him, but he always loved her and our family. Think of what he's done for you and your sisters."

Sheena felt her knees go weak and gripped his arm for balance.

He frowned at her. "Are you all right?"

"Just a pregnancy thing," she fibbed, stunned by the knowledge her father had just shared. Did he have any idea her mother and Gavin wrote letters to one another? That her mother sent him pictures?

"They kept in touch through the years, but I knew my Eileen was faithful to me, just as I was to her. It might not have been a perfect marriage, but we did our best."

In silence, they reached his room.

"Good night, Dad. Sweet dreams!" said Sheena giving him a hard hug. "Michael will pick you up for breakfast in the morning, so you can say goodbye to Darcy and Austin."

She kissed him and went on her way, feeling a huge lump in her throat. Her mother and her father had been faithful to one another, but had each been as happy as she and Tony? Darcy and Austin? Regan and Brian? She didn't think so. And she knew for certain Gavin hadn't been.

###

When the last of the breakfast guests had departed, Sheena sank onto the couch in the family room exhausted.

"Nice job, honey," said Tony. "I'm going to run down to the office to check in and see how sales are going. Bett said she'd meet me."

"Go ahead. Meaghan and Michael can help me straighten up. Then, I'm taking the rest of the day off. Tomorrow morning, I have a meeting with Casey, Nicole, and Graham to see how well we did with the wedding. We have a client's wedding in three weeks, and we want to be ready for it."

"You sit for a while before you even attempt to do anything." Tony went to the stairs and called up, "Michael? Meaghan? Come here, please."

When they appeared, he said, "Michael, we need you to clean up the lanai by straightening chairs and making sure all glasses, cups, and plates are brought inside. Meaghan, we need you to start loading the dishwasher and cleaning up the kitchen. Your mother is exhausted, and she needs us to step up and help."

The kids looked at her, hesitated, and then Michael said, "Okay, we're on it."

A flush of gratitude warmed her cheeks. "Thanks."

After a quiet day and a good night's sleep, Sheena felt more like her old self. Alone in the house after the kids left for school, she took a moment to reflect on the weekend. Holding the gold coin Uncle Gavin had given her as a child, she thought of what her father had told her about his marriage to her mother. They were good people who were true to one another. She now believed Gavin was not her father. But she was surer than ever her mother and Gavin had loved each other, not for one brief period of time in their lives, but always.

Putting the gold coin away, Sheena made a silent vow to herself to use it as a reminder to make her marriage a loving one, so neither she nor Tony would have any regrets. And someday, when it was appropriate, she'd pass the coin and the story behind it to one of her children, so they'd understand how important it was to love and be loved.

Sheena sat at a table in Gavin's with Nicole, waiting for Casey and Graham to appear for their meeting.

"Thank you so much for overseeing the arrangements for Darcy's wedding," Sheena said to her, then laughed. "I mean both Darcy's and Regan's weddings."

Nicole grinned. "It turned out so well. I'm happy for both of them."

Casey rushed in. "Sorry, I'm a little late. I was checking on The Key Hole. I've hired a good manager, but I won't feel comfortable until I see for myself all is in order."

He kissed Nicole on the cheek and took a seat next to her.

Graham appeared, wearing checked pants and a white T-shirt. When he and his staff started cooking, he'd slip on his chef's coat.

"Graham! The food for Darcy's and Regan's reception was fabulous!" exclaimed Sheena. "The few people who hadn't already eaten at Gavin's said they'd definitely make reservations. It's a great way to pick up local trade."

"Agreed," said Nicole. "And with destination weddings becoming more popular, you'll have a good way to build your reputation, Graham."

"As long as you don't leave us," warned Sheena in a teasing voice.

"I'm very grateful to be the chef here," said Graham in a surprisingly serious tone. "My Uncle Nick would be very proud of all of us for what we're building at Gavin's."

"Things appeared to go smoothly for the wedding reception," said Sheena. "But what can we do to make it better and easier on you and your staff?"

A lively discussion took place about flowers, music for the reception, dance floors, and wedding cakes.

"The bottom line is we need to develop a business relationship with a couple of wedding planners who would be willing to come into the hotel and restaurant and oversee weddings and receptions," said Nicole.

"Would it be easier to hire staff to do it?" Sheena asked.

Nicole shook her head. "Not unless you can find a professional to come in."

"And then, if you don't have weddings lined up, what do you do with her and her free time?" said Casey.

"What if we hire a coordinator who can also do other work for us."

"How about me?" said Nicole. "I can handle that and my marketing responsibilities."

"Can you do marketing for the hotel, Gavin's, Ventura, and The Key Hole?" asked Sheena.

"Yes, I think I can. They're all inter-related. That's what makes it so easy. And when we start to get really busy, we'll hire someone part-time to help me."

Sheena felt a smile cross her face. "How did we ever get lucky enough to bring you on board?"

Casey put an arm around Nicole. "Nicole and I are committed to staying here in Florida together, working for you."

"All right then. We'll ask Greg Ryan to draw up a contract with a good incentive program," said Sheena. "You can work our first wedding in a few weeks, and when Darcy is back, my sisters and I can make a final decision."

"Sounds good," said Nicole."

Graham spoke up. "As you asked, Sheena, I've put together three suggestions for wedding reception dinners with a selection of choices, along with a cost analysis of each one. In the future, we're going to need more staff to handle these occasions. I'd like to go ahead and hire and train at least six more service people on a part-time, as-needed basis, so they're ready for the next wedding. Then, they could be available on demand for future weddings or other banquet events."

Numbers flashed through Sheena's head. Every time she thought they could get ahead financially, new expenses arose. From her experience working in Tony's plumbing business in Boston, she knew better than her sisters how business ebbed and flowed. Things were looking better around the hotel, but it was costing more money than she'd thought.

"Okay, go ahead and hire them," she said to Graham. "Nicole, as long as you want to act as wedding coordinator, let's talk about bookings. We have three destination weddings booked so far. I realize we can't compete with the likes of the Don, the Vinoy, or any Ritz Carlton, but we can fill a niche for smaller, family-style weddings. Let's concentrate on those."

"Okay," said Nicole. "I'll get back to you on that."

After more discussion, they each left with more work to do.

Sheena sat in Rocky's truck between Rocky and her father, as quiet as the two of them. She'd visited Duncan on a couple of previous occasions. Each time she'd filled with sorrow at the life this man was forced to live.

She glanced at her father and realized from the rhythmic grinding of his teeth how nervous he was. Squeezing his hand, she gave him an encouraging smile. "I'm so glad you have the chance to meet Duncan. He may not react to you, but I'm convinced he'll know you're there."

"Gavin would be pleased to know you did this," Rocky said. "He saw to it every effort would be made to keep Duncan as comfortable as possible. He's well taken care of, but it's good for family to visit."

"His caregiver, Elena Garcia, is an extraordinary person who sees he has everything he needs, though there's no way he could tell her," said Sheena. "It's such a sad situation."

Patrick stirred restlessly. "I suppose it's just one of those things, though I've never heard of anything like this happening to the rest of our family."

Their conversation ended when Rocky pulled up to the small, red-brick house in Ybor City where Duncan lived with his caretaker.

Sheena followed her father out of the truck and stood a moment, bracing herself for the visit. She couldn't help thinking of the baby growing inside her and sent a private thank you to the heavens above that tests had shown her baby to be perfectly normal.

Elena greeted them at the door with a warm smile and then continued to study Patrick. "Rocky said you resembled Gavin. You two sure look like brothers."

Patrick bobbed his head. "I'm sorry, I didn't know about Duncan until recently."

"How is he today?" Sheena asked.

Her eyes filled with sadness. "Same as always, but do come in."

Sheena followed Patrick and Rocky inside. At the doorway to Duncan's room, her father's back stiffened as he looked into the room. Though he didn't cry out, Patrick's shoulders slumped, and he wrapped his arms around himself. After taking several deep breaths, Patrick walked forward and knelt in front of Duncan's chair.

Duncan's arms were mere stubs protruding from shoulders. His legs, almost as deformed, were hidden beneath a blanket. His eyes remained in a blank stare. Drool dripped from a mouth that hung open. He might have been a handsome man had he been given a chance, but nature's cruelty had taken that away from him.

For a brief moment, Duncan's gaze rested on Patrick as if he could see him. "Hello, Duncan," Patrick said, even though he understood Duncan couldn't hear. "I'm your Uncle Pat. You're a Sullivan, all right. You resemble my Dad."

"And he has my hair," said Sheena softly, standing next to her father.

Tears filled Patrick's eyes. He got to his feet and walked out of the room.

Sheena said, "Hi, Duncan. It's Sheena. Your two cousins, Darcy and Regan, got married a couple of days ago. I wish you could have joined us." She bent over and kissed the top of his head.

In the living room, her father sat on the couch, his face buried in his hands, his shoulders shaking.

Sheena went over to him and rubbed his back. "It's all right, Dad."

"No, Sheena," he said, shaking his head ferociously. "It isn't right at all. How can anyone live like that?"

She had no answer. She'd asked herself that same question over and over.

Sheena was at work in the office that afternoon when she got a phone call from Mary Lou Webster, the grandmother of their first bride.

"Our little private wedding has grown from eighteen to

thirty. Can you accommodate us at the hotel?" said the woman, panic rising in her voice.

Sheena did a quick review in her mind. With the twenty new rooms in the Egret Building opening soon, they'd have space. She checked the reservations chart and was dismayed but pleased as well to find that they'd be two rooms short. She'd read about hotels overbooking rooms because cancellations were inevitable, but she wanted to do it without disappointing any guests.

"We'd hate to have anything to go wrong now," Mary Lou said. "It's too late to change plans."

"Of course, we can accommodate you. Email us the list of names, and we'll put them into our system," said Sheena brightly. "With your permission, I'll add the deposit for their rooms to the account we've set up for you."

"No problem," said Mary Lou. "Just have the rooms ready."

After Sheena hung up the phone, she blocked off the rooms, double-booking two of them, turned on the emergency phone system, and ran to the Egret Building to check on the progress of the upstairs rooms.

New bedding and bedspreads were in place. Paintings were in the rooms but sitting on the floor, waiting for Rocky to hang them. Televisions were still in boxes in the rooms, but not yet mounted and hooked up. And a few rooms still had to have their phones installed. Chip Carson, who'd installed most of their computer systems, had promised to take care of these last few items.

Sheena sighed. Regan was usually good about following up on these kinds of things, but she'd been busy filming more ad campaigns for Arthur in addition to working on the renovation of the Sandpiper Suites Building.

In the office, Sheena called Rocky and Chip to make sure they'd finish their work. Then she called Tony.

"Hi, hon!" said Tony. "What's up?"

"I need you to make the final inspections on the plumbing and electricity before we bring in the building inspectors to approve the twenty top-floor rooms in the Egret Building for occupancy."

"Sheena, you know how busy I am with Brian away. Can it wait?"

"How about we have a light supper, and I'll help you with paperwork this evening?"

Tony was silent and then said, "Guess so. See you tonight."

"Thanks," said Sheena, well aware of the stress they both were under.

She hung up and looked up the schedule for the suites. They were due to be completed by April 1st. She studied the progress. They'd given the construction job to Brian and Tony's company, but their men were slow in getting the work done. Sheena decided to wait until Regan and Brian returned before discussing the situation with Tony. She didn't want to cause any friction between them.

After Sally came to relieve her, Sheena took some time to look around the property. The poolside bohio bar was built and awaiting installation of refrigerators, bar sinks, speed wells, and other bar equipment. Casey had already hired a couple of college kids to run it and to oversee distribution of towels and beach chairs from the pool storeroom.

She stood and gazed at the main building. A coat of fresh paint was being applied to the building in the back, where construction of the private patio for Gavin's people was mostly complete. She squinted at the roof. It looked fine, though they'd been warned it would need to be replaced. They'd scheduled that for next year hoping cash flow would pay for it.

There was a chill in the air as Sheena walked past the pool where a number of guests were lounging in the sun, protected from the slight breeze by tropical shrubbery surrounding the pool.

She approached the waterfront. A company was scheduled to rebuild the dock within the next two weeks. She and her sisters had decided to spend a little extra money by having them build benches at the widened and expanded end of the dock. The same company would build racks to hold kayaks, paddle boards, and a secure storage area for life preservers and paddles.

Sheena took a seat in one of the wooden Adirondack chairs and studied the gazebo and nearby trellis. Each provided a lovely setting for wedding pictures, as well as a location for an actual ceremony.

Closing her eyes, Sheena leaned back in the chair and lifted her face to the sun. The warm rays relaxed the tension she always felt after reviewing numbers for the hotel. Her thoughts turned to her family. Soon, Michael would hear whether he got into the college of his choice. Poor kid had really been torn up by his relationship with Kaylee. But, she reminded herself, he'd matured a lot because of it. He'd been extra gentle, extra helpful because of her pregnancy. Sheena patted her stomach. She'd already felt the baby move, making the idea of a new baby a firm reality. If the baby was a boy, she wanted to name him Gavin. She hoped her father would understand.

Thinking ahead, she decided to talk to Tony about giving Meaghan the use of her VW convertible. They'd need a bigger car to transport the baby and all the required gear. Having her own transportation would allow Meaghan to get around on her own and do errands for her.

Sheena opened her eyes and sat up. When she realized the person walking toward her was Maggie, she smiled and struggled to stand out of the awkward chair.

"Hey there!" Sheena called to her.

"Hi," said Maggie. "I saw you here and wanted to talk to you alone." She paused, sat next to Sheena an one of the chairs, and licked her lips nervously. "I wonder if you'd consider using me as a nanny after your baby is born. I'm trying to break away from my work in Gracie's. I know I can't renew my nursing license, but I want to work with patients of all ages as a nanny or an aide."

"Does Gracie know this is what you want to do?" Sheena asked. She'd never want to upset Gracie.

"Yes, she knows and understands," said Maggie. "We're having to expand our wait staff anyway, so she'll get someone to cover for me when it's needed."

Sheena looked into Maggie's eyes. She, like all of Gavin's people, had sad stories behind them. Hurt and disappointment still lingered on Maggie's face. She'd already been punished for helping her father with pain medications she'd felt forced to take from her employer.

"You as my nanny? That would be wonderful," Sheena said. "I'm sure I could use your help."

Tears sprang to Maggie's eyes. "Thank you!"

They stood and embraced, and then Sheena said, "Guess I'd better be going on my way. I've got more office work to do at home."

On her way home, Sheena thought of all it would take to continue her work at the hotel and wondered if she could meet the challenge.

CHAPTER FORTY

REGAN

Regan awoke with a smile. Today was the first day of the rest of her life as Mrs. Brian Harwood.

Lying beside her, Brian opened his eyes. A slow grin crossed his face. "How's my bride?"

"Happy," she replied, reaching over and trailing a hand down his body. He'd healed well, but she'd always wonder what might have happened if she hadn't gripped Brian's arm to warn him about the truck bearing down on their motorcycle. The scars on her face were less apparent, but would always be a reminder of the accident that had brought them together. The movement of her lip was slowly coming back, but it, too, would never be perfect again.

"Let's go to the pool before having breakfast," she suggested. "It'll be crowded later on, but we should be able to swim lengths now."

"What kind of breakfast were you talking about?" Brian asked, giving her a sly look.

At his teasing, Regan shook her head. "We'll have to see."

"What happened to the love and obey part?" he said in mock horror.

"I never said 'obey.' Remember?"

He laughed. "It wouldn't have mattered anyway."

"Got that right," she said, climbing out of their luxurious bed.

She put on her bathing suit and stood by watching as Brian

slid on his swim trunks. His brawny body was mostly brown from working in the sun. Staring at him, thinking of all that lay ahead, she hoped one day to have a son who would look like his handsome daddy.

"You ready?" said Brian, turning to her.

She grinned at him. She was ready for all of it. Her life had never seemed better.

Later, after an invigorating swim and a quick, light breakfast inside on the concierge level where Brian had booked their room, Regan suggested a walk along the beach.

"Okay, and then we can go paddle-boarding," said Brian.

Regan laughed. Brian liked to keep busy. "Then I want to lie in the sun and read. And maybe I should call Sheena and check on the hotel."

Brian waggled a finger at her. "No work. We're here to play."

"You're right. I wonder how Darcy and Austin are doing in London?"

Brian frowned at her.

"Just wondering," she said, chuckling. "C'mon, husband, let's take that walk."

Outside, the tropical air wrapped itself around her, inviting her to relax. At the beach, she took off her sandals and accepted the hand Brian offered her before stepping onto the sand. They walked to the water's edge and stood in the foamy edges of the waves feeling the water rush at their ankles and then ebb away.

"Seeing the endless movement of the waves, I feel like such a small part of the universe," Regan said. "How long has all this been here? How long will it remain?"

"We're lucky, you and I, to be alive and together in this

moment," said Brian.

Regan looked up into his face, feeling a surge of love for him. "I didn't realize you were such a romantic."

Brian gave her a sheepish look. "Now that you've found that out, I suppose I have to prove it to you." He pulled a small box out from a side pocket on his swim shorts.

"What's this?" Regan asked, stepping back in surprise.

"The jeweler where I bought our wedding rings helped me pick this out. I wanted it to be a perfect reminder of what you mean to me." He took the lid off the box and held it open to her.

Nestled on a background of turquoise velvet was a necklace. A white-gold symbol of a wave hung from a matching chain. Below the crest of the wave, a huge diamond sparkled at her.

"Brian, it's beautiful! Thank you," said Regan, placing a hand over her heart, stunned by his gift to her.

His smile lit his eyes. "The wave signifies all the swimming you did with me to help me heal. I love you so much, Regan."

"I love you too." Regan couldn't stop the tears forming in her eyes as she lifted the necklace out of the box and handed it to him with shaking fingers. "Will you help me?"

Brian hooked the necklace around her neck and stood back to look at it. "It's perfect!" He hugged her to him.

Regan laid her head against his hard chest. Brian would never know how grateful she was to have found such sweet love with him.

On the limousine ride back to the cottage on Kenton's property, Regan cuddled up next to Brian. Their short honeymoon had been fabulous, but that moment on the beach with Brian looking at the waves and learning the reasons behind his gift to her would stay with her forever.

"Back to the grindstone, eh?" Brian said.

Regan smiled and nodded. "I've got a lot to do before our first wedding celebration at the hotel."

"And I'm hoping we've sold a couple more houses," said Brian. "Bett and Taylor make a good team."

Regan sat up. "Taylor certainly works long hours. What do you think that's all about?"

Brian shrugged. "Who knows? It's all part of the real estate business."

Regan thought no more about it as the limo drove through the gates on Kenton's property and pulled to a stop beside the cottage.

The driver hurried to open the door for her. As Regan stepped onto the ground, she felt a dose of reality. She and Brian had a lot of work ahead of them.

After Brian paid the driver and tipped him, they headed inside. It seemed as if they'd been gone for several days, not two. Her thoughts flew to Darcy. London was a far cry from the Gulf Coast of Florida.

CHAPTER FORTY-ONE

DARCY

Darcy pulled her coat closer as she and Austin walked down the street toward Kensington Palace. After seeing Big Ben, the double-decker buses, and the black cabs particular to London, she felt as if she was in a storybook. Viewing these things through photos or film did not do justice to the city she'd wanted to see. She looked over at Austin and smiled.

"Just think! Princess Diana, Kate, William, and Harry have walked these same streets," she said, bubbling with enthusiasm.

Austin laughed. "They've certainly driven or been driven over the streets."

Much later, after touring the palace, they entered Brown's Hotel for their afternoon tea reservation.

"This is something my parents like to arrange for their small groups," Austin explained. "I've had tea here once before, and I know you'll like it."

They were shown to a table, and from that moment on, Darcy was lost in fanciful dreams of lords and ladies enjoying tea in their castles every afternoon.

Crisp linens, delicate china, layered tiers of sandwiches, fruits, sweets, and other delicacies spelled royalty to her. She reveled in it all.

"Quite a difference from Florida, huh?" said Austin, amusement in his voice.

Darcy laughed. "A royal difference. I wish my sisters could see me now. I'll send them a message with a selfie."

"Another one?" teased Austin.

Darcy couldn't hide her grin. "I'm going to share as much of my trip with them as possible. Who knows if I'll ever be here again?"

"If we accept my parents' company, you could come back here hundreds of times."

Darcy didn't answer him. They'd promised not to make any decisions until after the honeymoon. Besides, she wanted to think of this trip as hers alone with the man she loved with all her heart.

Sated, they left the hotel and headed to Harrods. Darcy hoped to pick up a few items to take back to Florida. Funny how thoughts of her sisters kept coming to her. She told herself not to worry about them and the hotel, but she couldn't help wondering how things were going.

CHAPTER FORTY-TWO

SHEENA

Sheena was in the hotel office waiting for the building inspector to show up when her phone rang.

"Sheena? It's Sally. I'm not feeling well today and can't relieve you. I'm sorry. I hope to be able to come into the office tomorrow."

"No worries. We'll work something out. Feel better, and, hopefully, we'll see you tomorrow." As Sheena hung up, the upbeat feeling she'd projected into the conversation collapsed with disappointment. She'd just put an ad in the paper for office help, but they needed someone today. On a whim, she called Lynn and explained the situation to her.

"I can help for a few hours this morning. But later, I'm driving Patrick to his house in The Villages. He wants me to stay and help him get settled. I've got a friend there who will put me up for the night."

"What? Wait! Dad is leaving today? I thought he was staying for two more days." Sheena felt as if someone had slapped her. She lifted a hand to her cheek.

"No, we're leaving this afternoon. I don't think he's coming back for a while, but you'd better talk to him. How soon do you want me at the office?"

"Can you walk over here now?" Sheena asked. She had to talk to her father. He'd turned down an invitation to join her and her family for dinner last night. Was it because he'd been with Lynn?

When Lynn showed up at the office, Sheena gave her a quick run-through of office procedure and headed over to the Egret Building to see her father.

On her way, she saw Patrick lounging at the pool and made a sharp turn through the gate into the pool area.

"Hi, Dad!" she said softly, hoping not to disturb the other hotel guests there.

He opened his eyes and smiled at her. "Hi, darlin'."

She sat in an empty chair beside him. "I just talked to Lynn. I understand you're going to leave us today, and she's going with you."

"Yeah, I've decided it's time to get my place in The Villages settled. Lynn's going to drive me and then help me set up the house."

"And she's staying with a friend?"

Patrick grinned at her like a naughty schoolboy. "Unless I can talk her into staying with me."

A sense of protectiveness washed over her. She knew how charming her father could be, how lonely he'd been, but she didn't want to see Lynn hurt. "Dad ..."

Patrick rose up on an elbow. "I know, I know. You want me to be careful. But at my age, you've got to move fast. I like Lynn a lot. She likes me. We want to see where it takes us. That's all."

"But, Dad, you've just met her."

Patrick let out a snort of disgust. "You think I don't know that? But like I said, we're just seeing if all these feelings are real or not. It's that chemistry thing, you know? It's there, all right. And poor Lynnie has been on her own for a while now."

Lynnie? Sheena opened her mouth to say more, then shut it. Her father was sixty-eight years old going on nineteen. "Just don't hurt her. Okay, Dad? You almost married Regina."

He gave her a steady look. "Like I said, Lynn and I, we like each other in a way I haven't felt before." He lifted a hand. "Don't mean to put your mother in a bad light."

"No, no," said Sheena. "I get it." She understood a lot more about her parents' marriage than he suspected.

"Well, your sisters might not get it, so I'd appreciate it if you kept quiet about it."

"Dad," said Sheena. "They'll know where you've gone and with whom. I'm not about to keep secrets from them."

"You're right. I just don't want Lynnie to get hurt."

At his words, Sheena relaxed. He was thinking of Lynn, after all.

Regan appeared. "Hi, I'm back. Hey! What's going on?"

"Hi, darlin'. Come talk to me," said Patrick.

"See you later, Dad. Safe trip." Sheena rose and kissed his cheek, then turned to Regan. "Hi! I'm going to check on things at the bohio bar, and then I'll head back to the office. Let's talk."

Sheena was on her way to the office when Regan appeared at her side.

"What's going on? Dad and Lynn?"

Sheena shrugged. "Let's go down to the waterfront. We'll talk about that, and then we need to discuss some other things."

They walked down to the grassy area beside the bay and settled in chairs facing one another.

"Dad told me he and Lynn are dating, that they're really serious," said Regan, scowling. "How can that be? They've only just met, and now they're traveling to The Villages together?"

"I know how surprised you are. I was too. When I talked to him, Dad told me he's very anxious not to hurt Lynn with a lot of talk about her going out of town with him," said Sheena. "Honestly, I've never seen anything like the glow of happiness he has on his face. Maybe, as he says, he's found what he's wanted all along."

"But Mom ..."

"He and Mom were faithful, but I don't think their love was anything like what I have with Tony, or you have with Brian."

Regan was quiet a moment. "Okay, I won't say anything more to either Dad or Lynn about their trip. What else did you want to talk about? How are things at the hotel? I know it's only been a couple of days, but it seems as if I've been gone forever."

"I'm waiting for the building inspector to approve a C.O. for the twenty top-floor rooms in the Egret Building. He should be here sometime this morning."

"Hold on!" said Regan. "Those rooms aren't ready. Tony needs to do an inspection of his own, televisions and phones need hooking up, and pictures have to be hung."

"I discovered that, and have taken care of all of it, but they aren't critical for a C.O. anyway. We can't lose income because of small details like this," said Sheena.

Regan gave her a crestfallen look. "You think I'm not doing a good job?"

"Nooo, I think you've had a lot on your plate, and I stepped in to help you."

"I hope you haven't gone ahead and messed with the suites. I've got that under control." The violet in Regan's eyes grew darker. "You do your job, and I'll do mine."

After handling the hotel the best way she could by herself, Sheena felt her cheeks grow hot with a flash of anger. "I appreciate your thanks for my doing your job, Regan. It isn't about egos; it's about working together to make the hotel a success."

Reining in her temper, Sheena rose out of her chair and headed toward the office, so frustrated she wanted to pound the ground with each step.

"Wait!" cried Regan.

Sheena slowed but kept walking.

Regan caught up with her. "Look, I'm sorry. I didn't mean to snap at you. I guess I should have asked for your help when I knew I was getting behind."

"It would've helped. Each room that remains unfinished means a loss of income. By the way, we're overbooked for our first wedding weekend, including the twenty upstairs rooms."

Regan's eyes widened. "All forty rooms?"

"Yes. We have to hope two people cancel, or we can get at least one suite done within eighteen days. I waited for you to come back. Now that you are here, the two of us need to talk to Tony and Brian together to make sure their crews are on the job each day. They're almost done, but we need them to finish their work in at least one of the suites, so the tile floors can be laid. And then we can move furniture and appliances in and do the final decorative touches."

"Okay, come to my house for dinner, and we'll talk to them tonight. Right now, I have a few phone calls I'd better make."

As Regan all but ran to the office, Sheena watched her with dismay. With both Regan and Darcy having plans of their own, it was very clear to Sheena her job at the hotel was going to get much harder.

That evening, Sheena and Tony drove through the gates of Kenton's property and pulled up in front of the cottage.

"I hope Regan is as good a cook as you," grumbled Tony. "I'm hungry, and I'm tired."

"Having dinner here is a nice way to have our business meeting," said Sheena. "Regan was sweet to invite us. We had a little disagreement this morning, and she's anxious to be in charge of the rooms renovation again."

Tony got out of the car and looked over at Kenton's house. "Nice digs, huh?"

"Regan showed it to me. It's beautiful inside."

"This cottage is something anyone would be happy to have," said Tony, studying it.

Brian stepped outside to greet them. "I thought I heard you drive up. Welcome to our little piece of paradise."

He clapped Tony on the back and gave Sheena a kiss on the cheek.

Regan appeared at Brian's side. "Dinner's in the oven, but let's go sit on the patio. It's always nice there until the sun goes down."

Inside the kitchen, Brian handed Tony a cold beer. "What can we get you, Sheena?"

"Just a glass of water. I can't seem to get enough of it," she said.

Brian fixed her a glass of water and handed a glass of red wine to Regan. "Well, now, let's enjoy the outdoors."

Regan led them out to the lanai. It was too cloudy to see a clear sunset, but the sky held a faint tinge of orange in and among the clouds.

"What's the meeting about?" said Tony after sitting and taking a sip of his beer.

Regan glanced at Sheena and cleared her throat. "Sheena and I need you guys to agree to complete work on the suites. It cannot be delayed any longer. As Sheena says, any empty room means a lack of income. And these rooms are empty because your part of the work hasn't been completed."

Into the silence that followed, Sheena said. "I walked through the rooms today. The walls in the main rooms and the bedrooms are painted, but the new crown molding we talked about needs to be installed and painted. And tile floors need to be put down in the kitchens and bathrooms, so installation of the toilets, sinks, and tubs can be done, and kitchen appliances can be placed and hooked up."

Regan studied the paper in her hand. "Also, the electrical fixtures including ceiling fans need to be hooked up in all the rooms. And the carpeting, for which you're not responsible, needs to be laid after you've completed your work. Then all the finishing decorating can be done. Have I missed anything, Sheena?"

"These suites all have new HVAC systems, but the thermostats are not set into the walls, they're just dangling on wires. It's that kind of clean-up work that needs to be done. We, more than most, know how busy you guys are, but we need your help on this. With a wedding coming up in a little over two weeks, it can't get messed up."

Tony and Brian looked at each other.

"Well, I'll be damned," said Brian. "You sound like one of our clients."

"This is one time where our relationships to you need to enter the equation," said Sheena. "Right, Regan?"

She looked at the men and nodded. "By the way, I just got word I'm to start work with another customer at the Ventura Village development. Congrats!"

"Thanks." Tony cleared his throat. "As far as the work at the hotel is concerned, if it's okay with Brian, I'll put together a crew tomorrow and take them over there for a rush job."

"Okay. Guess we'd better do it. I want to enjoy my new status of husband."

Tony looked at Sheena and grinned. "Me too. I like being able to go to bed with my wife."

They shared a good laugh.

Darkness sent them inside the house from the patio.

In the kitchen, Sheena sat back and enjoyed watching

Regan prepare and serve the meal. It was a treat to be a guest for once. She and Tony didn't have much more time before they'd either have to drag a baby with them or be required to stay home.

Later that evening, driving into their development, Sheena noticed Taylor's convertible at the show home. "Tony, pull to a stop. I want to check on something in Regan's office. I think the carpet sample we were talking about earlier is there."

Tony put on the brakes and stopped in front of the house. "Go ahead. I'll stay here."

Sheena got out of the car, walked up the driveway, and knocked on the door. She also wanted to check on Taylor. Something didn't seem right.

Through the front window, Sheena saw the sales office was empty. After testing the door, she opened it and stepped inside.

She started for Regan's office in the back of the house when she heard a noise upstairs. Wondering if she should call out, she hesitated. A hand touched her shoulder. She jumped and whirled around.

"For God's sake, Tony, you scared me. I thought you were going to stay in the car."

"Ssshh!" Tony waved her toward the stairway.

As they quietly climbed the stairs, Sheena heard more noises and suddenly understood what was happening.

Tony kept climbing, and now, Sheena knew, he understood too.

At the top of the stairs, they walked to the master bedroom suite and peered inside.

Taylor was lying naked atop the bed.

"C'mon, hurry! You paid for just one hour," she called to

the man standing naked beside the bed.

"I wouldn't, if I were you," Tony said, his voice low, angry.

"What the fuck!" The man turned to face them, his eyes bulging with surprise.

"Get dressed," Tony told him.

Sickened by what was going on in the house Tony and Brian had lovingly built, Sheena turned away.

"Make sure Taylor gets dressed while I call the cops," Tony said.

"No! Not the cops!" Taylor cried.

Tony ignored her as the man hastily dressed. The pulse at his temple indicated how furious he was.

The man bolted from the room. Tony followed, calling for him to stop.

Sheena stayed in the doorway as Taylor scrambled to her feet and reached for her clothes, which had been tossed on the floor. "I'm sorry. Look, it won't happen again."

"All those nights you were supposedly working late, this was going on?" Sheena said to her.

Taylor's eyes narrowed. "What do you know about struggling to make ends meet? You've got it all. A handsome, rich man, and a family, a hotel, everything. My husband left me nothing. All because of an affair I had."

"It wasn't just one, was it?" Sheena said, knowing the answer.

Taylor began to cry. Sheena knew a lot of women who struggled following a divorce, but they were nothing like this woman. Now Sheena understood why Taylor had gone after Tony, then Brian. She thought they were rich.

It was almost laughable. In construction work, what looked good on paper could evaporate in a hurry.

Brian and Regan showed up just as a policeman was leading Taylor away. Breaking and entering was the reason given for holding her, and though they knew the charges might not stick, it was as good a way as any to get her off the property and out of their lives.

Tony and Brian checked every room for damage or theft. Sheena and Regan went through things in both offices. A petty cash box held one dollar and nothing else. Sheena found a check for one hundred dollars written to Lortay Enterprises tucked inside an envelope marked private in one of the desk drawers.

"Lortay Enterprises?" said Regan when Sheena showed her. "Taylor couldn't think of a better fake name?"

"Her strongest assets didn't include her brain," said Brian, joining them.

"Guess we were all fooled by her," Tony said, shaking his head.

Sheena gave him a withering look. "Nooo. She fooled half of us. Regan and I never trusted her."

"That's right," said Regan. "I never liked her, but I didn't think she'd do anything like this."

"Well, lesson learned," said Brian. "The next person we hire to assist Bett has to meet with Sheena's and your approval."

Baby steps, Sheena thought. It took baby steps to make a good working relationship. But the four of them were coming together nicely for Ventura Village, LLC.

CHAPTER FORTY-THREE

DARCY

Vive la Paris! Darcy lifted her wine glass in a salute to Austin. Sitting inside a small, neighborhood bistro not too far from their hotel, Darcy thought Paris was every bit as wonderful as she'd hoped. After spending a couple of days sight-seeing, she was ready to have a quiet evening with a simple meal.

"What was your favorite thing today?" Austin asked her. His pleasure from her excitement was touching to see.

"Well, Le Louvre was as spectacular as I expected. But I couldn't believe how small the painting of Mona Lisa was. And I swear, when I moved around the room, her gaze followed me."

Austin chuckled. "Lots of people say that."

"All those famous works by Leonardo da Vinci, Rodin, things like the Venus de Milo and all the rest. I couldn't believe it was me seeing it for real. Do you have any idea what a special gift you've given me?"

He reached over and squeezed her hand. "And your gift to me? Priceless."'

"Sometimes I have to pinch myself to know this is all real—you, the trip, everything. If I die and go to heaven, I want to fill my little piece of it with the wine, bread, and cheese from France, and the artwork I've seen here."

Austin grinned. "We should enjoy every day and night we have here."

His brown-eyed gaze reached deep inside her to where she'd begun to store these precious times.

CHAPTER FORTY-FOUR

REGAN

Another postcard," said Regan, holding it up for Sheena to see. "Rome this time."

Sheena smiled. "I'm so glad she's having a fabulous time. Think of all the interesting things she's seen that she can put into her novels."

"I know. All of it within two weeks' time. One more week and she'll be home. Just in time to clean up after our wedding weekend. How'd your meeting go with Nicole and the wedding planner?" Regan asked. In just five days, the first wedding at the hotel would take place, and she was as nervous about it as Sheena.

Since the meeting they'd had a couple of weeks ago, Tony and Brian's crews had done their part, and the suites were ready for carpeting. Now it was left to her to see the rest would be done on time. Placement of furniture would follow, along with hanging pictures and adding other decorative touches.

The weather reports indicated rain during the week, but clear days on the weekend. Regan prayed they were right. Everything for the wedding was centered around the outdoors.

"Looks like some rain headed our way," said Sheena. "It's just as well. We'll get that out of the way."

Sheena turned to the woman they'd recently been training for the office. A retired schoolteacher who lived in Rosa and Paul's neighborhood, Jeanne Nance was a perfect fit. A heavy-set, jovial woman who'd taught kindergarten for years, Jeanne was a source of positive energy as she bustled around the office and greeted guests with a cheerfulness that was contagious. Teaching her the computer programs was another issue, but one they were slowly straightening out.

"Okay, if we leave you for a while, Jeanne?" said Regan. "I want to review the status of preparations for our outdoor wedding."

Jeanne gave them both a smile. "I'll be all right here. You two go tend to your duties elsewhere."

Regan exchanged an amused glance with Sheena.

Outside, they walked to the gazebo. The wedding planner had suggested stringing white silk flowers and mini-lights through the lattice work at the bottom of the gazebo. They'd paid Meaghan and two of her friends to do the tedious job.

The three-section trellis, covered with colorful bougainvillea, was mounted in the ground and would be the perfect backdrop for the bride and her small party.

The dock was finished, and though paddle boards had been ordered, they wouldn't arrive for another two days. The kayaks, however, were stored in the newly built racks.

Regan and Sheena stood and looked back at the hotel for a full view of the property. Plantings surrounded the buildings and were strategically placed to create color, shade, and interest. The buildings sparkled from the attention they'd received. The addition of the Bohio Bar, as it was now called, and Gavin's restaurant added an upscale look to the property.

"Wow! It sure looks a lot different from the place we first saw," said Regan.

"I sometimes wonder what Gavin would think of it. He had his own ideas about what he wanted, but I believe we've surpassed even those. It really looks nice. Refined and pleasant."

"I agree," said Regan. "It's perfect. Like our tagline says ... it's a quiet treasure."

"C'mon, girl," said Sheena taking her arm. "Let's go see what's happening at Gracie's. I heard Bebe is trying out a new design for the wedding cake. You know what that means!"

Regan smiled. "Cake!"

In the quiet that followed the closing of Gracie's, staff members normally relaxed inside the restaurant. Today, when Regan and Sheena joined them, they were sitting at tables eating the remains of the cake with which Bebe had been experimenting.

A short while later, Rocky hurried inside. "Hey, everybody! Looks like a bad storm heading our way. I need help stowing the pool and patio furniture."

Regan was surprised when Sam, a quiet man, spoke up. "Aw, Rocky, relax. We ain't supposed to get any serious rain until tomorrow."

"Well, this one's looking bad. And I can feel it in my bones."

Regan trusted Rocky's instincts on something like this. Rocky had spent a couple of years sailing with Gavin looking for gold, and though he resembled a pirate with his gold earring and dark curls, he was a sensible man.

Regan and Sheena quickly followed the others outside.

Dark clouds had gathered in the sky to the west. In a matter of moments, a strong wind kicked up, turning the clouds into a boiling mass. Then, like a finger pointing from the clouds, a rotating column of wind raced toward shore.

"Waterspout!" cried Rocky. "Get back inside."

As fascinating as it was to watch this phenomenon, Regan was quick to act. Rocky's voice held more than a warning; it was full of fear.

Back inside the restaurant, Rocky ordered, "Stay away from the windows. Go into the hallway."

"My God! This is like the tornadoes back home," said Maggie, holding Clyde's hand. He was whimpering softly.

"I was caught at the edge of one of these out on the water," said Rocky. "They usually stay at sea, but, even so, when it comes this close to shore, it can be dangerous stuff."

Flashes of lightning, the roll of thunder, and the pounding of rain on the roof kept them huddled inside. At one point, the whole building shook while it sounded as if a freight train was roaring by at high speed.

Then, as quickly as it had come, the storm lessened.

Sheena gave Regan a worried look as they followed Rocky outside.

Regan's jaw dropped at the sight of their landscaping. Hibiscus blossoms hung in shredded clumps. Palm fronds dotted the ground. The thatched roofing on the Bohio Bar now had gaping holes. A number of shingles from the roof of the main building lay on the ground like drowned seagulls.

"What a mess!" said Sheena to Regan. "We'd better check on the guests and the entire property. You start the tour, and I'll go to the office."

At the pool, several chairs had blown into the pool, chaise lounges were scattered, and two of the umbrellas had blown inside out. All else seemed okay. The flowering bushes around Gavin's were in bad shape.

As she approached the waterfront, Regan's heart stopped at the sight of the trellis. It looked like a giant creature had trampled on it, breaking it into small pieces and destroying the flowering vines that used to cover it.

The gazebo had withstood the wind and rain, but the bushes at the base of it would have to be replaced before the wedding.

Petey, the peacock, walked toward her looking as bedraggled as the plantings.

"Hey, Petey," said Regan. "You get rained on too?" He usually perched in one of the higher branches of the trees.

She didn't wait for a reply but hurried back to the office.

"How are things?" Sheena asked.

"It could've been worse. But, we'll have to put in a call to the landscapers. Ours isn't the only property hit around here, and they'll get busy."

"Okay," said Sheena. "And I'll call Tony to see if he can check on the roof for us. We don't want to have any leaks ruining the apartments for Gavin's people."

"We'd better check the Egret Building. We'll ask Bernice to have her cleaning crew go around to straighten and dry off furniture and check on the rooms. It appears the Sandpiper Suites Building and Gavin's restaurant are unscathed. I'll get a crew of Gavin's people over to the pool to help there."

Sheena took out her phone. "I'm calling Tony now."

After placing her calls, Regan helped Jeanne handle requests from hotel guests. Most were easy to handle—things like replacing broken patio furniture. Fortunately, none of the sliding glass doors had been damaged.

By the time she was free to go back outside, Tony had arrived. He stood beside Sheena and Rocky staring up at the roof.

"I'll get the ladder and go up to look at it," Tony said. "It may be as simple as replacing a few shingles. Once the high tourist season is over, we can reroof the entire building without interrupting guests."

"Okay," said Sheena. "Sounds like a good plan." She turned to Regan. "How did you do?"

"Jeanne and I started a list of rooms that need patio furniture replaced. Bernice is having four people on her staff survey all the rooms. They'll wipe down and clean off patios and sliding doors where needed."

"That's a lot of overtime pay, but it'll be worth it. What about the landscaping company?"

Regan shook her head. "I couldn't get through. Like you said, they're probably swamped with calls."

"I'll try them again. We have to get things back to normal, or as close to it as possible, by the time the wedding party arrives."

Regan and Sheena stared at each other with dismay. "I guess I should never have said how perfect everything was earlier."

"This is just one of those things that can happen. Not your fault."

Regan watched Sheena hurry away, thankful her big sister was around. When she'd seen all the damage, she'd wanted to break down and cry.

CHAPTER FORTY-FIVE

SHEENA

Sheena hung up the phone with a sigh. She hated confrontation, but she'd learned in business a squeaky wheel got attention. And with their first wedding party due to arrive in a matter of days, she was more than willing to "squeak" louder than normal. As a result, the landscapers agreed to appear tomorrow to do an assessment and to replant what was needed by the end of the next business day.

She opened the door to the office to head over to the main building when she noticed a crowd of people surrounding someone lying on the ground. A ladder had fallen onto the walkway behind the building.

Tony! Sheena's heart raced to keep up with her legs, which had found a sudden spurt of adrenaline.

Regan saw her and called out, "We've already called 911. He fell from the roof, but he says he's going to be all right."

Heart still pounding furiously, Sheena knelt beside Tony. "Where are you hurt? Tell me."

"I can't seem to get my breath, and my side hurts," he said, his words coming out in pain-filled puffs. "Damn ladder slid out from under me."

Memories from Sheena's high-school AP courses in nursing kicked in. *Broken ribs? Punctured lungs?*

"Just lie still until the EMTs arrive," Sheena said in a calm voice she didn't feel.

"We knew not to move him," Rocky said, standing aside.

"Thanks. That could have made things worse," said Sheena. She squeezed Tony's hand for encouragement.

It seemed hours, not minutes before the emergency crew arrived. After checking his vitals, the man who appeared to be in charge turned to her. "It doesn't seem to be life threatening. Of course, we'll take him on into the hospital and have him checked over there. I suspect bruises, scrapes, and a couple of broken ribs. And they'll need to make sure those ribs didn't puncture his lungs."

"Okay, let me get my car. I'll follow you to the hospital."

"I'll take you, Sheena," said Regan, putting an arm around her. "It's too stressful for you to drive."

"Thanks," Sheena said. She'd started to shake with cold fear and couldn't seem to stop.

Much later, Sheena sat in the backseat of Regan's Jeep with Tony beside her. X-rays had confirmed he had a couple of broken ribs, but Tony's lungs were in the clear. They'd given Tony something for the pain, advised him to be quiet for a couple of days, and told him to keep the deep scrapes on his right side clean.

"I'll drop you off at your house," said Regan.

"Thanks, that would be great," Sheena replied. "We can pick up our vehicles at the hotel later. It's been quite a day."

"The roof can be patched temporarily," Tony said, his voice slurring a bit from the medication. "Then we'll completely redo it sometime in May when your business slows down."

"Sounds good," said Regan. "I called Brian and told him what happened. He said for you, Tony, to take it easy and not worry about anything at work."

"Awww, I'll be fine," said Tony, stirring in his seat.

"Just relax," Sheena said. "You're not going back to work

for a day or two."

Tony swore softly and leaned back against the seat.

Sheena stared out the window wondering what she would've done if Tony had been seriously hurt. The plumbing business didn't have the dangers of construction work. But then, she reminded herself, anyone could be hurt any time. Brian had been badly injured in a motorcycle accident, not at work.

Three days later, Sheena stood with Regan in the office waiting for the first of the wedding guests to show up. Everyone had worked together to get the property presentable again. The trellis by the waterfront had been completely rebuilt; minor repairs had been made to the gazebo, and the roof on the main building repaired temporarily. Sadly, though plantings had been replaced, the new landscaping looked just like that—new. In an effort to add color and softness to the trellis, silk flowers had been added to the vines and flowers that twined up its slats.

"Let's pray Lea Webster's grandparents understand how much damage a storm can do," commented Regan. "They've called twice to check on our progress."

"I've tried to reassure them,' said Sheena, "but they're nervous about every little detail. I hope Lea knows how much her grandparents love her."

"It was a good idea to put them into one of the Sandpiper Suites. With Lea having the Bridal Suite in the Egret Building and sharing it with her maid of honor, eliminating two of the now three overbooked rooms, we're in better shape."

"Yes, one less room to worry about. If necessary, we'll ask Lea's parents to share their suite with Mary Lou and Bill and give them a discount."

Regan's eyes gleamed. "Who knew we'd ever be in the position of overbooking? The other suites should be finished in another week, and then we can rent those rooms out too."

Sheena returned Regan's smile, but she couldn't pretend her fingers weren't cold with apprehension. This, their first wedding, was a super-big deal. One of the editors of the social magazine was going to be a part of the photographer's team they'd arranged for Lea. The wedding would also be a test of Nicole's ability to handle these events for the hotel. Nicole was a hard worker, but along with marketing, could she handle bridezillas and their wedding parties?"

Before Sheena could worry any longer, Mary Lou and Bill Webster entered the office.

"Welcome," Sheena said, smiling. "This is going to be a great weekend for you and your granddaughter."

"I hope so," said Mary Lou, giving them a worried look. "We had our hearts set on coming here, but then her mother wanted us to book a bigger hotel on the east coast of Florida. But Lea decided she liked the idea of the Salty Key Inn better."

"She's a bit of a rebel," said Bill, smiling with affection, "but we both want her to have the wedding of her dreams."

"She's marrying a young man from a prominent, political family, which has her mother in a tizzy. But I understand. He and his family deserve a nice wedding too," Mary Lou asserted.

"Believe me, we'll do our best to accommodate you in every way we can," Sheena quickly assured them.

"You can call on Sheena, or me, or our wedding coordinator, Nicole Coleman, anytime," said Regan. "We've assigned you to a brand-new suite at no extra cost."

Mary Lou's eyes lit with pleasure. "Oh, lovely! Lea and her friend Caro are sharing the Bridal Suite. Right?"

"Oh, yes," said Sheena. "That's all arranged."

Nicole arrived as Mary Lou and Bill were ready to leave the office. Sheena made the introductions.

Nicole offered her hand and smiled warmly at them. "After talking to you so often on the phone, it's nice finally to meet you." She looked at Sheena and Regan. "I'll be glad to accompany them to their room." Regan held up the keys to the suite. "They'll be staying in Sandpiper Suite 101. I'll join you there."

After Nicole left with the Websters, Regan turned to her. "Oh, oh. Sounds as if this is going to be a very demanding wedding. I'll skip ahead and check to make sure the cookies and nuts we ordered are in the room, along with the small bottle of champagne and cheese tray."

"Thanks," said Sheena. "I'm going to try to get a final tab on the number of definite reservations for the rooms. It sounds like Lea's mother would not like to share a suite with anyone else."

By late afternoon, Sheena had been able to confirm all but one reservation. She left a message and hung up the phone, hoping Mr. and Mrs. Abbott, whoever they were, would not be able to come to Florida after all.

She looked up from the desk to see a young woman heading for the office. The short blonde was wearing torn denim shorts and a black tank top that showed bright purple bra straps. Dangling earrings and a small, delicate hoop threaded through her nose completed the picture of casual disdain for conformity.

Sheena checked her reservations list but had the niggling feeling she already knew who it was.

As the woman walked in, Sheena took a chance and said, "Hi, Lea! Welcome to the Salty Key Inn!"

The grin that crossed Lea's pretty face was full of satisfaction. "Guess my grandparents are already here, huh?"

Sheena laughed. "They told me you were coming. We're so happy to have you here and delighted to oversee your special occasion. Your grandmother said your mother wanted the wedding elsewhere. Why did you decide to have it here?"

"Image," said Lea. "So many weddings are all about image. I like the idea that the Salty Key Inn is a simple place—attractive and quiet. My fiancé, Dirk Bowen, is the son of Senator Chuck Bowen of Pennsylvania. That's why my mother thinks we should have chosen a fancier, more prestigious place. Luckily, Dirk was as unimpressed with that idea as I was. He knows how fake and insincere people can be to him because of his famous father."

Sheena did her best not to show her dismay. There'd been recent rumors Senator Chuck Bowen was going to be drafted as a presidential candidate for his party. Even at best, the Salty Key Inn couldn't be called glamorous, and now, after the storm, it had lost some of the luster they'd recently given the property.

"Neither your parents nor his are due to arrive until tomorrow. Is that correct?" Sheena asked, her mind spinning.

"Yes. Mine will be here in the morning, and Dirk's arrive tomorrow afternoon."

When Regan returned to the office, Sheena introduced Lea.

Regan smiled. "We have your grandparents in one of our new suites. I think you'll be pleased. And you're staying in the Bridal Suite, which has just been completed as well."

"Sounds good. Caro Parsons, my roomie, will be arriving shortly, but I might as well get settled in."

Regan smiled at her. "Okay. I'll take you there now."

After they left, Sheena collapsed in a chair, deep in thought. She knew pride could be a terrible thing, but, in this instance, it might serve them well. She picked up the phone and called Rocky.

After talking to and getting an agreement from him, she hung up and made a list of everything they'd need.

Next, she called Bernice.

"What are you doing?" Regan asked, entering the office.

"We've got to make some changes," Sheena said grimly. She explained the situation with Lea's parents and her fiancé's family. "I know we're waiting for some furniture and special-order items for the other suites, but I want to have two more of them ready by noon tomorrow. Chip completed the phone services and electronics for the building last week. I've just talked to Rocky about getting televisions brought in and hooked up, and Bernice is all set to send in cleaning crews. We need to fill in with furniture to replace those we've ordered, but haven't received yet. This is where you come in, Regan. You're going shopping."

Regan frowned. "Aren't you overreacting? Dirk's father is famous. So what?"

"A lot of this is Sullivan pride on my part, but, Regan, think of the publicity this wedding will give the hotel. Priceless!"

Regan's lips curved into a beaming smile. "Okay, then I'm going to have fun doing this. And, dear sister, if it seems like I've spent too much money, you can charge some of it to public relations."

Sheena laughed at the challenging look Regan shot her. "Do what you can to get good buys, and we'll pay whatever we have to for prompt delivery. But everything must be in place for the wedding party by noon tomorrow. We'll put both sets of parents in those suites."

"Okay," said Regan. "I'll take care of my share." She turned to go and then turned back to Sheena. "Why don't we decorate our two golf carts and have them available for the wedding party's use?"

"Great idea," said Sheena. "I'll ask Sam and Clyde to work

on them. You take the van and get going. And send me pictures of what you're buying."

At her sister's bossiness, Regan frowned and saluted.

Sheena knew she sounded like the demanding big sister, but it was time to pull out all the stops.

CHAPTER FORTY- SIX

DARCY

Darcy strolled down the winding cobblestone street hand in hand with Austin. As long as she lived, she mused, she would remember this honeymoon trip. She'd seen so many things she'd always longed to visit, tried new things to eat, and experienced a life of luxury she'd never known.

She'd found something to love in each city—London, Paris, Madrid, Rome, but having the opportunity to spend three nights in Italy's Tuscany countryside outside of Florence was something she and Austin were savoring like a gourmet meal. Seeing sights, experiencing different cultures was well and good, but living among the people in a small village was, Darcy decided, the way she wanted to experience traveling the rest of the world. And there was so much else for her to see. Thinking of the opportunity that awaited them by running Austin's parents' business, her pulse thrummed with happiness. It would be a dream come true to take it over.

"You're really enjoying this, aren't you?" Austin said, clasping her hand and smiling at her.

Darcy returned his smile and gave his hand a squeeze. "I've had the best time ever. And sharing it with you makes it perfect."

"So, are you seriously considering taking my parents' offer to run the business?" he asked, giving her a steady look.

"I think so. How about you? Is it something you want to do?"

Austin's brow furrowed. "I can't make up my mind. Taking the job would be exciting and fun, but exhausting and boring too."

Darcy turned to him with surprise. "Boring? How can you say that?" She elbowed him playfully. "You'd better not be bored with me."

He laughed. "Never. I promise."

Darcy thought of her sisters. Regan was building her own business, and Sheena was more than capable of handling the hotel herself. She'd be a fool not to take advantage of an offer to travel like this. Their accommodations had been first-class all the way, and their guided tours excellent.

"Let's wait until we get home before we make any decisions about this," Austin said.

Darcy smiled and nodded. She'd wait to tell him, but she'd already made up her mind.

As a neighbor walked by, she proudly said, "*Buonasera.*"

"Good evening" sounded so much better in Italian.

CHAPTER FORTY-SEVEN

REGAN

Regan studied the array of couches in front of her, pondering her choices. In her mind, she reviewed possible color schemes. The walls of the suites had been painted a soft, warm beige. The carpets were in a compatible tone, keeping the theme of casual beach. She trailed her hands over the woven fabric of two of the couches, liking the sturdy but soft texture and patterns of them. In warm tones of sea green, they would fit in nicely. She marked them as possibilities on her list.

From that section, she hurried over to where several chairs were displayed. The problem with sales items was they were so random. Regan needed to pull together the furnishings in the two suites to make them appear well-coordinated. She finally settled on overstuffed chairs covered in a light turquoise with a subtle, sea-coral design that added interest and a touch of coral to her theme. She would, she quickly decided, find some coral and turquoise pillows to place on the couches. Sheena had given her to the go-ahead to do what she wanted.

"How are you doing?" a saleswoman asked, approaching her. "You've been here a long time."

"I think I've found what I wanted. I just need you to promise me you will deliver them to my hotel tonight."

"As you asked, I checked with my boss," the woman assured her. "He said if you can take delivery after six o'clock and pay overtime to the driver and his assistant, he'll do it for you."

"That won't be a problem," said Regan. "I've chosen two couches and two chairs. Now I need side tables and lamps. We already have the rest."

Regan's head was spinning as she left the furniture store. While she still had colors and patterns memorized, she hurried to a Bed, Bath & Beyond store to buy bedspreads and bedding to coordinate with her new choices.

Later, the van filled with bedding, pillows, and decorative accent pieces, Regan headed back to the hotel. Maybe it was Sullivan pride on her part, but she'd done her best to make wise choices that would reflect good taste. As Mo had once told her, good taste wasn't about the amount of money spent on items but their quality and how she was able to coordinate them with each interior for a tasteful look.

When Brian met up with her that evening at the Sandpiper Suites Building, she was hanging pictures in the ground-floor hallway.

"Working a little late, aren't you?" He gave her a kiss that made her want to quit her job and take him home.

She smiled. "Sheena had the idea to move the parents of the bride and groom into suites. It seems the groom's father is Senator Chuck Bowen. She thinks it will bring us a lot of good publicity when it's announced his son was married here."

Brian gave her a thoughtful nod. "I agree. It's a good way to showcase the place. Maybe we can even get some mileage out of it for The Key Hole."

"I'll make sure they get extra coupons in their rooms," Regan assured him, hanging the last of the framed photographs of the early days of the hotel. She stepped back to make sure it was hung right.

"When are you going to be ready to go home, or should I meet you at The Key Hole?"

Regan checked her watch. "Give me fifteen minutes, and I'll be there. I want to check on Bernice's staff. They're close to being done cleaning the rooms."

"Okay," said Brian. "See you in a few. This will give me a chance to talk to our new manager. So far, so good, but it doesn't hurt to keep a careful eye on things at the bar."

Regan went inside one of the newly completed suites and looked around carefully. As she'd hoped, the recently purchased pieces of furniture looked as if they were supposed to have been there all along. Their casual style belied quality fabrics, colors, and patterns that complemented the walls and carpet perfectly. She continued her sweeping gaze of the suite. A large silk plant sat in one corner of the living room. A glass bowl filled with seashells and topped with air plants graced the coffee table. The lamps on the end tables were made from carved wood that looked like pieces of driftwood. The framed prints of underwater scenes were striking against the warm color of the walls. Yes, it worked. She checked the two bathrooms and the two bedrooms. Here, too, things seemed settled and compatible. Normally, families or long-term stays would occupy the suites, but for occasions like this, the suites provided flexible space to members of group events.

Sheena appeared in the doorway just as Regan was ready to leave. "Everything ready here?"

"All set. I'm going to meet Brian for dinner at The Key Hole, and then I'm going home to bed," said Regan, sighing. "If this is what hosting a wedding is going to be like, we'll both need all the rest we can get."

"I just finished work with Sam and Clyde decorating the golf carts. Tomorrow morning, we'll deliver one to Lea's grandparents, and save the other for Senator Bowen and his wife."

"How do they look?" Regan, looping a hand around Sheena's arm.

Sheena turned to her with a smile. "Adorable. I'm so glad you thought of it. It will be a nice touch for transporting the bride and guests to the beach and back."

Outside the building, Regan stood with Sheena a moment, watching people enter and leave Gavin's.

"Tomorrow, we'll double check the arrangements for the rehearsal dinner. I hope the Bowens will be happy with the restaurant," said Sheena.

"I'll be shocked if they aren't. Gavin's has become the number one place to eat here on the coast, even beating out The Key Pelican."

"Right, right," said Sheena. "I don't know why I'm so worried about this wedding."

"Maybe because it's our first one here at the hotel?" Regan said, and they both laughed.

But even as they chuckled together, Regan knew it was no laughing matter. A bad review from someone prominent could ruin their reputation.

CHAPTER FORTY-EIGHT

SHEENA

Fatigue dogged Sheena as she headed home. The fifteen-minute drive seemed to take forever. Maybe because she knew what awaited her—noisy, hungry kids demanding to be fed, a physically tired husband also waiting for a meal, and the mound of laundry she hadn't gotten to this morning.

Thinking of the months ahead when she'd have an infant to care for in addition to these three, Sheena questioned whether she'd be able to handle the hotel by herself. Then she reminded herself she'd have her sisters' help and told herself to stop worrying. Darcy would be home in two days, conveniently after the wedding party was packed up and gone. Then, maybe she, herself, could take some time off.

As soon as Sheena walked into the house, Michael greeted her with, "When's dinner? I'm hungry."

Meaghan followed Tony into the front hall. "What's for dinner?" she asked. "Remember, I have a cheer meeting tonight."

"Hi, honey." Tony gave her a kiss. "You're late."

The three of them lined up in front of her like hungry baby birds chirping for their mother to feed them.

Sheena pushed away her frustration. "How about ordering in? I'm thinking of Chinese food."

"Again? We had that last week," said Meaghan.

"The alternative is your cooking dinner," said Sheena more sharply than she'd intended.

Tony's look of surprise changed to one of sympathy. "Tough day, huh? Chinese take-out sounds fine. Meaghan and Michael can go together to pick it up."

"But ..." Michael began and stopped at the stern look Tony gave him.

Tony pulled the take-out menu from a kitchen drawer, and they quickly ordered what they wanted.

While the kids took off to get their order, Tony ushered Sheena outside to the lanai. "Have a seat. You look exhausted."

Sheena sank down into a lounge chair and let out a long sigh. "It's the wedding. We're trying to make everything perfect for the bride and groom, especially since we discovered the father of the groom is Senator Chuck Bowen."

Tony's eyebrows shot up. "Wow! No wonder you're nervous. I just saw an interview with him on the news. He's seriously thinking of running for president."

"Yes. That's why his having an enjoyable stay at the hotel is so crucial for us. Regan and I opened two more suites today, so the Bowens and the parents of the bride can stay in them."

"What about the rest of the suites?"

"We won't be able to open them for a week or so. We're waiting for things on back order to be delivered. We were able to steal patio furniture from the new lanai for Gavin's people, but we can't ask them to do without it for long. That wouldn't be fair. I told our suppliers we'll cancel our entire order if we don't get a response within the next couple of days. But it was an idle threat. We got that furniture for a such a good price, we can't replace it."

Tony gave her a thoughtful look. "I know how determined you are to have things right, but remember what the Salty Key Inn is all about—a quiet, unpretentious place where all are welcome. So what if Chuck Bowen might be president one day? You've told me from the beginning all guests need to be treated the same."

Sheena felt her eyes widen. "You're right. Every guest, not just one or two, needs to be treated as if he or she is special." She smiled at him with affection. "Thanks for reminding me."

He grinned. "You used to tell me the very same thing back when I had my own plumbing business." He leaned over and kissed her. "It'll work out. Now, let's go eat. I hear the kids coming through the door."

Sitting at the kitchen table with her family, Sheena told herself as busy as she was with the hotel, she shouldn't be too busy to enjoy her family. Michael had heard he'd been accepted at the University of Miami and would be off to college next year. Meaghan would follow three years later. Sheena gazed at Tony and tried to imagine what their new baby would be like. Michael had been easy-going, easy to entertain with a simple toy. Meaghan had been a fussy, active child who knew exactly what she wanted and when.

Meaghan broke through her thoughts. "The Spring Dance is in two weeks. I really need a new dress for it. Can we go shopping tomorrow, Mom?"

Sheena shook her head. "How about Monday, after the wedding at the hotel?"

Meaghan's lips formed a pout. "Awww, it's always about the hotel lately. What about me?"

Surprised by Meaghan's old "me-first" behavior, Sheena said, "I promise to take you shopping on Monday. Darcy will be back in town then, and I'm asking for the day off."

"Okay." Meaghan's hazel eyes shone with excitement. "I think Rob is going to ask me, and I want to look nice."

Sheena smiled. "You always look nice, sweetie." She turned to Michael. "Are you going to the dance? It's for seniors, too, isn't it?"

Michael shrugged. "Not many of us are going. Besides, I have no interest in asking anyone out."

Sheena studied him a moment. She understood his caution. It wasn't that long ago he thought he was about to be a father with someone he now didn't like at all.

After dinner, Sheena got up and stretched. "Who's turn is it to clean up?"

Meaghan frowned. "Mine."

"Thanks," said Sheena. She went into the laundry room and stared at the pile of dirty clothes. *Maybe later. Right now, I'm going to bed.*

As she settled in bed, Sheena knew she could've forced herself to do the laundry. But the idea was to ease her family into the transition that would take place with the arrival of a new baby. If Meaghan thought the hotel was competing for her attention, what did she think a new baby would do?

She had no idea what time it was when Tony crawled into bed beside her and drew her up against him.

"You awake?" he whispered in her ear.

"I am now," she said, turning to him.

His lips met hers in a soft, gentle kiss that told her he understood how tired she was. "You've been overdoing it. Maybe it's time to ease off work at the hotel a bit."

Sheena rolled over and faced him. "You know I can't do that. I'm the one who's been given the task of overseeing it. Uncle Gavin wanted me to be in charge. I can't let him or anyone else down."

Tony's lips curved. "I love when you get fired up about something, but, Sheena, it's okay to slow down."

"I'm worried about first impressions. Both sets of parents will arrive tomorrow, and then things will settle down, and I can let go of my jitters."

Tony cupped her face in his broad hands. "You're the best hotel owner I know. Now, go back to sleep."

She fit herself to the shape of his body and closed her eyes.

As she strode into the registration office the next morning, her late-night jitters seemed foolish. The sky was a beautiful blue, the temperature was in the low eighties, and the newly planted hibiscus and bougainvillea lifted their colorful heads to the sun. And the weather forecast showed more of the same.

Jeanne smiled at her from behind the registration desk. "I didn't expect you this early."

Sheena smiled. "This is a big day. We have a lot of guests arriving. Senator Bowen and his wife will arrive later in the day, but the parents of our bride should arrive mid-morning. I want to make sure everything is in order for them."

"Check-in isn't until three o'clock."

"Normally, that would be true, but for the wedding group, we promised early arrival times, and the bride's parents are staying in one of the suites, which is brand new and vacant. If you man the desk, I'll go check in with Bernice to see about her housekeeping crew."

Sheena left the office and crossed the lawn to the Egret Building, where Bernice had set up a small office in a section of what was, essentially, a maintenance room.

Sheena knocked on the door.

"Come in," came a musical alto voice.

Sheena opened the door and smiled when she saw Bernice at her desk. Mo Greene's cousin, Bernice Richmond, was a smaller version of him, with pretty features, bright eyes, and energy that was appealing.

"Hi, Sheena! Have a seat. What can I do for you?"

Sheena sat in a wooden chair in front of Bernice's desk. "I wanted to give you a heads-up about the two suites we got ready yesterday and explain the importance of having everything there perfect. Your crew finished up last night, but I thought you and I should check those rooms together. We also need to make sure any rooms are cleaned as soon as they are vacated. To accommodate our first wedding party, we've allowed some early check-ins."

"Yes, I got the memo and have scheduled an extra housekeeper for the entire weekend."

Sheena gave her a grateful smile. "Thanks. I don't know what we'd do without you."

Bernice's soft chuckle was musical. "Or me without you! Between the hotel, the restaurant, Gracie's, and the Key Hole, you've made my business get off to a roaring start."

"Mo and Regan were right to talk you into setting up your own company. How many people are on your staff now?"

"Including the other hotels we're now doing? Thirty-five." Bernice's note of pride was well-deserved. "And at some point, I'll be doing Kenton's house."

"Fantastic." Sheena stood. "Are you sure you have time for us?"

Bernice smiled at her. "Oh, yes. For the Salty Key Inn? Anything."

As they walked to the Sandpiper Suites Building, Sheena and Bernice chatted about their children. Bernice's daughter, Mercy, was one of the cutest little girls Sheena had ever seen. She had her mother's dark skin, snappy intelligence, and a natural sweetness to her that everyone loved.

"How is Mercy enjoying pre-school?" Sheena asked. "And are you happy with your nanny?"

Bernice laughed. "I figure Mercy will end up running the entire school in another couple of months. She's the leader of her class, that's for sure. Thank goodness, the teacher loves Mercy and can direct her nicely. And the nanny I've hired is great with her too."

"Maggie has asked if she can help with my baby. I'm so pleased, but I don't want to do anything to upset Gracie."

"From what I hear, that won't be a problem. With Lynn leaving the group, Gracie's begun to hire more people for the restaurant."

Sheena jerked to a halt and faced Bernice. "Wait! What did you say? Lynn is leaving the group?"

Bernice gave her a funny look. "You don't know?"

"Know what?" said Sheena, narrowing her eyes at Bernice. Suspicion rolled through her.

Bernice hesitated and shifted her feet.

"It's my father, right?" Sheena said.

Bernice looked uncomfortable. "I'm sorry. Maybe I shouldn't have said anything. I ran into Lynn at Gracie's, and she told me she's moving to The Villages."

"I see," said Sheena, furious Patrick hadn't told her, that she'd had to hear it from hotel staff first.

"Look, I don't want to make trouble," said Bernice, placing a hand on Sheena's arm.

"It's not you, Bernice. I'm just disappointed he didn't tell me." Sheena drew a breath and allowed a smile to form. "But I'm happy for Lynn and my father."

"Me too," said Bernice.

Sheena decided not to address the issue with Patrick until she'd had a chance to talk to her sisters. They would have as many concerns as she had. Maybe more.

"Ready?" Bernice said.

"Okay, let's see what, if anything, can be done to improve the three completed suites."

Later, after making a list of additional items to be added to the suites—things like soaps, lotions, extra towels, and items for the kitchens—Bernice and Sheena separated to go to their individual offices.

Sheena checked in with Jeanne, left a note for Regan, and headed out to the store to buy additional kitchen supplies for the suites.

CHAPTER FORTY-NINE

REGAN

Regan opened her eyes, rolled over, and nestled up against Brian's strong body. The warmth that exuded from him was welcome in the air-conditioned room.

Brian turned to her and drew her into his arms.

With her head lying on his chest, Regan inhaled the familiar manly smell of him and smiled. Marriage was more wonderful than her mother had ever led her to believe. Saving herself for the right man hadn't always been easy, but the reward for doing so was well worth it. The bond she'd forged with Brian was everything she'd ever hoped for, and better. The element of trust between them was real. She'd trusted him to show her what physical love was, and he'd trusted her enough to open his heart to the deep love she was willing to give him.

The sun hadn't yet risen, but Regan got out of bed. Brian's days were early and long.

"Hey, where are you going?" Brian murmured, rising on an elbow and giving her a sleepy look.

"I thought I'd surprise you with a nice, hot breakfast," she replied, resisting the urge to brush a blond-streaked, brown curl away from his forehead. She was on a mission.

Regan arrived at the hotel to find a line of guests waiting to be checked in. Cheeks flushed, Sheena stood with Jeanne behind the desk.

"Thank you for your patience, everyone," Sheena said. "We didn't expect so many early arrivals all at once."

Regan stepped up to the desk, leaned over, and said softly to Sheena. "I'll take guests to their rooms. Who do we have?"

Sheena's glance slid to the couple at the back of the line. "I believe Lea's parents are there. Can you go and talk to them? It's going to be several minutes before I can get them registered."

Putting a wide smile on her face, Regan approached them. "I believe you're the parents of the bride?"

"Yes, Ron and Julia Webster," said the fussily dressed woman. Her hair was over-sprayed and over-styled, unsuitable for the Florida humidity. "I must say, I'm already disappointed with the hotel."

Regan observed discomfort on Ron's face and wondered if Julia always ran the show. She observed Julia's lacy sundress, the diamonds in her earlobes, the oversized designer purse on her shoulder and had the distinct impression Julia was out to impress people. Unfortunately, her wardrobe did nothing to detract from the look of discontent on her face. The lines between her eyebrows were deep. Regan had the feeling they were seldom softened in pleasure. No wonder Lea was a little rebel.

"Lea and her grandparents have settled in nicely," Regan said. "We hope you enjoy your stay. We're putting you in one of our new suites."

Julia straightened and gave her a nod of approval. "That will do nicely. Do you have any idea where the Bowens will be staying?"

"Beside you, in the same building."

At this news, Julia's eyes lit. "Very good. You know Chuck and Evelyn and we are almost family now."

"Of sorts," Ron said, earning a frown from Julia. "Is Dirk here?"

"I'm not sure. I'll have to check at the front desk. Oh, here we go, you're up next. Excuse me; I have to show some guests to their rooms."

Feeling unsettled, Regan left Lea's parents. Julia Webster was bound to be trouble. She was as pretentious as anyone Regan had ever met. She dreaded meeting Chuck and Evelyn Bowen.

After showing two couples to their rooms in the Egret Building, Regan returned to the office in time to take Ron and Julia Webster to their suite.

As they walked past the patios of the suites, they passed Ron's parents.

Mary Lou waved. "Hi, Ron, Julia! Glad you arrived. You'll love it here, and the weather is perfect."

"Thanks, Mom. See you soon," said Ron.

Julia said nothing but marched along behind Regan.

Regan waved. "See you later!"

As they entered the building, Regan couldn't hide her anxiety at how Julia would react to her suite. People told her she was talented, but that old childhood feeling of being considered stupid still lingered in her mind from time to time.

"Here we are," said Regan, sliding the key card into the slot and turning the knob on the door. She handed Ron two key cards and stepped back.

Seeing it from a guest's point of view, Regan was pleased by the tropical colors and accents to the room.

"Thanks, this looks great," said Ron. "What do you say, Julia?"

Heart pounding, Regan waited for her answer.

"Nice, for this kind of place. Let's see the bedrooms." Julia left them and wandered into one of the bedrooms.

Ron gave her an apologetic look. "It may not sound like it, but Julia is pleased. You'd hear about it if she weren't."

Regan bobbed her head. "Please let me know if there's anything else you need. As you know, your parents are next door."

Back at the registration office, Regan and Sheena exchanged worried glances.

"I hope the Bowens are easier than Lea's parents," said Sheena. "Julia Webster is going to be very hard to please."

"Tell me about it," said Regan, plopping down in a chair. It wasn't even noon, and she already wanted to go home. "There's got to be some way we can check people in more quickly."

"I've already put in a call to Chip," said Sheena.

A tall, bespectacled man approached the office wearing khaki slacks and a buttoned-down, blue-striped shirt. The onshore breeze ruffled his red hair, but he didn't seem to notice as he talked on his cell phone.

He finished his call and entered the office.

"Hello," said Regan, admiring his blue eyes and the way the corners of them crinkled with goodwill.

"I'm here for the Webster/Bowen wedding," he said.

"And you are ...?"

A figure came running into the office and jumped up into his arms. "Dirk! You're here!"

Regan and Sheena looked at each other and laughed.

"Hi, Lea!" said Regan, still chuckling. She watched as Lea and Dirk exchanged kisses and knew, no matter how difficult Julia Webster could be, Lea and Dirk would be all right.

But later that afternoon, Regan had different thoughts when she met Dirk's parents. It was clear neither of them was thrilled to be there as part of the wedding.

Listening to them interact, Regan understood Chuck called the shots, and Evelyn made sure to please him. Maybe that's how people got ahead in politics, but Regan didn't like it.

After showing them to their suite, Regan asked if there was anything she could do.

"Does this hotel have a van?" asked Chuck. "I need a ride to the Don. I'm meeting a colleague of mine."

"Don't be late," warned Evelyn. "The rehearsal dinner starts with cocktails at six."

Chuck's glare quieted her. "It's on my schedule, Evie. You don't need to remind me." He turned to Regan. "Can you take care of the van for me? I'll meet a driver outside in five minutes."

"Sure," said Regan, relieved the van was available and in good working order. "I'll drive you myself."

As Regan hurried to the registration office, she realized they'd have to have drivers available in the future. She knew Michael would jump at the chance to earn some money, but they couldn't rely on him always to be available.

Regan took Sheena aside and told her about transporting Chuck Bowen. "We'll have to arrange for someone to pick him up. It can't be me. I'm helping Nicole with the dinner arrangements."

"Okay, I'll find someone to pick him up. Does he realize the dinner starts at six?"

Regan made a face. "Yes. He made that very clear to his wife. I'd hate to live with someone like him. Guess you have to be willing to pay the price for the kind of fame he wants."

"No wonder Dirk is attracted to someone like Lea. She's a free spirit and apparently unafraid to stand up for what she wants."

"I have a feeling she'd better stay strong because both sets of parents are difficult, and weddings bring out the best and worst in people." A shudder crossed Regan's shoulders at her doom-filled words.

"No matter what it takes, we have to make this wedding work," said Sheena.

"I wish Darcy was here. She'd make it seem a fun challenge," Regan said. There wasn't any doubt in her mind that the evening and following day were going to be difficult.

CHAPTER FIFTY

SHEENA

Sheena, wearing her best maternity dress, stood aside watching Evelyn and her son, Dirk, greet people as they entered the private dining room on the second floor of Gavin's. It had been set up to hold the forty guests comfortably. A bartender was serving refreshments from a bar at one end of the room, and most of the people were congregating there.

Chuck had yet to appear. Sheena knew through a series of texts with Michael that Chuck had kept him waiting at the Don in the van for over an hour.

Lea walked into the room with her parents. Dirk took hold of her hand and drew her to him while Evelyn looked on with interest.

"I'm so happy to be here," gushed Lea's mother, Julia, to Evelyn. "It's so exciting to be part of your family."

To Evelyn's credit, the look of surprise on her face quickly morphed into a smile that didn't meet her eyes. "Yes, we were as surprised as you by the news of the wedding. But we hope to welcome Lea into our house and our hearts."

Dirk saved the awkward moment by giving Julia a kiss on the cheek and turning to Ron. "It's a beautiful evening. Glad to see you again, sir."

When Mary Lou and Bill Webster walked into the room, both Lea and Dirk went to them. Observing the affection on the faces of all four, Sheena realized who'd supported the love between Lea and Dirk all along.

Moments later, Chuck Bowen's appearance caused every eye to focus on him. Smiling, he boomed, "Welcome to my party!"

A few nervous titters followed.

Evelyn stepped to his side and turned to the crowd. "Welcome to our party for Dirk and Lea."

Sheena exchanged glances with Regan, who'd followed Chuck into the room.

Chuck's voice boomed once more. "Yes, by all means! Let's drink to that!"

Conversation rose in the room once more, but Sheena overheard Chuck say to Evelyn in an undertone, "I don't like to be corrected in front of a group of people. Understand?"

"Sorry," Evelyn said, and turned to the group with a smile as if he'd spoken love words.

So that's how it's done, Sheena thought, disliking the senator even more.

Mary Lou and Bill were talking with Lea when Sheena approached them.

"Sheena, what a lovely party," said Lea's grandmother.

"Thanks. The wedding reception will be every bit as lovely." Sheena smiled at them, wishing she could warn Lea about the kind of family she was joining.

"Aren't my grandparents the best?" said Lea, beaming at them. "They're the people Dirk and I trust most to allow us to be ourselves." She glanced at the Bowens. "Dirk isn't anything like them."

"And you're not like your mother," said Mary Lou. She clapped a hand over her mouth. "Sorry, I shouldn't have said that. It must be the wine talking."

"Or the truth," murmured Bill as Julia approached.

"Such a lovely occasion with the Bowens," Julia said

happily. "I can't wait to tell my friends how lovely they are." She smiled at Lea. "You've done well for yourself, dear."

Lea's frown marred her delicate features. "Excuse me. I'd better go and save Dirk. He looks distressed."

"Hopefully Lea will become a little more suitable in her appearance," Julia said. "No rings and the like ... " her voice trailed off.

"She's lovely as she is," Mary Lou said with an unmistakable annoyance in her voice.

Julia glanced across the room at her daughter. "If she cleaned up her act, she would look just like my mother, rest her soul."

Sheena gave Mary Lou a sympathetic look. "Is there anything I can do for you? We've got things set for the wedding and reception, but if you need anything else, please let me know. We're delighted to have you and Bill here."

Feeling as if she was leaving a lamb standing next to a lioness, Sheena left them to speak to Casey, who was talking to the bartender.

After making sure everything was in order, Sheena decided to go home. Casey had assured her that her presence wasn't needed, and it being a Friday night, Meaghan and Michael would be busy with their friends, and Tony would be at home relaxing.

On the way to her house, Sheena thought of the complications of a wedding. Sometimes, as in the case of Lea and Dirk, it seemed improbable the two families would ever blend. But she knew how much adding a baby to the mixture could change things. She'd been fortunate from the beginning that Tony's parents had been kind and loving to her and her family.

###

Early the next morning, Sheena was in the kitchen sipping her coffee when her cell rang. She checked caller ID. *Regan.* "Hi! What's up?"

"I'm sick," said Regan. "It must have been something I ate, but I can't come into work this morning. I'll try for this afternoon, but no promises. Sorry."

"Something you ate made you sick? Promise me it wasn't anything served to the guests at the rehearsal dinner."

"I don't know if that is the case or not. Nicole and I ate some of the leftovers. Maybe we shouldn't have."

Sheena fought the panic that had begun to chill her bones. "I'll check to make sure everyone else is fine. Pray they are. Hope you feel better soon. We're going to need you at the wedding."

Sheena clicked off the call and phoned Nicole. "Hi, there! Are you set for today?" Sheena asked, forcing a cheerful note into her voice.

"Ugh, I'm not feeling well. I hope I'll be better enough to get to the hotel, but there's no way I can leave my apartment without knowing if or when I'm going to throw up."

"Regan's sick too. What do you think it was? Food from the rehearsal dinner?"

"We didn't eat any of the food prepared for them. Just leftovers in the kitchen."

"Oh, my God! Did the other staff members eat them?"

"I'm not sure. Casey is fine. He left for work earlier."

"Keep in touch with me, and make every effort to get to the hotel. You're important to us, Nicole." Sheena knew she should have been more sympathetic, but she was scared. How were they going to make this the perfect wedding the Salty Key Inn needed to establish its reputation as a destination for weddings?

###

At the hotel, Sheena manned the registration office. Jeanne would replace her in the afternoon, but for now, it was left to her to answer questions, make sure the pool and beach activities were overseen, and ensure the waterside sports area was operational.

As scheduled, Dirk and Lea's friends from the University of North Carolina arrived in two separate vans from the Tampa airport. Their excitement was contagious. Soon, the hotel was filled with activity on the bay, in the pool, and even on the bocce ball court. Michael, handling the water sports, called to tell her they needed more paddle boards, and two kayaks were not enough for this crowd.

The Bohio Bar became busy, adding to the sounds of pre-wedding fun. Sheena watched to make sure their regular guests weren't annoyed by all the activity. It seemed, though, everyone loved a wedding.

By late afternoon, things quieted. Sheena took advantage of this time to eat the lunch she'd picked up earlier from Gracie's. Neither Regan nor Nicole had shown up, but each had called to say they were struggling to make it.

As Sheena finished the last of her sandwich in the back office, she heard a voice calling to someone from the front office and rose to check it out.

Julia Webster faced her with an angry look. "I looked for Nicole and couldn't find her. I thought chairs were to be set up on the beach for everyone at the wedding."

Sheena held back a sigh. "Nicole's not feeling well, and I'm taking over for her. When I spoke to Lea this morning, she said there was no need to do that. It's going to be a short ceremony with the group gathered around."

"In light of who she's marrying, I think it should be a much more dignified ceremony than that," said Julia. "I'd think you'd know that and understand."

"My job is to do as I was asked. This wedding is being set up according to the bride's specifications and your mother-in-law's."

Julia narrowed her lips. "I knew we should have gone somewhere else."

Sheena wished she had, but refrained from saying so.

"I'll speak to Mary Lou and get back to you," Julia huffed, turning and leaving the office with forceful steps.

Moments later, Sheena received a phone call. "This is Mary Lou Webster. Sheena? I want you to know we're going to stick to our original plans of no chairs at the wedding ceremony. Lea and I decided that's what we wanted."

"Okay," said Sheena. "May I ask a personal question?"

"Yes, go ahead," said Mary Lou.

"Is there a reason you and Lea have excluded Julia from the plans? And should we ignore her suggestions?" In the silence that followed, Sheena wondered if she'd overstepped common courtesy.

"Julia and Lea got into a huge fight about wedding plans, with Lea threatening to elope. In a panic, Julia asked for my help. Bill and I decided the only way it would work would be for us to take care of the wedding with both Lea's and Dirk's input. We respect their wishes and are excited by what the four of us have agreed on. I'm sure you understand how difficult some family situations are."

"Oh, yes," Sheena assured her. "I just wanted to know how best to handle things for you."

"Thanks," said Mary Lou. "I appreciate that. These two kids are worth fighting for."

As Sheena was leading guests to the beach for the ceremony, Regan joined her looking unusually wan but still lovely in a pale lavender dress perfect for a wedding.

"Sorry I couldn't get here earlier. How's it going?" she asked Sheena.

"We've had several rough patches, but I believe everything is in order now. Nicole is back, and she and Casey are making sure the reception is set up properly."

"Good," said Regan. She smiled at Sheena. "You look beautiful in that new dress."

"Thanks." When she'd put it on, she'd been dismayed by the way her body filled the navy maternity dress with three months to go before the baby came.

The guests all gathered by the same portable altar that had been used for Darcy's wedding. Dirk and his father stood next to it, beside the minister. Looking at it, Sheena thought back to Darcy's special day. It had been wonderful to see her sister so happy, so in love. The three weeks since then had flown by. She knew from the many postcards Darcy had sent and her Facebook posts how fantastic the honeymoon trip had been for her, but she hoped once Darcy returned, she'd be ready to settle in to work at the hotel once more.

Regan grabbed hold of Sheena's arm and whispered, "Here comes the bride!"

Sheena looked up to see Lea coming toward them like a sprite, wearing a smile that was both impish and emotional. A tiny tiara sat among the strands of blond hair that billowed playfully in the breeze. Her white wedding gown reached only to her ankles. The dress with a sweetheart neckline and sleeveless bodice was stunning in its simplicity.

Tears came to Sheena's eyes. She'd hoped for a perfect wedding for them, and though things hadn't always gone smoothly, this moment, this couple were perfect.

CHAPTER FIFTY-ONE

DARCY

Darcy stepped into the warm, humid air outside the airport terminal and inhaled the salty aroma with a sense of satisfaction. As Austin had told her, he loved traveling, but he always loved coming home.

She turned to him now. "Feel good?"

He put his arm around her. "And how. Where's the van that's supposed to pick us up?"

Darcy frowned. "I don't know. I thought my sisters would be here to greet us."

"I'll call," said Austin.

While he phoned the hotel, Darcy gathered her new purse to her chest. *Italian leather was so soft.*

Austin turned to her with a worried look. "My grandfather is picking us up. No one from the hotel could do it."

Darcy felt her eyes widen. "Is everything all right? Let me call Sheena."

Darcy punched in Sheena's number and heard a voicemail message. "This is Sheena. Sorry, I'm unable to take your call. Please leave me a message, and I'll get back to you as soon as I can."

Darcy clicked off the call and phoned Regan. A similar message came on.

"Okay," Darcy said into the phone. "I've tried Sheena's number and now yours, Regan. I'm worried about you. Call me. We're at the Tampa Airport waiting for a ride."

Darcy disconnected the call and turned to Austin. "I hope you don't mind, but I want your grandfather to drop us off at the hotel instead of taking us to the condo. I'm worried about my sisters. They always take phone calls."

"Okay, hon. We'll see what's happening there, have a drink, and grab dinner before going to the condo and collapsing."

She smiled and squeezed his arm affectionately. "Thanks for understanding."

They were standing outside the terminal with their luggage when Austin's grandfather drove up. Darcy warmed to his wide smile. Bill Blakely was one of her favorite people.

He got out of the car and came over to them. Throwing his arms around Darcy, he said, "So good to have you kids back home. I missed you, you know."

Darcy laughed. "Wait until you hear about our trip. We saw everything!"

Bill and Austin exchanged back slaps. "Good trip, then?"

Austin grinned. "The best."

They loaded the luggage into the car and took off.

"We need to go to the hotel," Austin explained. "Neither Sheena nor Regan answered their phones, and Darcy's worried about them. If you drop us off there, we'll treat you to dinner."

Bill nodded agreeably. "Sounds good."

As she'd done on her first trip to the Salty Key Inn, Darcy opened the car window beside her to inhale the sweet smell of home. She hadn't known what to expect on that first trip, Now, she couldn't wait to see the hotel Uncle Gavin had once envisioned.

As they drove through the entrance to the hotel, Darcy let out a gasp. Two police cars sat in the driveway, their lights flashing a blue and red that spelled trouble. A white ambulance with flashing red lights was parked in front of the police cars, its back door open.

"Stop!" cried Darcy. Bill slammed on his brakes. Before the car had fully stopped, Darcy jumped out of it and began running.

A crowd had gathered around a man lying on a gurney on the ground.

Seeing her sisters among the group of people, she rushed over to them. "What happened? Who is it?"

Sheena turned to her with moist eyes and cheeks gone white. "It's Senator Bowen. He collapsed after going for a swim. They're trying to stabilize him, but he's not responding."

"I don't think he's going to make it," whispered Regan, staring wide-eyed at the inert figure.

"Oh, my God!" Senator Bowen?" said Darcy, realizing who it was. "Is that his wife beside him?"

"Yes," said Sheena. "She was on the beach when this happened."

Austin came up beside Darcy and put an arm around her. She quickly filled him in on the details.

"Okay, everyone! Stand back," ordered one of the policemen. "Give the EMTs room. We're transporting him to the hospital. The State Police are clearing the way for us."

As the medics lifted the gurney with the senator on it and rolled it into the back of the ambulance, Sheena hurried to his wife's side. "Do you want me to drive you to the hospital?"

"That would be nice," said Evelyn. "I need to be with him. And we'll have to be in touch with Dirk. Can you call him for me?"

"Yes," said Sheena. "We'll see he and Lea get the message. I don't believe their flight to Barbados has left yet."

Sheena waved Regan and Darcy over to her. "Regan, call Dirk and Lea and tell them what's happened. Tell them also

I'm taking Evelyn to Tampa General Hospital, and ask them to meet us there."

Regan turned to Darcy. "You help break up the crowd. We don't want a lot of publicity. If reporters find out what has happened, they'll flock to the scene." Regan hurried away, leaving Darcy to handle the curious crowd.

The ambulance left with its siren blaring, along with the two police cars. Sheena and Evelyn followed behind in the hotel van.

"Wow! Some homecoming," said Austin, giving Darcy a troubled look.

"I'd better get to work." She walked into the crowd of milling people. "Everything is being taken care of for the senator. Why don't you carry on with whatever you were doing? We'll keep you informed."

"What if he dies?" said an older woman. "What will that do to the political scene?"

Darcy shook her head. "I don't even want to talk of him dying. Let's keep our hopes up, shall we?"

As people began to go their ways, a man walked over to her. "Hi, Darcy. I'm Jim Waters from the *Tampa Bay Times*. I heard there was some trouble here with Senator Bowen. What happened?"

As sympathetic as she was to someone reporting the news, Darcy shook her head. "I honestly am not sure. I just arrived here myself. Give me your card, and I'll call you tomorrow."

"Aw, you know I can't wait until tomorrow," he said, giving her a pleading look.

"I'd tell you if I could, but all I know is he's on his way to the hospital. Maybe you can find out more there. Sorry."

Feeling jarred by the scene, the time change, and the shock of what had happened, Darcy lowered her head into her hands.

"You okay?" asked Austin, approaching her.

"I will be. Right now, I have to see what I can do to help Regan."

"I'll have my grandfather drop me and the luggage off at the condo, get my car, and come back for you."

"Thanks, that's probably best." She lifted her face to receive Austin's kiss. London seemed an entire lifetime away.

CHAPTER FIFTY-TWO

SHEENA

Filled with dread, Sheena sat with Evelyn Bowen in the surgical waiting room. The scene with the EMTs trying to work on Chuck replayed over and over in her mind. She wasn't sure how long they'd been waiting when a doctor wearing green scrubs approached them.

"I'm so sorry, Mrs. Bowen. We tried to save your husband, but were unable to do so."

Evelyn burst into tears.

Sheena placed her arms around Evelyn's shaking body. She looked up at the doctor. "What was the situation? Heart?"

He shook his head. "Brain aneurysm. There was really nothing we could do. And if it's any comfort to the family, he would not have done well as a survivor."

Dirk and Lea hurried into the room. Evelyn cried out and scrambled to her feet as Dirk's arms reached out to her.

Lea stood back, watching them, tears in her eyes. Dirk pulled her to his side, and the three of them huddled and cried together.

Later, when emotions had calmed, Sheena asked what she could do to help.

Evelyn immediately straightened. "We'll need to draw up a press release. Chuck's staff in Washington can do that for me if you give them the facts. Will you call the office?"

"Yes, I can, but they will also need a statement from the doctor. Agreed?"

Evelyn turned to Lea and Dirk. "And we'll want it stated we were in Florida for a very happy occasion."

"Thank you," said Lea softly. She'd removed the ring from her nose for the ceremony and hadn't replaced it, making her appearance much more in keeping with this political family.

The doctor who'd remained quiet and in the background stepped forward. "Why don't we go into my office? We can take care of things there." He glanced at Sheena. "You can have the senator's staff call me here at the hospital. They'll page me."

Approaching Evelyn, Sheena gave her a long hug. "I'm so sorry for your loss. If there's anything more I can do for you, simply ask. As soon as I get back to the hotel, I'll call the senator's staff as you requested."

Evelyn reached into her purse, pulled out a small pad of paper and a pen, and wrote down a number. "Steve will handle it." Her eyes filled. "Thank you so much for your help."

"Yes," said Dirk. "Thanks for everything. The wedding too."

He and Lea exchanged sad looks, and then Evelyn, accompanied by the newlyweds, left the room.

As Sheena drove into the parking lot of the hotel, she saw a small crowd still lingered outside Gracie's. A truck from a local television station pulled in beside her.

Nerves on high alert, Sheena got out of the van and hurried toward the registration office.

"Wait!" a young woman called to her.

Sheena picked up her pace. Publicity at this point could help or hurt them, and she wanted it to be right for the senator's family.

Regan and Darcy were in the office when Sheena burst through the door. "I have to make a phone call to the senator's staff. Where's Nicole? We need her here now."

"I'll call her," said Regan. "What's happened?"

Sheena turned to them, her emotion too strong to hold back any longer. "Senator Bowen is dead." Tears ran down her cheeks. "He died of a brain aneurysm."

"Oh my God! That's awful!" said Regan. "This morning, he seemed so relaxed, so happy even."

"When the public finds out he died here at the Salty Key Inn, what will that mean for the hotel?" said Darcy.

"That's why we need Nicole," said Sheena. "We need help in protecting the hotel's reputation. It's not fancy, but we can't let the press make it seem as if it's not a nice place. You know how judgmental they can be."

Sheena went into the back office, closed the door, and punched in the number Evelyn had given her. A man's voice came on the line almost immediately.

Sheena explained who she was and why she was calling.

"All right, we'll get on this right away. You say we can reach the doctor at the hospital?"

"Yes, Tampa General Hospital. He's waiting for your call. And, Steve, Evelyn wanted you to know she and Chuck were staying at the Salty Key Inn for a very happy reason. Yesterday, their son, Dirk, married Lea Webster here on the beach."

"Ah, nice touch. I'll be sure to work that in. Thank you, Sheena. If we need anything else, I'll call." His voice cracked. "Chuck was a helluva guy. A guy's guy."

"Yes, he seemed to be," said Sheena. "We're so sorry his life ended this way. Please give our condolences to all the staff." Feeling drained, Sheena sat in her chair, unable to move. Life was one surprise after another.

CHAPTER FIFTY-THREE

SHEENA

Sheena and her sisters could never have imagined what the story of Chuck Bowen's death would do for the hotel. Once it became known he had stayed there because of his son's wedding, it seemed as if every young, engaged woman on the east coast wanted to have her wedding at the Salty Key Inn.

Taking on a bigger role in marketing, Nicole hired a full-time wedding coordinator, whom both Sheena and she agreed to oversee. As part of the bigger program, Sheena arranged special deals with suppliers and service providers like florists, photographers, and others. Regan became busy with new upgrades to the suites and function rooms, making sure themes were carried out in all areas. Darcy upgraded their website and worked with photographers to present videos, photograph albums, and personal stories for the brides and their families,

On the waterfront, Michael was given the task of adding sports equipment and manning the dock area with assistance from others. The gazebo was upgraded to have better flexibility in lighting and was wired for music. Comfortable lounge chairs were added in small conversation groups in several shaded areas along the perimeter of the property, along with additional tropical flowers and palm trees.

The hotel wasn't the only business going through changes. The Key Hole Bar worked up special menus and options for bachelor parties and now offered personalized "morning-after" meals for wedding parties. Bebe was now devoting much of her time to designing and baking wedding cakes, which meant new staff had to be hired for Gracie's. Casey hired an event manager at Gavin's, who worked closely with Nicole and the wedding coordinator. She also ran smaller events that ranged from birthday parties, to anniversary parties, to class reunions as more and more people discovered Gavin's and the hotel.

The part-time staff who manned the Bohio Bar on the property also shared duties driving the hotel van when necessary.

After one wedding in late May, Sheena sat with her sisters in the office reviewing their performance.

"It seems like we finally have weddings down to a routine," said Regan.

"It's taken all of us working together to make it happen," Sheena said, rubbing a hand over her swollen stomach.

"I wasn't going to tell you, but now I will," Darcy said. "When I came back to Florida from Europe, I had every intention of telling you that I was quitting the hotel business. Austin and I were offered the chance to take over his parents' travel business, and I was all for it. Then, with Senator Bowen's death, everything changed. And now, I know I could never leave the Salty Key Inn. It's where I want to be ... with you."

Sheena glanced at the way Regan's eyes were filling and felt her own eyes well with tears. The last few months had been both exhausting and exhilarating. She could never have done it without her sisters.

Lifting her glass of water, Sheena said, "Here's to the

Sullivan sisters!"

She didn't mind that tears slid down her cheeks. Her sisters were crying too.

CHAPTER FIFTY-FOUR

SHEENA

Sheena and her sisters were in the office one morning when Rocky knocked on the door and opened it. Startled at seeing him, they grew silent.

"I've got some sad news," Rocky said, continuing to stand in the entrance of the room, looking ill-at-ease. "Well, actually it's not all sad, I mean ..."

"What are you trying to say," Sheena asked gently, unaccustomed to seeing Rocky so emotional.

"It's Duncan. He died this morning." Tears glistened in his eyes. "Poor guy, he had no real life at all, but, dammit, he was Gavin's son, and now it's like losing Gavin all over again."

"How did it happen?" Sheena asked.

"I think his heart finally gave out. It's a miracle he lived as long as he did."

"We'll have a service for him, won't we?" Regan asked. "I know you're in charge, but I think Gavin would want his family and friends to give Duncan a nice service and burial."

Rocky let out a long sigh. "You're right. And Elena agrees."

"What will happen to her?" Sheena said. Elena Garcia and her family had taken care of Duncan for his entire, pitiful life. Unable to speak or hear, and without normal arms and legs, he hadn't ever been able to thank her for all she'd done for him, much less smile, or laugh, or play.

"Elena will be fine. She's already been given the house in which Duncan stayed and enough money that she won't ever have to worry."

"I'm glad," said Darcy. "She's one of my angels."

He shuffled his feet. "I'd like your permission to give Duncan's brain to science. A group of doctors has been following his life, wondering how it is that he lived so long. Gavin had wanted to do this, but never signed the papers for it. Now, I can. What do you think?'

A shudder passed through Sheena, but she gave Rocky a steady look. "If it helps others, I think we should do it. That would give meaning to Duncan's life."

Darcy and Regan glanced at her and silently gave their assent.

"This might be of great importance to medicine," said Darcy.

Rocky sniffed. "Thanks. I was hoping you'd see it this way. I'll let you know when the service will be. Will you tell your father?"

"Sure," said Sheena. "He'll want to be part of this too. After all, Duncan was his nephew."

After Rocky left, Darcy got to her feet with an air of determination. "Sheena, will you call Dad? I want to write a few words for Duncan's ceremony."

"And I'll see about having a reception at Gracie's," said Regan. "We want to make it really nice."

Left alone, Sheena thought about the miracle of life. Automatically, she caressed her rounded stomach with gratitude. All the tests had shown that her baby was normal and was due any day.

Sheena and her sisters helped Rocky make the arrangements for Duncan's memorial service. Rather than holding it indoors, they decided to have a service outside at the gazebo. There, the sun and fresh breezes would give the impression of a sense of freedom for the spirit of the man who was bound so cruelly by his life on earth.

The minister who'd married Darcy and Regan agreed to handle the simple service.

On this sunny, warm day in early June, he stood in the gazebo with a small group of family and friends gathered around him. He read some passages from the Bible and then stepped aside.

Darcy, her red curls tossing in the summer breeze, stood before them holding a piece of paper in her hand.

"Most of you know and have even read my stories about angels. How could I pass up the opportunity to tell you about another?

"Duncan Patrick Sullivan fought to come into the world just as he struggled with life every day. He was not your ordinary person. He didn't have normal arms or legs, and he was deaf and unable to speak. At first sight of him, I grew dizzy with disbelief and, yes, horror. Questions circled in my mind. How could any human being live like this? What was his purpose? Why had this happened? I, of course, had no answers at the time.

"But with each quiet visit I made to him, mostly with Rocky, I came to see not the being I'd first encountered, but the soul, if you will, within the man. There were times he looked right at me for a mini-second, a time when a corner of his lip once twitched into what I hoped was a smile. Duncan lived, ladies and gentlemen. It wasn't a life any of us would want, but Gavin, out of love, made sure his son was well taken care of. If Duncan wasn't able to show love, he knew love through the gentle care given by Elena and her family and through the faithful visits of his father, Rocky, and other family members. Now he has a chance, I believe, to be free from the constraints of his life—to be able to walk and talk and laugh. More than that, all the information about him will be shared with medical professionals and scientists, giving a chance of better lives to others."

Tears glistened in Darcy's eyes. "Did his life have meaning? Oh yes. Think of how he's brought us all together. Our families have blended—Gavin's and ours. I will never know why his gift to us was given in such a tortured way, but I know the heavens above hear me."

She lifted her face to the sky and shouted, "Bless you, Duncan Sullivan. You're free now!"

Sheena was as startled as the others by Darcy's loud cry of anguish. And then, while her words settled around the family, they tearfully bowed their heads.

Later, as Sheena was crossing the hotel grounds with Tony and the kids to join the others at Gracie's, she let out a groan. "Oh no!"

Ahead of her, Michael and Meaghan whirled around and stared at the wet mess that was forming on Sheena's sandals.

"Is it the baby?" Meaghan asked, looking aghast.

"My water has broken!"

Michael's face turned white. "Is it coming right now?"

"Hold on! We'll get you to the hospital," Tony said. His face, too, had lost some color.

Hearing the commotion, Regan and Darcy trotted over to Sheena and Tony.

"What's the matter?" asked Regan.

"Oh my Gawd! It's the baby," Darcy said.

Tony tossed Darcy a set of car keys. "Bring the van around to the front. I'll help Sheena to it. You kids better stay here for now. We'll call you as soon as we can."

"I'm sorry. I don't want to interrupt the family party," Sheena said, as if she could control the baby's decision to join the family.

"Oh, hon! Does it hurt?" Regan said, taking hold of Sheena's free arm.

"Not as much as it's going to," she murmured, stopping to catch her breath as a wave of pain filled her.

As they approached the parking lot, Tony dropped her arm to open the door for her.

Darcy came around the van. "Good luck with everything."

When Sheena couldn't hold back a long, low moan, Darcy gave her a wavering smile of encouragement. She'd never wanted to be a nurse as Sheena had. Things like blood and pain upset her.

Tony got behind the wheel, gave Sheena a worried look, and said, "Hold on! Let's not have our baby in the van."

Sheena grimaced as another pain struck. "Then, hurry!"

Through her haze of worry and pain, Sheena caught glimpses of Tony hunched over the wheel as he swerved around slower traffic, beeping the horn. It was almost laughable, but Sheena was as worried as he.

The hospital emergency room entrance appeared in Sheena's vision. While Tony raced inside to get help, she managed to get out of the car. A nurse's aide arrived, pushing a wheelchair. Sheena gratefully sank down into it and grabbed hold as she was hastily wheeled inside. By her calculations, the pains were just two to three minutes apart.

Tony stayed behind to help complete the online forms while the aide wheeled Sheena to the maternity ward.

Sheena had been placed in a birthing room and was wearing a specially designed hospital gown for mothers-to-be when Tony arrived.

"How are we doing?" Tony said.

As another pain hit her, Sheena said, "*We* are holding on. Want to take over for me?" *She knew she sounded cross, but really? We?*

Tony gave her a sheepish look. "Okay, I get it. But I'm here to encourage you." He took hold of Sheena's hand and kissed her cheek. Mollified, Sheena gripped his hand as tightly as she could as she rode the next wave of pain.

Later, one of the nurses checked to see how far along she was and said, "You're getting close hon. Oh, the baby's head has crowned. Here we go!"

Another pain ripped through Sheena, and amid her scream, she heard a voice say, "Grab hold of the shoulders, and let's see what we've got."

"It's a boy!" cried Tony. "We've got a boy!'

Beaming at him, even as tears remained on her cheeks from the pain, Sheena said, "Let me see my baby!"

Umbilical cord still attached, the baby was placed on her stomach, and Sheena looked down into a red, scrunched-up Sullivan face. Tears of joy mixed with her previous tears. Gavin Patrick Morelli gazed at his mother with dark eyes full of wonder.

Tony called Michael and Meaghan to give them the news and asked them to come to the hospital to see their new brother.

The baby and Sheena were cleaned up by the time the kids arrived. Little Gavin was wide awake after trying to nurse. Wrapped in a blanket, he lay on his back looking at his surroundings with curiosity.

"Oh-h-h, can I hold him?" Meaghan said, staring at him with awe.

Sheena handed him to her, and Meaghan held him close.

"Does he have all his fingers and toes," asked Michael hesitantly.

"Yes, he's perfect. In fact, Michael, he has broad shoulders like you and Dad."

"And he's going to have auburn hair like us, Mom," said Meaghan, smiling at Sheena. She gently fingered the strands of hair on his head. "It already has a little red in it."

"We'll see," Sheena said, returning her smile.

"Now, can I hold him?" Michael asked.

Sheena smiled, touched by his request, and watched as he took the baby from Meaghan, handling Gavin as if he was a china doll about to break. Watching him with the baby, Sheena knew he'd be a good father someday. He glanced at her, and Sheena understood the pain on his face. Meaghan patted his arm.

"When are you coming home?" Meaghan asked.

"Probably tomorrow. They don't keep mothers in the hospital as long as they used to when I had you two."

Tony smiled at his family. "Let's ask a nurse to take a picture of our new family. It seems unreal this little guy is finally here with us."

"It's going to seem real when he's screaming in the night," said Michael. "I'm glad my bedroom is upstairs."

Sheena laughed. "There will be other ways you can help, Michael."

"I know," he said easily.

After Michael and Meaghan left to go and have dinner, Tony sat beside Sheena on the bed holding Gavin, who was sound asleep. Gently, he traced the baby's cheeks and then lifted him closer to give him a kiss.

"I'm glad we had him, Sheena," he said. "We're settled in a way we couldn't be when we were younger and struggling with the plumbing business."

"Yes, I want to enjoy this baby. It seems so fitting he's named Gavin."

There was a knock at the door. Paul and Rosa entered, carrying a blue Teddy Bear and a vase with yellow roses.

"Got your message. We're here to see our new grandson," said Rosa. "I'm dying to hold him."

Tony handed the baby to her.

Paul stood beside her, and the two of them smiled with pride as they studied the little boy who bore the Morelli name.

Rosa's eyes welled. "He's such a beautiful baby—a combination of the two of you."

"Yup, a handsome boy. And big too," said Paul. "Eight pounds, like Michael."

Regan and Darcy knocked and entered the room.

"Let's see that boy!" said Regan.

"You all right?" Darcy asked, hugging Sheena.

"I'm fine," said Sheena smiling. "It was a much faster delivery than my other two."

"Everyone at the reception for Duncan is anxious to see the new addition," said Regan.

"And we all love you've named him Gavin. It seems so right."

"Bebe is baking a cake in his honor, Maggie is knitting him a blanket, Gracie and Sally have already put together a gift basket for Gavin from the rest of Uncle Gavin's people," said Darcy.

Patrick Sullivan and Lynn entered the room. "Had to see my new grandson," said Patrick. "I hear he was named for me."

"You and Gavin," Sheena corrected. "His full name is Gavin Patrick Morelli, so each family is honored."

Patrick grinned at her. "Sounds good. I think my brother would be very pleased."

"I love that both Gavin and Patrick, two fine men, have a namesake," said Lynn.

Sheena exchanged glances of amusement with her sisters. Lynn was crazy about their father.

As Gavin began to cry, a hush filled the room.

"Babies really are a miracle," said Regan softly. "I'm so glad he's the newest member of the family."

Sheena smiled and drew the baby closer to her, feeling the heat of his body, loving the shape of him, the smell of him. She thought of Duncan and Gavin's people at the hotel and how they'd added to her family and said a silent prayer of thanks for all she'd been given.

As Darcy said, they were all family. In time, some would leave, and others would join them. But of all the gifts Gavin and his son, Duncan, had given them, finding family was, and would continue to be, a treasure beyond measure.

Thank you for reading *Finding Family*. If you enjoyed this book, please help other readers discover it by leaving a review on Amazon, Goodreads, or your favorite site. It's such a nice thing to do.

Enjoy an excerpt from my book, *Going Home* – Book 1 in The Chandler Hill Inn Series:

CHAPTER ONE

Some people's lives unfold in the most unusual ways.

In 1970, the only things Violet Hawkins wanted for her eighteenth birthday were to escape the Dayton, Ohio, foster-care system in which she'd been raised and to make her way to San Francisco. There, she hoped to enjoy a mellow lifestyle and find the love that had always been absent in her life.

Though she made it to San Francisco easily enough, she soon discovered she couldn't afford a clean, safe place in which to settle down. At first, it hadn't seemed to matter. Caught up in the excitement and freedom of living in a large city where free love and openness to so many things reigned, she almost forgot about eating and sleeping. One couch, one futon was as good as any other as long as grass or other drugs were available, and others didn't mind giving her a place to sleep. But after spending four months there, the dollars she'd carefully saved, which had seemed so many in Dayton, were nothing but a mere pittance in a city where decent living was too expensive for her. She took to wandering the streets with her backpack until she came upon a friendly group willing to give her a sleeping space inside or a bite to eat.

One June day, feeling discouraged, she'd just sunk down

onto the steps outside a row house when a young man emerged. He smiled down at her. "Tired?"

She was more than tired. She was exhausted and hungry. "Looking for work. I need to eat."

He gave her a long, steady, blue-eyed look. "What's your name?"

"Violet Hawkins. But call me Lettie."

His eyebrows shot up. "With all that red hair, no flowery name for you?"

She shook her head. She'd always hated both her hair and her name. The red in her hair was a faded color, almost pink, and the name Violet indicated a delicate flower. She'd never had the luxury of being the least bit frail.

He sat down beside her and studied her. "You don't look like the hippie type. What are you doing in a place like this?"

"On my eighteenth birthday, I left Dayton, Ohio, to come here. It sounded like a great plan—all this freedom."

"How long have you been here?"

"Four months. I thought it would be different. I don't know ... easier, maybe."

He got to his feet. "How about I fix you a sandwich, and then I'll tell you about a job, if you want it. It's at a vineyard in Oregon. I'm heading there later today."

Her glance slid over his well-built body, rugged facial features, and clean, shoulder-length, light-brown hair. He didn't fit into the usual crowd she'd been with, which made her cautious. "Who are you? And why would you do this for me?"

"Kenton Chandler." His lips curved into the same warm smile he'd given her earlier. "I'm heading to Oregon, and, frankly, I could use the company. Keeps me from falling asleep."

"Yeah? And what is this vineyard?"

He shrugged. "A couple of years ago, my dad bought a small inn with 75 acres in the Willamette Valley south of Portland. He's planted most of the land with grapes. He doesn't know that much about making wine and wants me to learn. That's why I'm in San Francisco. I've been working at a vineyard in Napa Valley just north of here, learning the ropes." He grinned. "Or maybe I should say, learning the vines."

"What kind of sandwich?" she asked, warming toward him and his wacky humor. Her stomach rumbled loud enough for them both to hear it.

"How does ham and Swiss sound?" he said, giving her a knowing look.

"Okay." Lettie didn't want him to think she couldn't manage on her own. That was dangerous. She'd learned it the hard way, fighting off a guy who thought he could have her just because he gave her a puff of weed. She'd been careful ever since to stay away from situations and guys like that.

"Well?" He waved her toward the door.

Lettie checked to see if others were within hearing range if she needed them. Plenty of people were hanging around nearby. Thinking it was safe, Lettie climbed the stairs behind Kenton. He didn't know about the knife tucked into one of the pockets of her jeans.

Inside, she found the same kind of contrast between this clean house and others she'd been in. It wasn't sparkling clean, but it was tidier than most.

He led her into the kitchen. "Sit down. It'll only take me a minute to make your sandwich." He handed her a glass of water. "Mustard? Mayo?"

"Both," she replied primly, sitting down at a small pine table in the eating area of the room.

She sat quietly, becoming uncomfortable with the idea that

he was waiting on her. She wasn't used to such a gesture. She was usually the one waiting on others both in her foster home and at the church where she'd spent hours each week attending services and events with her foster family. Thinking of them now, a shiver raced across her shoulders like a frightened centipede. It had been her experience that supposedly outstanding members of a church weren't always kind to those they'd taken into foster care primarily for the money.

"Ready!" said Kenton, jarring her out of thoughts of the past. He placed a plate with the sandwich in front of her and took a seat opposite her.

She lifted the sandwich to her face and inhaled the aroma of the ham. Keeping her eyes on Kenton, she bit into the bread, savoring the taste of fresh food.

He beamed at her with satisfaction when she quickly took another bite.

"Who lives here? Lettie asked.

"A friend of mine," said Kenton. His gaze remained on her. "You don't look eighteen."

She swallowed, and her breath puffed out with dismay. "But I am."

"And you're not into drugs and all the free-love stuff everyone talks about?"

Lettie shook her head. "Not really. I tried weed a couple of times, but it wasn't for me." Her strict upbringing had had a greater influence on her than she'd thought.

"Good. Like I said, if you want to ride to Oregon with me, there's a job waiting for you at the Chandler Hill Inn. We're looking for help. It would be a lot better than walking the streets of Haight-Ashbury. Safer too."

She narrowed her eyes at him. "And if I don't like it?"

He shrugged. "You can leave. One of the staff recently left

for L.A. That's why my father called me to ask if I knew anyone who could come and work there. You're my only choice."

Lettie's heart pounded with hope. Acting as nonchalant as she could, she said, "Sounds like something I'd like to try."

The ride to Oregon was mostly quiet as an easy camaraderie continued between them. Kenton answered any questions she had about him, the inn, and the way he thought about things. Lettie was surprised to learn he hadn't joined in a lot of the anti-war protests.

"My best friend died in 'Nam. He believed in serving our country. I want to honor him," he said to Lettie.

"A boy in my high school was drafted. His parents weren't happy about it."

"Well, if I'm drafted, I'm going," Kenton said. "I don't want to, but I will. I don't really have a choice."

As they talked, they agreed that John Wayne was great in the movie *True Grit*.

"And I love the Beatles," said Lettie.

"Yeah, me too. Too bad they just broke up."

"And what about the new group, The Jackson 5?" Lettie said.

"They're great. And I like Simon and Garfunkel and their music too."

At one point, Lettie turned to Kenton. "Sometimes you seem so serious, like an old man. How old are you, anyway?"

He gave her a sheepish look. "Twenty-two."

They shared a laugh, and in that moment, Lettie knew she'd found a person with whom she could be herself.

Lettie woke to someone shaking her shoulder. She stared

into the blue-gray eyes of a stranger and stiffened.

"Lettie, we're here," said a male voice.

As she came fully awake, she realized Kenton was talking to her.

"Here at Chandler Hill?" she asked, rubbing the sleep from her eyes.

She looked out through the windshield of the Ford Pinto and gaped at the huge, white-clapboard house sitting on the top of a knoll like a queen overlooking her realm.

Lettie scrambled out of the car and stood gazing at the clean lines of the two-story building. Across the front, four windows offset by green shutters were lined up with identical windows below. Beneath a small, protective, curved roof, glass panels bracketed a wide front door, welcoming guests. To one side, a two-story wing had been added to the house.

Green, leafy bushes offset by an assortment of colorful flowers she didn't recognize softened the front of the building. As she walked closer, she realized between the main house and the addition a small, stone patio and private garden had been installed.

"Come on in," said Kenton. "There's a beautiful view from the back porch."

Feeling as if she were Alice in a different kind of Wonderland, Lettie entered the house. As she tiptoed behind Kenton, her gaze darted from the polished surfaces of furniture to gilt-edged mirrors to a massive floral bouquet sitting on a large dining-room table. It all seemed so grand.

Kenton led her to a wide porch lining the back of the house. Observing the rolling land before her and, in the distance, the hills crouching in deepening colors of green, Lettie's breath caught. The sun was rising, spreading a gold topping on the hills like icing on cake.

"Nice, huh?"

Lettie smiled and answered, "I've never seen anything so beautiful, so peaceful."

At the sound of footsteps behind her, she whirled around.

A tall, gray-haired man with striking features similar to Kenton's said, "Welcome home, son."

They shook hands, and then the older gentleman turned to her. "And who is this?"

Shy, she stared at the man who seemed so familiar to her.

Kenton nudged Lettie.

Minding her manners, Lettie held out her hand as she'd been taught. "Lettie Hawkins. I've come for a job." A niggling feeling kept her eyes on him longer than necessary. When she could no longer stop herself, she blurted, "Aren't you Rex Chandler, the movie star?"

He smiled. "Yes, I am. But I've changed professions."

Lettie held back a chuckle of delight. A friend's mother had privately adored him.

"Why don't the two of you come into the kitchen," said Rex. "Mrs. Morley will want to talk to Lettie, and I need to talk to you, Kenton."

As Lettie followed the men into the kitchen, a woman hurried toward them, crying, "Kenton! Kenton! You're home at last!"

Laughing, Kenton allowed the woman to hug him. "You'd think I've been gone a year, Mrs. Morley."

"You almost were," she said, smiling and pinching his cheek. "And look at you! More handsome than ever."

Looking as if he couldn't wait for her to focus her attention elsewhere, Kenton said, "Mrs. Morley, I'd like you to meet Lettie Hawkins. She's here for a job."

Mrs. Morley's gaze settled on Lettie. "So, you like to work?"

"She likes to eat," said Kenton, bringing a smile to Mrs. Morley's full face.

"By the looks of it, Lettie, you could use more food," said Mrs. Morley. "Let's you and I talk about what kind of jobs you could do around here. I'm short-handed at the moment."

Kenton and Rex left the kitchen.

Mrs. Morley waved Lettie over to a desk in a small alcove in the kitchen. After lowering her considerable bulk into a chair, Mrs. Morley faced her. Her green eyes exuded kindness as she studied Lettie. Her gray-streaked brown hair was pulled back from her face and banded together in a ponytail, giving Lettie a good look at her pleasing features.

"Have a seat, dear."

Lettie sat in the chair indicated for her and clutched her hands. After seeing the small inn and the beautiful countryside, she desperately wanted the job.

"Where are you from, Lettie? And why in the world do you want to work here in the country? I'd think a pretty, young girl like you would want to be in a city having fun."

Lettie paused, unsure how to answer her. She'd thought she'd like living in the city, being free to do whatever she wanted. But after four months of doing just that, the excitement had worn off. She liked to know where she was going to sleep at night and when she'd next eat.

"Maybe I'm just a country girl at heart," she answered lamely. Her two best friends at home would scoff at her, but right now, that's how she felt.

"Well, that's what you'll be if you stay on. A lot of activity is taking place around here, what with people buying up turkey farms and the like, turning them into vineyards, but it *is* country. I hope it always will be." She leaned forward. "Know anything about cooking? Cleaning?"

"Yes," said Lettie. "I used to do both in my foster home. I was the oldest of eight kids there."

"Eight? My land, that's a lot of kids to take in," said Mrs.

Morley.

"It's a lot of money," Lettie said, unable to hide her disgust. "That's why they did it."

"I see," said Mrs. Morley, studying her. "So how long have you been on your own?"

"Four months," she replied. "I was in San Francisco when I met Kenton."

"Such a good, young man. I've known him for a while now," Mrs. Morley sighed with affection. "You're lucky he found you. Why don't we start in housekeeping, see how it goes, and then maybe you can give me a hand in the kitchen."

"Okay," Lettie said, jumping to her feet. "Where should I put my things? I need to get them from the car."

Mrs. Morley gave her an approving look. "I like your eagerness. Let me show you to your room and then I'll give you a tour."

The north half of the front of the house consisted of a large, paneled dining room she'd seen earlier. The long mahogany table that sat in the middle of the room held seats for twelve. A summer flower arrangement consisted of pink roses and pink hydrangeas interspersed with white daisies and sat in a cut-glass vase in the middle of the table. Along one wall, above a service counter, an open cupboard made of dark wood stored coffee mugs, extra wine goblets, and water glasses. A coffee maker and a burner holding a pot of hot water sat on the marble counter. A bowl of sugar, a pitcher of cream, and a dish of lemon slices were displayed nearby. At the other end of the counter, a large plate of homemade, chocolate-chip cookies invited guests to take one.

"How many guests do you usually have?" Lettie asked.

"We have six guest rooms, so we have as many as twelve people for the breakfast we serve. During the day, people come and go on their own, tasting wine at nearby vineyards or sightseeing. We offer a simple dinner to those not wishing to travel to restaurants at night." A look of pride crossed Mrs. Morley's face. "Sometimes my husband, Pat, grills out, or Rita Lopez cooks up Mexican food. Guests like these homestyle meals. In fact, we're becoming known for them."

Lettie's mouth watered. It all sounded so good.

Mrs. Morley led her to a sideboard, opened its drawers, and gave her a smile. "Let's see how well you polish silver."

Later, after being shown how, Lettie was working on the silverware when Kenton walked into the kitchen.

"Well? Are you going to stay?" he asked.

"Yes," Lettie said with determination. The whole time she'd been cleaning the silver she'd been able to gaze at the rolling hills outside. This, she'd decided, is where she wanted to be. It felt right.

About the Author

A ***USA Today*** **Best-Selling Author,** Judith Keim is a hybrid author who both has a publisher and self-publishes. Ms. Keim writes heart-warming novels about women who face unexpected challenges, meet them with strength, and find love and happiness along the way—stories with heart. Her best-selling books are based, in part, on many of the places she's lived or visited, and on the interesting people she's met, creating believable characters and realistic settings her many loyal readers love.

She enjoyed her childhood and young adult years in Elmira, New York, and now makes her home in Boise, Idaho, with her husband, Peter, and their lovable miniature Dachshund, Wally, and other members of her family.

While growing up, she was drawn to the idea of writing stories from a young age. Books were always present, being read, ready to go back to the library, or about to be discovered. All in her family shared information from the books in general conversation, giving them a wealth of knowledge and vivid imaginations.

Ms. Keim loves to hear from her readers and appreciates their enthusiasm for her stories.

“I hope you’ve enjoyed this book. If you have, please help other readers discover it by leaving a review on Amazon, BookBub, Goodreads, or the site of your choice. And please check out my other books and series:

The Hartwell Women Series
The Beach House Hotel Series
The Fat Fridays Group
The Salty Key Inn Series
The Chandler Hill Inn Series
Seashell Cottage Books
The Desert Sage Inn Series
Soul Sisters at Cedar Mountain Lodge
The Sanderling Cove Inn Series
The Lilac Lake Inn Series

ALL THE BOOKS ARE NOW AVAILABLE IN AUDIO on Audible, iTunes, Findaway, Kobo, and Google Play! So fun to have these characters come alive!”

Ms. Keim can be reached at **www.judithkeim.com**

And to like her author page on Facebook and keep up with the news, go to: **http://bit.ly/2pZWDgA**

To receive notices about new books, follow her on Book Bub:

https://www.bookbub.com/authors/judith-keim

Sign up for my newsletter and get a free story. I keep my newsletters short and fun with giveaways, recipes, and the latest must-have news about me and my books. Welcome! Here’s the link:

https://BookHip.com/RRGJKGN

She is also on Twitter @judithkeim, LinkedIn, and Goodreads. Come say hello!

Acknowledgments

There are so many people to thank for supporting me. My writing friends, especially those in the Women's Fiction Fans group and the Women's Fiction Writers Association, provide me with knowledge and inspiration. My readers give me the encouragement to keep writing just one more story, another, and another. My review team shows the world their support. I have Lynn Mapp and my husband Peter to thank for their work in editing my novels. Peter is my rock both within the business and in life. Love you all!